The 14 Point Method for Beating the Market

The 14 Point Method for Beating the Market

William P. O'Connor, Jr.

Henry Regnery Company • Chicago

Published by Henry Regnery Company
114 West Illinois Street, Chicago, Illinois 60610
Manufactured in the United States of America
Library of Congress Catalog Card Number: 72-80933

Contents

Preface

Acknowledgments

1   Investor Purposes   1

2   Capitalism and Investors   3

3   Quality Measurement of Stocks   10

4   Debt, a Quality Defect   35

5   Quality of Accounting: When Should Profits Be Recognized?   54

6   Growth Forecasts   73

7   Cyclical Industries   109

8   Staples Industries   132

9   Growth Industries   167

10   Emerging Growth Companies   201

11   Stock Prices and Returns to Investor   213

12   Imaginary Information and Values   264

13   Money Markets, Interest Rates, and Stock Prices   274

14   Portfolio Suggestions   282

     Appendix   291

     Glossary   313

     Index   327

Preface

STOCK investing, like game-type contests, should be a matter of knowledge and applied skills. People who do not have the skills to engage in such contests call them games of chance; when the participants have studied and trained for the contests, they call them tests of skill.

People who do well with stock investments are those who integrate good methods with their personal styles, effectively applying their combined talents. This book is intended for the investor who seeks good methods and wants to make the most of personal talent. It aims to give the inexperienced investor a guide to what he or she ought to know to make sensible decisions about stocks. At the same time, it presents to the experienced investor new ideas that should improve methods he already has found helpful. In the stock market, most of us are somewhere between novice and expert investor.

The methods described in this book were developed because I needed simple measures to use in rating a big choice of common stocks. Being responsible for the work of many analysts, I need simple tools to help me review their findings and forecasts. I must be able to take a company's annual report, make a quality appraisal from the figures in the report, estimate the growth energy of the company, and then judge at what prices the stock could be expected to sell. The techniques I use must be readily understood by anyone familiar with financial reports of American corporations; therefore, I have to translate any complicated formula I use in my work into simple terms so that it will be useful to others.

Quality is the first thing an investor should look for in a stock. Risks and rewards relate to quality. I have found that it is easier to make a universally useful quality measurement when I look at a large number of factors than when I try to rely on merely a few things. Do not be taken aback when you find that there are 14 factors in the quality measurement system I present in this book. Using an annual report and one of the popular stock manuals, you can do a quality study of a stock in about an hour.

The next major subject we need to appraise is possible future *growth* for a company. Therefore, I have included a number of graphs and tables that depict growth, and I explain what I see in them. Also included are explanations of how I got the numbers on the graphs and why they may be useful.

Three chapters on industries cover what I call staple, cyclical, and growth industries. These interpret the strengths and weaknesses of various American industries and suggest how the quality and growth measures can be applied.

The final portions of the book concern stock prices, which are really what we want to know about. In theory, quality and growth should control stock prices. What we know about stock prices came from examination of past behavior. I try to explain, among other things, what investors have gained in rate of return from investments in this century. I also include measures that can be used to determine whether stock prices are relatively high or low.

The book ends with a discussion of money market cycles and the stock market as well as a general explanation of how to use the techniques presented in this book.

Acknowledgments

I drew on the research and statistical work of my associates in preparation of this text. All the graphs were prepared by Sandra Ferrer and Julia Cox, including the statistical computations behind them. Ira Hersch made the first overall editorial review. Interpretation of the drug industry was supplied by George Sacic. Research in the computer products and services was provided by Theo Otis and Robert K. O'Connor. Ernest Levenstein was the source of information on the recreational businesses. Carl De Biase is our interpreter of consumer services businesses, and Scott Nichols consulted on transportation. I drew on the work of Robert Hinckley for petroleum and Roland Moreno for construction-related businesses, while Robert Pollack supplied a number of facts in electronics and aerospace. The consumables industry information was based on the work of Allen Kaplan. The manuscript language was streamlined by Diane O'Connor.

It is hard to be specific about the help from investment professionals in our industry at various stages. It is easy to give credit to those who favor our work. Equally useful have been the critiques from investors on aspects of my work that should be improved or abandoned. Stock-broker analysts and professional investors also participate in a cooperative effort to get improved performance for the owners and beneficiaries of institutional portfolios.

A great deal of patience concerning the use of leisure time for the preparation of this book was shown by my wife, who became convinced of the advantages of the quality approach for her own investments.

1

Investor Purposes

Words mean various things to different people. To an investor or a businessman, *conservatism* does not mean sticking to old things or old ways. More specifically, it means control of the resources necessary to supply some services or goods that are modern, marketable, and of excellent quality. *Forward looking* denotes more than a concentration on new invention; it also means foreseeing trouble either from adversity or from overzealous exploitation of opportunity.

An ambitious course of action has a better possibility of success than an overcautious one if it is based on a realistic appraisal rather than on an overoptimistic projection. Two important principles for investor attention are: (1) proven money-makers are most likely to do well with future programs; (2) rarely will a business organization drastically alter its profit-making ability to the plus side. Investor success tends to be proportionate to the quality of the stocks selected; profit-making ability tends to conform to quality.

Rewards and Risks

We start with the fact that a person who holds U.S. dollars in cash will see his money dwindle at the rate of approximately 4 percent a year thanks to inflation. This is not an aggressive assertion; it is attested to by Washington. We can get 5 percent interest in a savings bank, but taxes must be paid on that 5 percent. To get any net return at all we must take some risks. This book is intended to shed some light on the problem of balancing risks and promised rewards.

In two of the decades since 1930, investors en masse attained their desired gains through ownership of property, as represented by stocks, and in two decades they did not. The 1930s and the 1960s were disappointing decades for stock investors. In either of the 20-year periods 1930-1950 or 1950-1970, stock investors averaged returns on their money of 8 to 9 percent. The 9 percent came from about 4 percent cash dividends and 5 percent average growth. Prior to the late 1960s and early 1970s, current dividend yields were competitive with the 4 percent to 5 percent interest rates on bonds; in addition, retained earnings were almost as large as the dividends that increased corporation assets. The average increase of about 5 percent in the dividends and the earnings assets that supported them brought gain in market value that offset the inflation of U.S. currency. (In Chapter 11, the effect of 7 percent bond interest on stock values is discussed.)

Making Capital Grow

Preservation of capital in the United States in the 1970s requires a return on investment of 10 percent. The savings bank interest is now 5 percent. Inflation is assumed at 4 percent. Data, which I will introduce later as proof for the capital preservations formula, show that about 14 percent return has been achieved through ownership of just highest quality stocks. The 14 percent return is 5 to 6 percent higher than the usual return from ownership of stocks in general.

The quality approach is the best method for achieving above-average investment results. Quest for a 25 percent annual investment return is aggressive and means more risk. This book will explain methods that should work very well for the investor who seeks to achieve a return in the 10- to 15-percent-a-year range. For the investor in pursuit of a 25 percent annual return, the techniques described should be useful, but such a return comes to those with unusual skill as well as a willingness to use proven tools.

2

Capitalism and Investors

Our investments have to be made against a background of an economic society that tolerates rather than enthuses over capitalism. In our world, a hot debate exists between those who believe in individualistic capitalism, in which all property is private, and those who think the stress on individualism is a hindrance to the useful management of the environment. The historical fact is that some humans have always sought, by capitalist-type actions, to free themselves from the limitations of the environment. The instincts of leader types are to expand their capitalist potential from a basic individual property.

Humans organized into tribes or other social groups when certain individuals recognized that the environment could be exploited more effectively for everyone's benefit if people worked in a cooperative and regulated fashion. In the initial stages, the leader persuades others to cooperate, and he divides up the product of the group effort. After a while, the leader's program becomes more complex, and leadership must be shared. In the longer trend, the leaders become interested in wider horizons.

Empire building, whose purpose is to enhance and protect the capital of the leader, comes in various stages. When benefits are shared and there is less drudgery, the advantages of cooperation seem attractive to the leader's closely related followers.

Business Leadership

Armies have a motto that there are no good regiments and no bad regiments; rather, there are good colonels and poor colonels. What this means is that the assortment of soldiers in a given country's army is capable of becoming an effective fighting force when properly led. In theory, leadership in publicly owned stock companies is not greatly different. Businessmen use the French word *entrepreneur* to indicate the self-starting owner-manager type. *Enterpriser* in English means the same thing. Literally, either word means "to seize entry."

One may ask if the take-charge type is doing so merely for his own benefit or if he will do some good for other investors. An individual need not have public stockholders to be a good entrepreneur, but in our large-scale economy many entrepreneurs need public investors to supply the capital for their business projects. Good business enterprisers know how to function in the environment, to make good product judgments, to stimulate their sales force, to control expenses, and to do a good job for stockholders.

The more one studies corporations, the more obvious it becomes that their great growth eras are almost always associated with the careers of master builders. However, it is more important to identify the proprietor-capitalist-leader than it is to know about management succession and depth. The key man may have been the founder, or he may have emerged and built a new business on an old structure.

For the stock investor, the problem is to identify the leader and the stock while the entrepreneur is in charge. When he leaves the scene, the stock may not be such a good investment. How do you find such a man? Here are a few things he can be expected to do.

1. He seeks to operate in a commercial environment that has not been exploited, where the industry growth potential of two to three times in a decade is considered favorable. In any event, he should perform in a business that has a growth prospect rate at least twice that of the general economy.

2. He stresses new products and operating techniques in his business plan. He likes to try things that have not been done before, but not recklessly.

3. He maintains company profits at a higher percent of capital than is usual for industry in general.

4. He has a plan for the future, spelled out in some detail, which he consistently revises.

Environments and Leader Opportunities

In addition to identifying the leadership attributes of companies, we need to look at environmental factors.

Investors should be concerned with the development of values from unorganized resources of the environment. Just keep in mind that at all times values in the world are rising and decaying. Most investors are aware that some nations are improving as capitalistic environments while others are deteriorating. Rarely does a nation entirely alter its character with respect to capitalism. Wherever capital property has been converted to state ownership, individual capitalism either had not been the tradition before or had not been aggressive. Overthrow of a military government, though, is often the precursor of a flowering of enterprise capitalism. West Germany and Japan are recent examples of this replacement of warriors with entrepreneurs. Among national capitalist environments, certain European countries have vigor. The present generation of young adults in Great Britain, France, and Germany, as well as Russia, is the first to mature in this century without having been decimated on the battlefield. In Britain we can see the painful efforts to remove the grip of trade unionism.

Some people think that the United States is deteriorating as a capitalist environment. In my judgment, plenty of capitalist entrepreneurial energy still exists in the American economy. The question is whether forces hostile to the effective functioning of the entrepreneur are seriously limiting the possibilities for capitalism as practiced by ambitious individual owners. Admittedly, mature industries tend to be more restricted by socialist tendencies than do younger growth industries. It is critical for American investors to have a good fix on the state of the entrepreneurial environment.

So many industries offer limited or no entrepreneurial scope that the impression of dying capitalism is created. In certain conditions, leader-type young men are repelled from entering specific fields of endeavor.

In the 1970s, ambitious young men are as discriminating about business opportunities as were such men in the 1940s. Then, considering the financial condition of the railroads, the effects of ICC regulation, and government subsidies for barges, truckers, and the young airline industry, none was interested in a railroad career. In 1940, young men were attracted to businesses in which new invention could be positive and marketing really could make a difference. Process industries were attractive because of the many new synthetics being invented and the opportunities for process improvements. Nylon had just been invented, and wood products with new synthetic adhesives and coatings were becoming more interesting. Aspiring leaders discriminated among consumer products, preferring industries whose items were used rather promptly and raw materials either were minor cost components or were tending to decline in price. They were shy of industries where strong union activity complicated life.

Labor Unions

Strong unionism is likely to indicate industry dependence on low-cost labor as a major production cost. When an industry is growing strongly with modern products, it usually is also efficient in the use of labor and can pay workers well enough to obviate their need for expensive union representation. Although some companies do have unions and high profits with growth, such cases are exceptional.

About one-fourth of the American workers are unionized, and they are mainly in mature industries, such as metals, transportation, building, motor products, and machinery. To deal with the remaining three-fourths, employers need not negotiate through union representatives. In the future, as in the past, ambitious young business leaders probably will tend to avoid industries in which it is necessary to employ militant unionized workers.

Labor Costs

The impact of militant unions is more important when employment costs are high relative to net sales, as is shown in Table 2-A, compiled by Standard & Poor's. From 1965 through 1970, industries with severe labor cost pressures were air transport, cars and trucks, building materials, publishing, and trucking. Conversely, retail trade, with lower labor cost ratios, was able to pass on costs. In the oil industry, other cost variables were much more important than labor.

TABLE 2–A
RECORD OF EMPLOYMENT COSTS BY GROUPS
(based on S&P annual surveys)

	Salaries and Wages as Percent of Net Sales			
	1965	*1968*	*1969*	*1970*
Aerospace	41.4	39.9	41.7	38.2
Air transport	37.0	39.6	40.1	45.9
Automobiles and trucks	27.8	26.5	28.2	33.4
Auto parts and accessories. . .	33.5	34.3	35.3	37.0
Brewing and distilling	22.2	19.6	20.9	19.8
Building materials.	31.4	31.5	30.9	34.2
Chemicals	27.6	27.0	26.9	28.4
Containers (metal and glass). .	35.0	35.1	34.2	35.3
Drugs and cosmetics	25.5	25.6	26.2	25.1
Electrical products	39.3	39.2	39.8	39.4
Food products	15.5	17.6	18.1	18.3
Home furnishings.	33.0	31.3	28.5	32.4
Leisure time	−	36.0	36.1	38.0
Machinery — agricultural. . . .	34.4	35.7	36.0	35.7
Machinery — industrial	34.1	34.3	33.9	34.9
Meats and dairy products . . .	14.6	18.3	15.1	13.7
Metal fabricating	22.3	26.1	21.9	38.8
Metals — nonferrous	34.1	35.5	31.4	32.9
Miscellaneous	32.3	32.7	33.1	33.8
Office equipment	37.8	35.9	42.0	32.9
Oil	11.9	11.8	12.4	12.4
Paper and paper containers . .	28.4	30.0	28.8	30.9
Printing and publishing.	31.2	35.8	34.2	35.4
Rail equipment	36.6	34.5	33.4	40.4
Retail trade	13.5	13.9	14.0	16.4
Steel and iron	36.8	37.8	39.1	40.1
Textiles.	26.9	28.2	29.9	28.9
Tires and rubber goods.	32.7	31.0	31.7	32.0
Trucking and leasing	−	20.9	35.3	32.0
3 Average.	27.1	28.0	27.8	27.9

In utilities, the difference between electric and telephone system labor costs is spectacular.

Salaries and Wages
as percent of Net Sales
Electric utilities 13.4
Telephone companies 61.3

Environmental Problem Industries

In the 1960s, Americans finally recognized that the process of satisfying demands of the opulent society at minimum cost was damaging the environment. Very few people understand that we cannot have electric power at 1960 price rates and also avoid air pollution and landscape spoliation because of coal extraction. The costs of clean air and primeval landscapes must be paid for in the price of power. In view of this general lack of understanding, it is ironic that auto buyers who opt for $1,000 worth of extras for performance, comfort, and decoration object to the expense of motor tune-ups for efficient fuel consumption.

Some manufacturers cannot rebuild their plants to overcome pollution problems at costs that will permit them to operate with competitive product prices. To the extent that old plants have been generating cash flow, the owners experience some loss. When closings of polluting plants reduce the supply of commodities, the possibility of price increases exists. To finance expansion required to replace the commodity supply lost from pollution shutdowns, owners need higher profits from plants that continue to operate.

Pollution is a whole new factor for investors to consider. Companies that have to find the money to correct environmental degradation operate under handicaps from the viewpoint of common stock investors. Pollution problems also are causing aspiring young managers to give some second thoughts to entering or continuing in industries where pollution problems are severe.

Many investors favor the suppliers of equipment and materials for pollution abatement. This field does look attractive to young men in search of a business with potentials. Some drawbacks are obvious, the worst being that no one really wants to buy pollution-abatement products since they do not add much value or significant technical input to a company's products or services. The bulk of antipollution money is being spent on fairly simple products commonly used in engineering construction.

Industry Opportunities for Entrepreneurs

Certain industries are not attractive for entrepreneurial managers to operate with public stockholder capital. These industries, whose service charges and markets are government regulated, have lower rates of return on total capital than do most investor-owned industries. To secure a competitive return on stockholder capital, they usually have to operate with borrowed capital. Major regulated industries do not earn sufficient cash flow to finance their own growth. An exception is life insurance, which is required to charge premium rates high enough to assure meeting its commitments. Airlines have a double jeopardy in that rates are regulated and the government has enforced uneconomical competition by route duplication. A few business builders do exist among regulated industries, mainly in banking.

Certain business categories in which public stockholder capital is needed do offer a good scope for entrepreneurs. For example, computer-based services are already a $1 billion group that was growing 20 percent a year in 1971 (see Chapter 9). Very small business computers represent an infant market. Although hazardous, businesses that manufacture semiconductor computer memories have attracted numerous entrepreneurs in recent years. Another dynamic investment area recently has been modular housing.

3

Quality Measurement
of Stocks

Our records show that quality stocks beat the market. Greater profits have been made from stocks of companies with the quality strengths, and if we can make a correct analysis of quality most other questions about stocks become easier to answer.

Our ability to forecast the price of the stock is affected by past performance. When company performance has been erratic, investors also may be erratic in their decisions to buy or sell a stock. When we understand quality well, we can forecast prices better, and we will be less apt to pay too much or to make the mistake of selling at the bottom of a bear market.

The 14-point quality measurement method was designed to help analysts in fitting growth forecasts for earnings together with prices of stocks. It was originally designed to help with comparative valuation between proven stocks and promising younger company stocks. Because many young stocks do not attain their goals, the successful ones would have had to carry the klunkers. The overall performance of a broad sample of unproven growth stocks may not equal the earnings growth and stock price appreciation of a major growth stock.

We must pay a lower price multiple for a dollar of a young growth company's earnings than for one of a high quality growth company's earnings in order to compensate for the failures among the younger company stocks. In order to measure differences, we must have a method to give credit for positive factors in the top grade company record.

The measures must be those available from annual reports and popular statistical manuals. If a statistical factor is to have influence on investor opinions about stocks, it must be something that many investors know about and consider important. The beauty of the method is that it requires us to examine most of the points that should be looked at in the study of a stock. That the method includes 14 points makes it easier. If we are a little off on a couple of measures, the distortion will not be so great as it will be when only three or four measures are used for quality rating. After a little practice, you can measure the quality of one stock in an hour.

Testing the System

In 1970 I made a test to determine whether selection of stocks based on this quality measurement would have brought better performance for the investor starting from 1960. It was assumed that the buyers of a stock made purchases at the average price in a year. At the end of five years, the stock was sold at the average price. The value of dividends received was added to the gain in price. The compounded annual gain from the original purchase was calculated. (We call this gain *investment return* or *total return*.)

The particular stocks were selected from my records of quality ratings in the years when purchases would have been made. Six consecutive five-year periods were available for the test. Table 3-A, which includes five years through 1971, shows the remarkable results. The Grade I stocks consistently returned more to the investor than lesser grade stocks or the market averages. Only 0.1 percent of the New York Stock Exchange listed stocks qualify as Grade I. They are much greater in terms of market value. Examples of such stocks are IBM, Eastman Kodak, Avon Products, 3M Company, Coca-Cola, and Merck. Even though in each period several stocks declined in quality, the whole group performed nevertheless. (The 1971 Grade I stocks are listed at the end of the chapter.)

TABLE 3–A
PERCENTAGE INVESTMENT RETURNS BY QUALITY GRADE

Grade	1960-65	1961-66	1962-67	1963-68	1964-69	1965-70	1966-71
I	17.0	14.4	16.1	16.9	14.3	10.0	16.3
II	14.0	8.2	15.9	16.3	14.6	8.1	8.7
III . . .	9.9	9.1	13.2	12.3	10.5	-0.3	6.6
IV . . .	15.0	9.7	11.0	10.2	4.4	-1.5	2.7
V	6.7	3.1	9.1	14.2	8.1	-1.5	-1.2
S&P 425 Industrials Average							
	12.4	7.7	11.1	8.5	6.8	2.2	6.7
Dow Jones Industrials							
	11.0	8.7	9.1	8.7	4.6	0	2.5

Over the various five-year periods, Grade I stocks outperformed stocks in the other grades. The average return of Grade I stocks was 14.6; Grade II, 12.7; Grade III, 9.1; Grade IV, 7.7; Grade V, 7.6.

In seven periods, all the samples changed, and yet Grade I stocks had the most uniform and highest return because they are more profitable and grow faster than lower grades, and none of the high grades suffer severe declines in profits. In lower grades, a number of stocks proved serious disappointments. Investors are more tolerant about sluggish periods for high grade stocks, while the greater volatility of low grade stocks tends to work against the average investor. The reason is that in bull markets low grade stocks tend to become more overpriced than high grade stocks.

Quality Measurement System

The purpose of a corporation is to employ the stockholders' capital in an effective manner. If it is successful, presumably it has learned how to cope with its environment — social, political, economic, and physical. (It is worth noting that in 1970 corporations began to talk about service to society as coming ahead of profits. Companies that express this goal usually are telling stockholders that they must pay for the past sins of failing to consider the environment, and so on. In the long run, it is cheaper to attend early to the general welfare considerations.)

Investors want to own the stocks of companies that get the best returns on capital.

The heart of stock analysis is quality measurement. It helps one to decide how much confidence to put in a growth projection, and it also indicates how much premium or discount is warranted in the price of a stock.

Because we mainly rely on data for information, the process of judging quality should be statistical and detailed since so many factors bear on it. The procedure is something like scoring a track meet, in which a team can win by scoring well in the flat races while gaining only a few points in field events or vice versa. The scoring method provides a possible 70 points, 5 on each of 14 questions.

Industry	Company	Financial	Market
1. Industry dynamism	4. Management	8. Return on equity	13. Volatility
2. Stability	5. Organization depth	9. Plowback	14. Acceptance
3. Service rating	6. Research	10. Debt/equity	
	7. Plant	11. Persistence	
		12. Dividends	

Each of these items is given a number value for measurement of overall quality. The importance of a type of measurement has weighting both in the main list and in the way points are measured. A score of 60 out of 70 is extremely high. The Dow Jones Industrial Average scores 34 points.

How Quality Is Measured

The procedure for scoring the points is shown in a questionnaire. A 200-stock sample in the Appendix shows how the stocks rated. You may find the why more challenging after you look at some of my conclusions about the quality of stocks.

Industry
Question 1.   Dynamism of Industry versus Maturity

How fast does the industry grow? High scores are given to industries that grow fast, because growth in the industry gives a boost to all companies, something that may save a few weaker outfits and give powerful acceleration to the good company. However, companies in slow-moving industries must be alert and aggressive every hour every day or be run down by the hustlers.

In 1971, industries were rated on dynamism approximately as shown in Table 3-B. Growth rates are averages for a period of years. Some companies are in more than one industry, and for these you have to work out some kind of average.

TABLE 3–B
INDUSTRY GROWTH RATES

Very Fast 10%	Fast 8%	Active 6%
Business services	Consumer services	Banking
Electronic data processing	Recreation	Chemicals
Nuclear power	Electronic instruments	Containers and packaging
Electric photography	Canadian petroleum	Cosmetics
Precision optics	Photography	Publishing and printing
Medical service	Office equipment	Hotel chains
Protection	Integrated circuitry	Telephone
Fast food service		Electric power
		Aluminum
		Drugs
		Electronic components
		Broadcasting
		Air transport
		Department stores

Above Average 4.5%	Same as Economy 3%	Stagnant
Household products	Aircraft	Public transportation
Consumer credit	Housing	Lead–zinc
Machinery	Grocery	Carbohydrate foods
Wood products	Auto and trucks	Tobacco
Specialty foods	Petroleum–U.S.	Railroad
Food service	Meat	
Appliance	Building	
	Steel	
	Textile	
	Apparel	

The effect of inflation may cause dollar growth to exceed the growth rates given here. Where possible, I have used unit of product growth. For banks, the dollar value of loans is the growth; for electric power, it is kilowatt hour consumption; for oil, barrels. But a pill count for drugs is impossible.

In some industries, the nature of the product changes. Although the quantities of lumber sold in the United States have been on a flat trend for decades, plywood sales have provided much of the growth for forest products. Growth in paper sales has slowed as plastic packaging has become popular. We may think that food sales must have more than 3 percent growth. Some companies increase sales partly from the addition of convenience features — either packaging or partial preparation.

Question 2.   Industry Stability Preferred over Cyclicality

Investors prefer stocks in industries that suffer only mild buffeting from recessions. They like the freedom from worry about when the business should enjoy above-average profitability, because one of the prices of stability is more intense competition in some instances. In the case of utility companies, stability means regulation of profits. No other company in the utility industry provides such a high return on stockholder investment as General Motors, but GM stockholders see earnings irregularly.

Examples of industry stability include the following:

Aerospace — low stability
Chemicals — cyclical
Electric power — very stable
Machinery — cyclical but progressive
General merchandise retailing — relatively stable
Banking — cycle resistance
Drugs — mostly consistent   *Drug Stores*
Computing products — consistent, thanks to rental income
Electric and electronic components sales — irregular
Entertainment — erratic

Cyclical but Progressive. Machinery makers provide tools for increasing the productivity of workers, and they are always engaged in some amount of new invention. Their customers buy machinery with capital rather than with consumption dollars. Decisions to buy machines are related to expectations for sales of the customer's products or services as well as to the availability of capital to the buyer. Capital spending is more cyclical than consumption of end products in our economy.

Stable. Industries with stable sales supply things that are used up in a short time. Electric power really cannot be stored at all. Apparel wears out, and we do not defer its replacement very long. Banking is consistent in profits because it can change the rate of interest paid for deposits even when there are big changes in the demand for loans.

The prices of stocks in stable industries were more volatile in 1970 than in most previous market cycles. Concern over ability to adapt to inflation and high interest rates led investors to the question of adaptability in some industries. In 1971, investors recognized that retail merchants had the easiest time in adapting to inflation, and high interest rates slowed store expansion. Electric utilities, though, were hurt by rising fuel costs and higher interest costs, while rate increases were resisted by regulatory commissions. Bank stocks in 1970 and 1971 actually were less volatile than the market. Over many decades, the cycle-resisting stocks have been more stable along their growth trends, and they will be in the future.

Question 3. Industry Reputation with Statistical Services

The best way for the investor to get information on this question is to study the advice given by prominent investment advisory services such as Standard & Poor's, Moody's, and Value Line. This is not a formal qualitative measure, but the attitudes of these organizations, as well as investment management organizations, have some influence on the quality rating of a stock. Some new industries are not yet recognized in standard industry classification, which is a lack. The list below incorporates most of the recognized industries and rates them on a five-point scale.

Five Points

Business data processing	Soft drinks	Life insurance
	Photography	Proprietary drugs

Four Points

Hospital supply	Medical automation	Household products
Precision instruments	Services	Ethical drugs
Cosmetics and toiletries	Office supplies	Packaged foods
Telephone		

Three Points

Grocers	Chemicals (diversified)	Antipollution
Finance	Electronic components	Uranium
Banking	Business and	Petroleum
Utility equipment	educational publishing	Office machines
Aluminum and nickel	Department stores	Gas pipelines
Industrial controls	Electric utilities	

Two Points

Building materials	General merchandise	Air transport
Chemicals (raw materials)	retailing	Food service
Machinery	Consumer appliances	Trucking

One Point

Mobile homes	Contracting for	Public transportation
Textiles and apparel	defense department	Publishing of periodicals
Automobiles	Construction contracting	Ocean freight
Steel		

Not Recognized

Independent vendor computer services

The publishing services and prominent investor magazines such as *Forbes* and *Barron's* have wide readership and therefore great influence on the attitudes of investors. Since we invest in environments controlled by other people's opinions, it is important to know what the majority of investors may be thinking about the industries we study. Evaluations about industries change, and the points I used in the list above may not be valid some time later.

Question 4.   Company Top Management

While the financial measures included in the quality analysis also express top management ability, this rating is included to permit the analyst to allow for experience. When a management has gotten performance out of an organization for a number of years, the whole team has acquired habits that are reflected in results. A brand new team can perform for a year or two without having acquired the habit of repeated success.

The problem in rating a top management team is to avoid subjectivity on the part of the analyst. In the mid-1960s, a number of capable young managers developed substantial earnings in companies built up by exploitation of novel technical products or by financial transactions that increased the earnings bases of older companies. Although the progress achieved by such company managements rivals even IBM and Kodak, they have not sustained themselves under adversity on a repetitive basis. This is the difference that the top management rating is intended to score.

We can look at what has happened in the application of computerized business information. In the last two decades, the cost of filing data for quick retrieval has declined 90 percent. Managements were severely tested in the adaptation of this new capability to mature business operations. Usually, the business is not getting 10 times as much value from its ability to store and manipulate data at low cost per item. Often, we have simply complicated our lives and possibly enhanced the competitive advantage of those with the greatest skills.

Credit expansion can be used to illustrate the way that physics applied through computers led to more business and less profit. Because personal expenditures in cash are less than they were a generation ago, merchants, services, and suppliers are trusting their customers for accuracy in record keeping and credit equal to purchases. Most of us know that we hardly ever have more money than we think we have, and we often have less. Historically, retail stores extended credit when they knew the customers, but changes occurred in the 1950s and 1960s when computers enabled credit organizations to process enormous quantities of credit card charges, and the majority of citizens were found to be credit worthy. Bank policies in extending credit changed as the banks became able to handle many more transactions on a credit basis.

The new quick credit led individuals to incur more debt relative to income than they would have under the old system, by which credit at least had to be requested. Retailers and services acquired more receivables accounts relative to sales than was normal. Inevitably, they were slower in paying suppliers and carried higher than usual bank loans. Suppliers therefore had more overdue accounts receivable and used up bank credit. In general, business experienced more credit losses and paid higher interest.

The credit losses and interest threw a lot of smaller business firms into the red, exhausted their capital and borrowing ability, and led to more failures. When analysts examined bank annual reports, they found that losses in 1970 were about triple what they had been in 1969. It was the first time since the 1930s that loan write-offs greatly exceeded the normal allowance for loan losses.

Large company managements often have been responsible for what amounts to misuse of invention. Some may have oversold equipment and methods; others have let competitive urgency lead them further into new things than previous testing and experience warranted. Companies must take advantage of new applications of science, but it is possible to minimize misuse of new inventions and methods and avoid bad fallout from engineering projects.

In general, the highest quality companies do not mess up the environment. Most of the organizations that spoil the landscapes and watercourses are sloppy operators. Almost all of the oil spilled on the ocean can be traced to human faults. Subordinate personnel work to the standards enforced by the management. If the workers think that the boss would rather chance oil spills than incur the expense of accident prevention, they work that way.

In the application of the top management measure, I suggest the use of statistics as a guide. You will find problem areas, as when a company continued to market less than safe products because consumers refused to buy the safer or more reliable products, insisting on the lesser quality things.

Question 5.   Organization Depth

This measure is designed to favor the large company, which has advantages in our competitive economy. The large company has many well-trained executives who in the process of protecting their jobs can keep it on even keel without strong leadership. It is quite possible that a company may score higher on depth than on top management effectiveness.

The efforts of well-trained lower echelons of management have kept some companies in condition so that they could be redeveloped. Coca-Cola had gotten sleepy until a new top management was installed in the mid-1950s. But the existence of a good organization, as well as the independent bottling companies, made possible Coca-Cola's rather quick improvement.

The existence of very large organizations of operating employees was the basis for believing that a number of companies could be restored to high profitability. Among Detroit companies, Chrysler is still struggling, but Burroughs and Kresge made dazzling turnabouts. Atlantic Richfield is still striving to turn three slow-moving companies (Sinclair is the third) into an aggressive North American oil development company.

Question 6.   Product Development Impact on Sales

By specifying that 80 percent of a business must result from the company's product development in the last 10 years, this research rating measure has been deliberately loaded to single out those very special companies whose existence is attributable to the creativity of key people who are leaders of their organizations. In rare cases, large old companies developed entirely new product lines internally, where the bulk of sales are made in such new products. The test is the importance of innovation for current sales. Burroughs Corporation is a conspicuous example of this point. Wonderful new products in small divisions do not earn these points, because often the success of a small division is not material in the total company profits.

Recognition of merchandising finesse is covered with some scoring allocations.

The quality point on top management stressed responsibility for control of applied science to avoid misuse of technology. In rating product development, lean in favor of the technical achievement. While engineers are paid to invent better things through technical work, it is up to management to set the standards of what may be offered to customers and what qualities must be met in manufacturing plants or other facilities. The engineer gets paid to build a good 1,000-foot-high building. He may question whether it is a good idea to put up such a building, but the management has the responsibility.

We can sympathize with the wizards who were designing the Boeing Super Sonic Transport, but in this case the Congress was the board of directors that decided the product was not suitable for the environment. Boeing's management erred in making its commitment to the SST. However, in an earlier stage of SST development the engineering staff of Boeing was remiss when it said it could build a swing wing SST, which would have been able to fly at subsonic speeds. They misled the management and the customer.

Product development in a company should be the process whereby new things are developed and become primary profit sources. Henry Ford II gave some insights into this problem in the 1970 annual report of Ford Motor Company. He implied that the $60 million that Ford was spending on exhaust emission problems could not offset the emissions caused by misfiring spark plugs in cars that are tuned only once every 25,000 miles. Profit from new technology is secured by application of a group of skills in coordinated fashion. Ford, or another company with a technical problem, will come up with a profitable product development only if it figures how to turn the problem solution into a source of profit.

Question 7.   Physical Assets

The analyst can rely on numbers to a considerable degree in appraising the modernity of a company's physical assets. It is rare indeed that a company that has increased the book value of its fixed assets by 100 percent in the last 7 years does not have efficient plants to that degree. Company reports normally provide descriptions of facilities, and most companies will provide brochures describing their facilities.

Even when a company and its industry have become over-expanded, those with the newest plants will fare better during periods when capacity is excessive. The company with old facilities may not survive a recession or will have to drop some product lines.

Financial

These five measures account for the largest part of the difference among companies, particularly in similar businesses. The points were designed to give credit for superior statistical performance. Certain companies have high profit rates, consistency, and conservatism. We want to show these qualitative factors.

Most of the five points in some way relate to book value of stockholder equity. Return on equity is a ratio of profits to book value. We are interested in the plowback of earnings as an indication of the internally generated growth of assets. In the quality test, we use a cash plowback measure that is compared to gross operating assets. Usually, retained earnings as percent of book value for a company is about the same as the cash plowback.

Book value per share refers to the net assets of the company after deduction of all liabilities and senior capital. It came into being in the form of paid-in capital by stockholders and reinvestment of profits over the years. Many investment people aver that it is not of material concern for decisions about the merits of stocks. They say that valuation of earnings is the way to judge stocks.

This is like taking a meal at a restaurant and then agreeing to purchase the establishment without looking at the kitchen. Profits do not come out of the air; they arise according to the quality of success in sales of goods and services through employment of the stockholder capital. Business decisions are constantly being made on the basis of estimates of adequacy of capital and the projected profits to be earned from employing it in certain ways.

When you are the manager of a business organization, you are more concerned with the capital in the company than with what the stock market says the stock is worth. It happens that for the great majority of listed stocks the market prices are greater than the book values of the stocks. Listed stocks sell for more than book value because they earn sufficient profits on capital to impress investors and are readily marketable. Investors usually will accept lower yields when their investments are marketable than when their capital is locked into private business or property.

Investors often are confused about market prices in relation to earnings because they are not sufficiently conversant with the quality of earnings. Numerous people say they would not pay a price equal to 30 times earnings and that maybe a stock growing at 12 percent a year might be worth 20 times earnings.

The simplest way to appraise the quality of earnings is by studying their relation to book value. Table 3-C shows a sample of stocks by quality, return on book equity, and price compared to book value. The qualities of the stocks are measured by the

TABLE 3—C

Stock	Grade	Earned on Book Equity	Median 1969—1970 Price ÷ Book Equity
Eastman Kodak	I	21%	6.0
Coca-Cola	I	24	9.0
American Home Products	II	35%	8.0
Simplicity Pattern	II	24	8.0
Georgia-Pacific	III	15%	4.0
Texaco	III	14	1.6
Ford Motor	IV	10%	1.0
Ex-Cell-O	IV	11	1.25
Bethlehem Steel	V	7%	0.65
Allied Stores	V	7	0.6

method explained in this chapter. Most investors will know the reputation of Eastman Kodak for excellence and firm growth, and the plight of steel companies is regularly in the news; but I doubt that most investors have thought of the ratio of stock price to book equity. In the market, a dollar of book equity for Eastman Kodak is worth 10 times as much as a dollar of book equity for Bethlehem Steel.

Question 8.   Earned on Net Worth (Book Equity)

If you had no information about 10 stocks other than return on net worth, you would make much more long-term gain from the 5 stocks with the highest return than from the 5 with the lowest return. Earned on net worth is derived by calculating the net income for the year in question as a percent of stockholder's equity at January 1 for the same year.

For most companies, per share data can be used. If there are preferred stock issues, these are taken into account, and any substantial mergers must be accounted for.

Question 9. Cash Plowback Return

Because this measure of ability to generate growth from retained cash flow is not a measure usually interpreted to investors, the arithmetic is displayed here.

Percent of plowback =

$$\frac{\text{Cash flow} - \text{dividends}}{\text{Gross plant} + \text{net working capital \& investments} + \text{other assets}}$$

DERIVATION OF CASH PLOWBACK ($ MILLIONS)

Depreciation and other reserve additions	$ 2.00
Net income	3.00
Cash flow	$ 5.00
Less dividends	1.50
Cash flow minus dividends	$ 3.50

Gross Plant Plus Net Working Capital Plus Other Assets
(January 1 data)

Net plant (usual balance sheet entry).	$15.00
Reserve for depreciation (from notes)	5.00
Gross plant	$20.00
Total current assets	$10.00
Minus total current liabilities	4.00
Net working capital	$ 6.00
Add investments	4.00
Add value of gross plant	20.00
Gross plant + working capital + investments.	$30.00

Solution of cash plowback return equation: $\dfrac{\$\ 3.50}{\$30.00} = 11.7\%$

In deciding on a rating measure for cash plowback, I set the minimum at 6 percent, which is 1 percent above the plowback of the Dow-Jones Industrials index. The top score applies at 12 percent, which is about the highest plowback for large growth companies. Because of circumstances that may have been beyond the complete control of management, companies often complete large plants at the wrong time for current profits. Operation of such plants may throw off large depreciation accruals, which may be building up the liquidity of the business or paying off debt.

The sum net working capital, gross fixed assets, and investments represents the amount of money that has been invested up to the beginning of any year, and if cash plowback return equals 8 percent of the asset figure, the company is now generating enough cash to sustain an 8 percent annual addition to working assets or replacement of obsolescent facilities.

If cash plowback is from 8 percent up, it is usually helpful in projecting long-term growth, but when plowback is lower, replacement of old facilities may absorb much of the plowback. In other words, *the cash flow plowed back is significant only in relation to the assets on which it is earned.* We find that if the cash plowback ratio is low as a percent of assets, usually there are a lot of unprofitable old facilities. This is generally true of regulated industries that must sell new bond and stock issues to build new plants; depreciation is never sufficient.

When business is turning up after a recession, investors may look for companies with earnings leverage because of ownership of underutilized fixed assets. Numerous corporations usually earn a rather low return on capital invested in chemical, paper, metals, or textiles plants. The theory is that when good times arrive they can run such plants near capacity and experience earnings leverage. A similar concept applies to hotel chains, airlines, store chains, and durable goods for consumers and business.

Investor experience over the years has been that less profit is earned from businesses that sell their goods by the ton or other bulk measure than from businesses in which an effective marketing organization places end products directly in the hands of users for current consumption. Marketing is more important than assets ownership in the generation of cash flow for a business. Not that it will work if you do not have something good to sell. Procter & Gamble soap must be excellent if it is to be pulled through retail stores by promotional effort. When Du Pont had new wonder fibers and plastic films, it put them across by merchandising. When the laboratories went dry, it kept going with merchandising innovations.

To some extent, new products are part of the marketing function. There have been some dramatic failures as well as successes in computing, for example, when the supplier did or did not understand what the customers wanted and would use. Several computer products put on the market were fashioned the way inventors and engineers thought interesting, but prospective customers were not consulted in sufficient depth.

Marketing effectiveness also has its hazards, as may be seen in the aircraft industry. The product is really a ride on an airplane, but the aircraft builders and their customers get more excited over new planes than do their riders. The first round of jets proved overwhelmingly popular, and the airlines and plane builders mutually snowed themselves with the prospects for continuing growth in riders at 15 percent a year. They thought they were capable of creating demand through merchandising, and in the 1960s they tapped a travel market that was ready and waiting to be served with jet flights. Once this market had been saturated, by about 1967, the aviation industry was unable to create new demand as fast as they had seats available.

Hotel chains require marketing as much as does the merchandise business. A comparison of room occupancy levels of Marriott Corporation hotels and competing chains during 1970 shows that Marriott had average occupancy 15 percent higher than Hilton and Holiday Inns. Each chain had sales people around the United States to solicit conventions and other patronage, but Marriott had three times as many salesmen relative to available rooms as did competitors — a vivid example of more adequate salesmanship to provide the patronage for cash flow in a capital intensive business.

Question 10.   Debt as Percent of Capital

Debt ratio has long been a subject of debate; many managers argue that a company's failure to grow is attributable to unwillingness to use borrowed capital to speed up growth. Debt as a temporary expedient may be productive, but the evidence is so overwhelmingly in favor of companies that operate with minimal debt that the negative rating applied to heavy borrowers in the quality measure may not be hard enough. Among growth companies, the real goers earn profits high enough to finance a strong rate of growth internally.

There is a widely propounded theory that capital structure leverage results in a higher rate of return on equity capital. The burden of proof is on those who hold this theory, and examples of earnings problems and disappointing growth are more numerous among highly leveraged companies, than among companies with little debt. It is easier to demonstrate that companies with little debt grow faster than comparable borrowing companies. Petrie Stores Corporation has grown some 20 percent a year with no debt and had cash in the bank equal to its whole earned surplus. Allowance in the measure is made for the normal debt ratios of utilities, albeit with growing skepticism. Short-term debt should be treated the same as long-term debt in capitalization when a company continues to borrow over several years. For instance, lessors of computing equipment must eventually obtain long-term financing proportionate to the current debt used to finance machinery on rental.

Question 11.   Persistence — Regular Earnings Gains Every Year For 10 Years

This measure, which may seem rough, was intended to give a break to the consistent earnings growth of certain electric utilities. Very few industrial companies are able to maintain a 10-year stream of earnings increases on a precise trend line. However, industrials can generate prodigies in the research department, whereas a growth utility really cannot do much about product development, since most of its research is supplied by General Electric and other equipment firms. But the utility can organize itself to derive a very even growth in earnings per share. Several companies, such as Texas Utilities, had the full score until clipped by the surtax in 1968, and several continued to warrant four points in spite of this tax. In recent years, I have become more impressed with the persistence measure as a guide in appraising younger growth companies; the good ones do not have earnings setbacks.

Question 12.   Dividend Payments and Quality

Investor acceptance of stocks depends in part on the record of dividend payments. In the judgment of investors, ability to pay dividends is evidence of some degree of financial accomplishment. While some people consider reinvestment of all earnings to be a more constructive use of profits, investors usually prefer evidence that a company can pay as well as grow.

Most prized are stocks that have a record of yearly dividend increases at a high rate — for instance, 10 percent or more a year. For such a record, investors usually pay a high premium as measured by current yield, which means that the dividend may be equal to under 2 percent on the market price. Prize examples of the high rate of dividend increase are the great growth stocks such as Avon Products, IBM, and Eastman Kodak. During a string of 15 years (1955-70), the dividend of IBM increased at 24 percent compounded. Avon Products pays about 70 percent of its profits in cash dividends and earnings, and dividends increased 17-18 percent a year.

Second is a group of regular dividend-paying stocks that make increases intermittently at 5-7 percent average growth rate. These stocks are valued for income, and the freedom from dividend cuts makes them competitive with bonds and preferred stock. Investors usually look at the growth factor plus the dividend yield as the expected total return. In other words, 5 percent growth plus 4 percent yield gives the theoretical return of 9 percent. Such stocks, in effect, provide returns comparable to market averages at a given time. Most of the time the stocks in this class sell at about the same total return basis of the whole market.

A large number of dividend-paying stocks have variable earnings and occasionally may fail to earn their dividends. Typical of this group are stocks with variable extra dividends. Usually, investors demand a higher current yield on such stocks than for the averages.

A short dividend record is most often evidence that the company became strong enough in recent years to keep up its growth and also pay dividends. As often as not, the prices of such stocks are determined by investor judgment about quality and growth potentials. Seldom is the yield competitive with income invest-ments. The dividend does enhance the value in investor eyes and is given some quality credits.

In the 1960s, many companies reduced the percent of earnings or cash flow paid in cash dividends. This reduction was most common in the computer office equipment field, where several companies became lessors of a major fraction of equipment delivered to customers. A declining payout means that the company's ability to pay is weaker for the time being. Such stocks rate in the middle classification.

Current dividend yields for a number of stocks usually are 2 percent to 3 percent higher than the concurrent yields of the majority of stocks. In such examples, the dividend usually is not safe because earnings are undependable or the payout is too large a portion of cash flow. (The quality scoring section shows the method of rating dividends.)

Market

Question 13.   *Volatility Measure*

When the price of a stock makes violent moves up and down, so that its low is only 50 percent of its high in a year, speculators are attracted and investors are repelled to some extent, thus making the stock unstable. If investors think the stock is speculative, there is an effect on its quality rating. (In 1971, professional investors began to use the term *beta* to describe volatility or price sensitivity. My 12-year-old method measures the factor about as well as the more popular technique.)

Question 14. Institutional Investor Acceptance

The information required in this measure is published in Standard & Poor's Stock Guide. In all, 1,800 institutional investors with published holdings are canvased, and both the number of holders and the number of shares held are shown in the *Stock Guide*.

Ownership of a stock by a large number of professional investors can lead to price stability. Pension funds, life insurance companies, and investment companies receive new money each year or at intervals during the year. It is their custom to buy stocks from an approved list on a dollar-averaging or timing basis. Such investors are willing to disregard cyclical fluctuations to some degree on the theory that the dollar-averaging method will compensate for recessions. Such buying must tend to stabilize the market. Performance-oriented large investors may destabilize a stock when a period of disappointing earnings impends or support it when restoration of the company's prosperity is probable.

The critical approach of institutional investors tends to influence prices in another way. It is normal for them to be aware of developments in companies sooner than most investors, and for that reason they act before a trend becomes evident to the public.

Quality Scoring

The factors described in this chapter are reduced to a single number to describe the quality of any stock we select, and the numbers will have valid comparability.

For each of the 14 measures, from 0 to 5 points are possible. Data concerning a stock is applied to each measure; the investor figures a value for each and finally totals the value for a quality score.

Measure	*Points*
1. Dynamism of industry versus maturity	
Industry growth in volume:	
10% a year	5
8% a year	4

Measure   *Points*

    6% a year 3

    4.5% a year.................................... 2

    3% a year 1

2. Stability preferred over cyclicality in sales of industry

    Gain in sales every year for the industry 5

    No sales decline in any year 4

    3% maximum sales decline in any year 3

    6% maximum sales decline in any year 2

    9% maximum sales decline in any year 1

3. Reputation with publishing services

    Strong regular growth industry 5

    Moderately irregular but generally dependable
       growth industry 4

    Consistent good industry 3

    Cyclical but growing or partly proven 2

    Erratic though mature or new and untested 1

4. Top management

    20 years uniformly good statistical performance 5

    10 years uniformly good performance 4

    Long adequate record, or hit high standard in last
       10 years 3

    Sustains industry position or reached high standard
       in last 5 years 2

    Record of capability just evidenced 1

5. Organization depth

    Operating organization is so well trained that
       company could go on for years with ineffectual
       top management 5

    Employs 10,000 people and had above-average
       profit rate over last decade 4

    Employs 10,000 people and had no operating loss
       in decade, or 20,000 but had trouble 3

    Employs 5,000 and had no loss, or employs 10,000
       and had loss 2

    Employs 1,000 and had no loss in decade, or employs
       5,000 and had loss 1

6. Product development impact on sales

    80% novel products from own research last 10 years . 5

    60% novel products of research in last 10 years 4

    60% advances in art or innovations 3

    80% improvements or merchandising innovations ... 2

    60% improvements or merchandising innovations ... 1

Measure   *Points*

7. Physical assets
    Unique revolutionary new process that works 5
    All modern and lowest cost in industry 4
    50% new last 7 years and equal to lowest cost 3
    In lowest cost one-half of industry 2
    Capable of profitable operations in any conditions .. 1
8. Earned on net worth
    Above 20% in each of 5 consecutive years 5
    Above 17% in each of 5 consecutive years 4
    Above 15% in each of 5 consecutive years 3
    Above 13% in each of 5 consecutive years 2
    Above 11% in each of 5 consecutive years 1
9. Cash plowback return
    At least 12% in each of 5 consecutive years 5
    At least 10% in each of 5 consecutive years 4
    At least 8% in each of 5 consecutive years 3
    At least 7% in each of 5 consecutive years 2
    At least 6% in each of 5 consecutive years 1
10. Debt as percent of capital
    No debt 5 years (30% for a utility) 5
    Under 15% debt 3 years (40% for a utility) 4
    Under 25% debt 5 years (50% for a utility) 3
    Under 25% debt 2 years (60% for a utility) 2
    Under 40% debt 5 years (70% for a utility) 1
        Debt equity position for banks:
        10% capital: deposits = no debt
        5% capital: deposits = 50% debt
11. Persistence of growth in EPS (10-year record)
    No year with less than 30% of 10-year average gain .. 5
    No year with less than 15% of 10-year average gain .. 4
    No year with earnings less than year before 3
    No year off over 10% from year before in earnings ... 2
    No year off over 20% from year before in earnings ... 1
12. Dividend record
    Long record, with annual increases averaging at
        least 10% a year for decade; some increase
        every year 5
    Long dividend record, with irregular increases
        averaging 10%, or yearly increases of less than 10% . 4
    Dividend record free of cuts and with average gains
        above 5%, not yearly, though 3

Measure	*Points*
Long dividend record but with little or no growth trend in dividend payments, or paid dividends for 5 years on rising trend	2
Long but irregular dividend record with no evident trend of growth; began paying dividends in last 3 years	1

13. Volatility of stock price
Volatility measure: Highest 1969-71 cash yield as
percent of lowest cash yield

Highest cash dividend yield 130% of lowest	5
Highest cash dividend yield 140% of lowest	4
Highest cash dividend yield 150% of lowest	3
Highest cash dividend yield 175% of lowest	2
Highest cash dividend yield 200% of lowest	1
No dividend	0

14. Institutional investor acceptance

400 holders or 2,000,000 shares	5
300 holders or 1,000,000 shares	4
200 holders or 500,000 shares	3
100 holders or 300,000 shares	2
50 holders or 100,000 shares	1

Quality Grade Limits

The stocks are divided into five quality grades for convenience.

Grade	Points
I	Above 50
II	43 — 50
III	34 — 42
IV	26 — 33
V	Below 26

About 60 percent of the stocks measured scored between 40 percent and 60 percent of the possible quality points (between 29 and 42), and 20 percent scored less than 29 points. Another 20 percent scored over 42 points, with a range up to 63 (IBM). Dividing these top stocks at 52, midway between 42 and 62, about 7 percent with the highest scores fall in Grade I and 12 percent in Grade II.

Our sample is weighted with larger companies or more dynamic lesser companies. If all stocks listed on exchanges were graded, the Grade V would be a much more numerous group, but the number of Grade I stocks would not change. There are very few highest grade stocks, but the combined market value of these superior stocks is very large. IBM alone was valued at $35 billion, which was comparable to the value of the whole Amex list in the spring of 1971.

The quality measurement gives enormous range on quality points. Numerous listed stocks score only one-fourth as many points as Kodak or IBM. Within Grade III, for example, the low end scores are only 80 percent of the top end. Whether a stock scores high or low within its grade should be considered.

Cutting grades at a point score, an arbitrary but necessary step, means that the top of Grade II, for instance, is closer to the lowest Grade I than to the lowest Grade II stock. As in all other areas in investment valuation, the market does not agree with objective ratings in a consistent manner.

Sample Scores

The lists of stocks in Tables 3-D and 3-E give a broad sample of quality scores so that you actually could conduct an investment program using this group and would be able to use all different quality grades.

TABLE 3–D
THE HIGHEST QUALITY

	Quality Measure														Total	Grade
	1	2	3	4	5	6	7	8	9	10	11	12	13	14		
IBM	5	5	5	5	5	4	4	5	5	3	5	5	2	5	63	I
Eastman Kodak . . .	4	5	5	5	5	3	3	5	5	5	4	5	3	5	62	I
Minnesota Mining																
& Manufacturing .	3	4	3	5	5	4	4	5	5	5	5	5	3	5	61	I
Coca-Cola	3	4	4	5	5	1	4	5	5	5	5	5	4	5	60	I
Avon Products . . .	3	5	3	5	5	2	4	5	5	4	5	5	3	5	59	I
Merck	3	4	3	5	5	4	4	5	4	5	2	5	3	5	57	I

These six stocks stand out from the rest of the list. It is noteworthy that they score most of the points on financial operations. Avoidance of cyclical environments is typical, and they benefit from institutional endorsement.

TABLE 3—E
Sample of Quality Ratings

	1	2	3	4	5	6	7	8	9	10	11	12	13	14	Total	Grade
								Quality Measure								
Dow Chemical . . .	3	4	3	4	5	2	4	2	4	0	1	4	2	5	43	II
Monsanto Chemical.	3	4	3	2	5	2	3	0	2	0	0	3	1	5	33	IV
Sterling Drug	3	4	4	5	4	2	3	5	4	4	1	2	2	5	48	II
Syntex	3	4	4	2	2	3	4	2	4	5	0	2	0	3	38	III
Kresge, S. S.	3	4	3	5	5	2	4	4	4	1	3	3	1	5	47	II
Penney, J. C..	4	4	3	5	5	1	4	4	4	1	2	3	3	5	48	II
Woolworth.	3	4	3	3	5	1	2	0	2	3	2	2	2	5	37	III
Hewlett-Packard . .	4	3	3	4	3	4	4	1	5	4	2	2	0	4	43	II
Motorola	3	1	3	3	4	3	4	0	3	2	0	4	0	5	35	III
Whirlpool	3	2	3	3	4	2	4	3	3	0	0	3	3	4	37	III
Boeing	2	0	1	3	5	3	0	0	0	0	1	1	1	4	23	V
TRW	3	1	2	4	5	3	3	2	3	0	1	1	2	4	34	III
Emerson Electric . .	3	2	3	5	4	2	4	5	4	3	4	4	2	4	49	II
General Electric. . .	3	2	3	4	5	2	3	1	3	1	0	2	2	5	36	III
Raytheon	3	2	2	4	5	3	3	2	3	1	0	3	1	5	37	III
Texas Instruments .	2	3	3	5	5	5	4	1	3	1	0	3	0	4	39	III
Kennecott	1	0	1	2	3	0	3	0	0	1	0	1	0	5	17	V
National Steel	1	1	1	2	5	1	3	0	0	0	0	1	4	5	24	IV
Burlington Industries	1	1	1	3	5	2	3	0	0	0	0	3	2	5	26	IV
Atlantic Richfield. .	2	4	3	4	4	1	2	0	1	0	2	3	0	5	31	IV
Gulf Oil	2	4	3	3	5	1	2	0	1	1	2	1	2	5	32	IV
Louisiana Land & Exploration. . . .	3	4	4	4	2	2	4	5	5	3	4	4	1	5	50	II
Texaco	2	4	3	3	5	1	3	2	3	3	2	3	2	5	41	III
Dome Petroleum . .	4	5	2	2	1	3	3	2	5	1	0	0	0	5	33	IV
Imperial Oil	3	5	2	4	4	3	3	1	0	3	2	3	2	5	40	III
Automatic Data. . .	5	5	2	5	3	3	4	5	5	4	5	0	1	3	50	II
Planning Research. .	5	3	1	3	2	3	3	2	4	0	0	0	0	2	28	IV
Black & Decker . . .	3	2	2	5	4	3	4	4	3	0	5	4	3	4	46	II
Caterpillar Tractor .	3	2	2	4	5	3	4	2	1	2	0	4	2	5	39	III
General Foods	2	4	3	3	5	3	4	3	2	1	3	4	4	5	46	II
Procter & Gamble. .	2	4	3	5	5	2	4	2	3	4	5	4	4	5	52	I
Standard Brands . .	2	4	3	4	4	1	3	1	2	0	5	4	2	3	38	III
International Tel. & Tel.	3	4	3	3	4	2	3	5	5	0	5	4	1	5	47	II
Simplicity Pattern .	4	5	3	4	2	2	4	5	5	5	5	3	2	2	51	I
American Can	2	2	3	2	5	1	3	0	0	0	0	2	4	4	28	IV
Continental Can. . .	2	2	3	4	5	1	4	2	3	2	2	4	2	5	41	III
American Broadcasting	3	3	2	2	3	1	3	0	1	0	0	1	1	5	25	V
Walt Disney	3	4	2	4	3	3	4	1	5	1	3	0	4	38	III

(Continued on next page)

TABLE 3–E *(Continued)*

	Quality Measure														Total	Grade
	1	2	3	4	5	6	7	8	9	10	11	12	13	14		
Bank of America . .	3	4	3	3	5	2	3	2	2	0	4	2	5	5	43	II
First National City .	2	4	3	4	5	2	3	1	1	2	4	4	4	5	44	II
Burroughs	5	5	5	5	5	4	4	2	5	0	2	2	0	5	49	II
Control Data	3	2	3	2	4	2	4	0	0	0	0	0	0	5	25	V
Honeywell	4	4	4	4	5	3	4	1	5	0	0	3	0	5	42	III
Chrysler	1	0	1	1	5	1	3	0	0	1	0	1	0	5	19	V
General Motors . . .	1	0	1	4	5	2	3	0	0	4	0	1	4	5	30	IV
Purolator.	2	3	2	4	3	2	4	5	5	0	4	3	2	1	40	III
American Express .	3	4	3	5	5	2	3	5	0	5	5	5	2	4	51	I
Howard Johnson . .	2	4	2	4	4	2	4	1	5	4	2	1	1	4	40	III
Carrier	3	3	3	3	4	3	3	0	0	1	2	2	4	5	36	III
Georgia-Pacific . . .	2	1	3	3	4	2	4	2	0	0	1	3	2	5	32	IV
U.S. Gypsum	1	1	1	1	3	1	2	0	0	4	0	1	3	5	23	V

Appendix lists 200 quality ratings.

4

Debt, a Quality Defect

ALTHOUGH business school students are taught that the stockholder should benefit when borrowed money is used to increase the assets working for him, the record shows that most of the time long-term debt is bad for stockholders. It is not easy to provide absolute proof for this statement, particularly when theoretical statistics can demonstrate that the opposite conclusion is more probable, but the examples used in this chapter will show that the tendency among established companies is to build white-elephant assets with borrowed money.

There are, of course, good examples of smaller companies built on credit, and they seem to contradict the argument against debt. However, the records of listed stocks do not show the small companies that never made the grade with borrowed capital. A further problem is that even when debt is used to an advantage, the stock price suffers.

The quality measurement is predicated on the theory that the companies that prosper with no debt are those that undertake only the most promising projects, and that the concentration of attention on fewer *good* things nets more profit. Borrowers often acquire more stores, factories, airplanes, or products than they can exploit. Often, they invest in diversifications with debt. Somehow the new area can look easier than the established business for which they would be reluctant to borrow. Many companies believe that they should attempt to supply all the goods that can be sold in boom years, and they borrow to expand capacity. They usually end up with new plants coming on-stream just as business turns down.

The Effect of Excess Debt

The American economy generates enough business and personal savings to finance its growth. Most mature nonregulated industries have enough cash flow to build all the plants they really need. When established industries add a lot of borrowed capital, they create excess capacity and divert capital from where it is really needed, as the following examples show.

Boeing

Boeing's experience with debt is easy to follow. Until the late 1950s it had no debt and earned over 20 percent on capital. In 1958, it borrowed $70 million, and profits slumped; the percent profit on net worth also collapsed. When debt reached a temporary peak, in 1963, profits hit a low for the 1960s. As the percent of debt declined, profits came back. In 1966, Boeing went heavily into debt to 45 percent of capital, and in the next 3 years profits declined 85 percent after a short-lived uptilt. In 1969, debt again went to 44 percent, and profits disappeared. Whatever the excuse may be made for the Boeing 747, it was financed with borrowed capital and destroyed Boeing stockholders' market value.

In all probability, had The Boeing Company never borrowed money it still could have delivered aircraft at a pace that would have been sufficient for the airlines.

Pan American World Airways

For the investor, Pan Am's aggressive use of borrowed capital has proven useless. In only a handful of years were profits really good. The growth in the business could have been handled with moderation and less debt so that stockholders might have

TABLE 4—A
BOEING COMPANY

	Debt as Percent of Capital (%)	Net Income ($ millions)	Earned on Capital (%)
1955	0	30	25
1956	0	32	22
1957	0	38	21
1958	26	29	12
1959	25	12	6
1960	23	25	9
1961	20	36	12
1962	19	27	9
1963	29	22	7
1964	27	45	12
1965	21	78	18
1966	45	76	10
1967	39	84	9
1968	36	83	9
1969	45	10	4
1970	44	22	5
1971	41	23	5

TABLE 4—B
PAN AMERICAN WORLD AIRWAYS

	Debt as Percent of Capital (%)	Net Income ($ millions)	Earned on Capital (%)
1954 . . . . :	30	10	9
1955	32	10	7
1956	39	14	8
1957	40	8	6
1958	55	5	3
1959	64	8	3
1960	69	7	4
1961	67	9	6
1962	64	15	7
1963	53	34	13
1964	53	37	10
1965	52	47	11
1966	53	72	11
1967	58	66	9
1968	59	49	7
1969	65	def. 26	2
1970	70	def. 48	1
1971	71	def. 46	1

enjoyed more lasting growth. Instead, the very survival of the common stock investment was threatened in the early 1970s.

Trans World Airlines

Stockholders of TWA can only beg for mercy; they have been used simply as a borrowing base for management's meglomania. Whenever the prosperity of the airline business permitted this volatile company to get some profits from past gambles, TWA again plunged for a borrowing spree, wiping out profits. Although the big years have been exhilarating for stockholders, subsequent capital spending orgies have promptly wiped out the illusion of prosperity.

TABLE 4–C
TRANS WORLD AIRLINES

	Debt as Percent of Capital (%)	Net Income ($ millions)	Earned on Capital (%)
1954	22	10	14
1955	34	5	6
1956	49	def. 2	–
1957	36	def. 2	1
1958	38	def. 2	1
1959	22	9	8
1960	64	7	3
1961	76	def. 15	1
1962	80	def. 6	4
1963	74	20	10
1964	69	37	12
1965	55	50	13
1966	59	30	8
1967	62	41	7
1968	63	22	5
1969	68	20	4
1970	73	def. 64	–

Competitive Pressures

During the 1960s, chemical manufacturers were big capital spenders. As a group, they plunged into debt, and everyone was affected.

In this group, the most aggressive borrowers did have bigger sales gains; Celanese, for example, raised a major part of its capital through convertible debentures. However, the gain in

TABLE 4–D
HISTORIES OF SIX MAJOR CHEMICAL MANUFACTURERS
($ millions)

	Funded Debt		Net Income		Sales	
	1962	1970	1962	1970	1962	1970
Celanese Corp. . .	$ 113	$ 550	$ 28	$ 52	$ 317	$1,035
Dow Chemical. . .	126	950	73	131	926	1,915
Hercules	0	203	31	50	455	799
Monsanto Co. . . .	361	602	78	78	1,063	1,971
Rohm & Haas . . .	0	37	24	25	261	455
Union Carbide	457	990	160	160	1,631	3,026
	$1,057	$3,332	$394	$496	$4,653	$9,191
Percent of Change		+215%		+24%		+98%

per-share profits at only 20 percent was not in proportion to the overall gain. Everyone's profit margins suffered somewhat. In 1970, Dow had a $29 million loss on its synthetic fiber joint venture, Dow Badische, which is not reflected here. Deducting the $29 million loss, Dow should have reported $102 million profit and the 6-company group $457 million, reducing the gain to 16 percent.

The chemical industry is an integral part of the United States economy, and it illustrates the effects of excessive capital spending. In this example, we see the effects from both overestimating future markets and attempting to increase share of markets by expansion in established product categories. During the 1960s, this group raised debt from 18 percent of capital to over 35 percent and contributed to an overheated boom and the subsequent recession that shows in the 1970 figures. The chemical industry generates enough cash flow to finance its growth, and there a big increase in debt inevitably leads to overexpansion.

Carl Gerstacker, Chairman of Dow Chemical, had been an aggressive exponent of debt to finance a growth effort, and Dow came out relatively better than the industry. Yet, Dow consistently fell short of its profits targets between 1962 and 1970. Moreover, Dow contributed to industry excess capacity and also encouraged others to follow its lead in borrowing.

Texas Instruments

Texas Instruments does not depend greatly on borrowed capital, but it would have been better off with *no* borrowed

$ millions

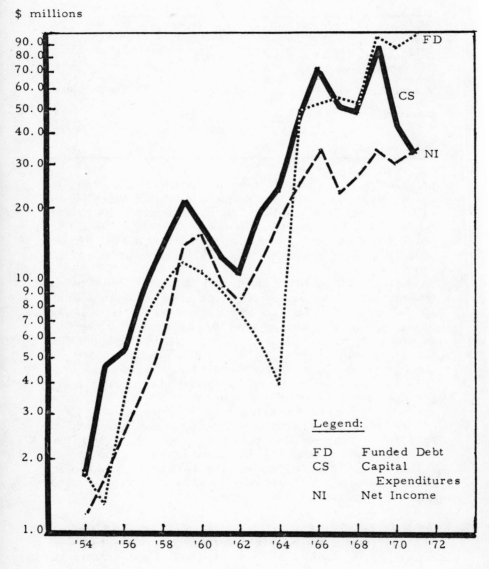

Figure 4-1

capital. Records indicate that Texas Instruments tends to borrow or raise equity capital in the middle of a prosperous period and thus overexpand; it doubled capital spending in 1959 and watched earnings slump until five years later. In 1965-66, years of buoyant prosperity, Texas Instruments took the capital spending plunge again and through 1971 had not yet achieved earnings equal to 1966. Debt and spending were accelerated in 1969, and in 1970 Texas Instruments spent the year pulling in its horns. Fortunately, it had good control and managed to increase cash by $60 million. By the end of 1971 it had $180 million in cash, confirming that it had raised more capital than needed.

McLean Trucking and Roadway Express

These two companies have had substantial growth since the mid-1950s. Roadway used debt in its early years but steadily reduced its dependence on debt in the 1960s. McLean has remained consistently aggressive in the use of borrowed money. The return-on-capital record shows that Roadway always achieved higher profit rates on capital, confirming that the low-debt companies are usually more profitable and do not need to borrow. In 1970, McLean suffered from the recession with a 30 percent profit setback, while Roadway improved on its growth trend and ran away from McLean in 1971. Thus, without debt dependence Roadway has managed to cut back the effect cycles can — and usually do — have on debt-dependent companies (McLean).

TABLE 4–E
MCLEAN TRUCKING AND ROADWAY EXPRESS

	Percent Earned on Total Capital									
Roadway..	15	14	16	16	21	21	20	16	17	23
McLean...	10	13	9	9	14	13	13	14	12	15
	Debt as Percent of Capital									
Roadway..	48	45	36	40	23	6	2	2	1	0
McLean...	38	33	47	74	63	68	63	56	51	48
	1954	*1956*	*1958*	*1960*	*1962*	*1964*	*1966*	*1968*	*1970*	*1971*

Net Income $ Millions

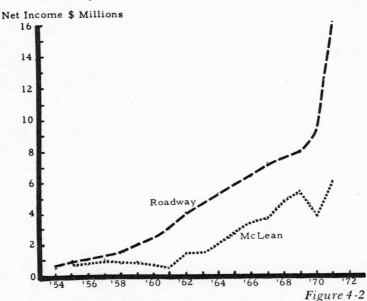

Figure 4-2

Debt Expansion and Change in Business

The previous examples showed cases of business becoming less profitable after debt expansion. In the case of Dome Petroleum, an oil- and gas-producing company that was nearly self-financing through plowed back cash flow was transformed into a heavy borrowing company that had greatly altered its business. The 10-year record from the 1970 annual report is shown in Table 4-F.

In the late 1960s through 1970, although gross income increased, cash income after interest stopped growing, and net income actually decreased. In 1970, extraordinary items were $2 million, and long-term debt tripled in those years. The item "Additions to plants, pipelines, and related facilities" represented expenditures on the construction of plants to process gas and oil and for transportation of products. By 1971, almost half of the capital investments were in facilities other than those concerned with oil and gas production. In earlier years, the company had been successful in oil and gas discovery and production, and most of its investments were in that area.

The other items in capital expenditures relate to oil and gas production, and they continued in amount about equal to the cash income shown. Expenditures concerned with land seem to indicate a big increase in acreage compared to cost; the bulk of the acreage increase was in the Arctic Islands, where the prices are low. Acreage in active oil and gas production areas is more valuable. Over the period, oil and gas reserves increased satisfactorily. Discovery of supplies tends to come in surges. Confidential reserves in the Zama Field of Alberta, first disclosed in 1969, constituted the bulk of the increase in reserves shown near the end of the decade, and it does appear that Dome was in a dry period. The Zama discoveries were made in 1966 and 1967.

Analysts are faced with the problem of forecasting whether the change in the company's business, represented by the big fixed assets additions, will lead to a new profits expansion.

The balance sheet and the source and application statement show more of the picture. The last item for 1969, "Current assets and liabilities," indicates that Dome Petroleum had no

TABLE 4–F
DOME PETROLEUM
($ millions)

	1961	1962	1963	1964	1965	1966	1967	1968	1969	1970
Gross income . .	8.0	10.2	12.2	13.7	15.2	17.8	21.8	24.6	23.6	28.6
Cash income after interest	4.3	6.3	7.6	8.7	9.0	9.7	12.1	14.5	12.8	13.1
Net income . .	1.7	2.2	3.4	4.1	5.8	6.4	8.4	10.0	8.4	8.0
Long-term debt .	18.9	13.1	14.5	18.1	21.3	23.4	29.3	38.2	42.6	74.4
Additions to plants, pipelines, and related facilities	.5	3.3	1.8	1.8	4.1	1.8	4.9	4.1	14.0	30.9
Exploration, development, and land rental costs	2.9	5.0	5.7	5.3	7.7	9.2	12.9	10.5	10.5	5.7
Net acreage held (millions) . . .	3.5	4.0	4.2	4.2	3.8	5.2	11.0	15.9	19.1	17.2
Land acquisitions cost ($ millions)	.8	1.8	1.0	5.6	.9	2.5	3.6	3.7	4.3	2.3
Estimated liquid reserves (millions barrels)	52	45	48	51	54	59	62	73	117	114
Estimated gas reserves (trillions cubic feet) . . .	.8	.8	.8	.8	.8	.9	1.0	1.1	1.2	1.3

working capital at the end of 1968 and that a year later current liabilities were $12 million greater than current assets. Bank loans went up $9 million, and current maturities of long-term debt rose $4 million.

When a statement says "working capital decreased," the natural assumption is that there was extra cash to be drawn on. In this example, the $12 million cash flow is less than the short-term debt, and there is no spare cash. Dome Petroleum clearly needed long-term capital just to fix up its balance sheet. In 1970, it added $32 million to its debts. To drill the extra wells and to provide pumps, storage, and pipelines, a producing oil and gas company in Canada requires more money than the amount needed to discover oil.

At the end of 1970, Dome Petroleum had gross property of $204 million (gross property is fixed assets at cost). In the first 6 months of 1971, cash flow had increased to a $17 million annual rate, 8.5 percent of the fixed assets. Because some money must be spent to replace oil and gas extracted, we cannot assume that all of this cash plowback is available for growth. Dome was not generating cash flow sufficient for its expansion.

There are certain rules of thumb for valuing reserves. I usually apply a 10 percent discount to the projected receipts over the 15 to 20 years when the primary reserve would be produced. Primary reserve is what oil engineers say can be produced through flow and pumping. With stimulation techniques, the ultimate production is more than the primary reserve; the 10 percent discount could be marginal, but such reserves can be sold to other oil companies on this basis. With a 10 percent discount, reserves would have present values of 75 cents a 42-gallon barrel for oil and 5 cents a thousand cubic feet for natural gas. On these measures, the values of Dome reserves were as shown in Table 4-G.

TABLE 4–G
DOME RESERVES VALUATION–1970
($ millions)

Oil	$ 88
Gas	65
	$153
Net investment in oil and gas properties	$ 78
Difference	$ 75

The reserves of oil and gas are actually marketable at such values, and the borrowing capacity is in proportion. Adding the $75 million to the $167 million net property figure gives a total of $240 million to carry the $92 million of short- and long-term debt. These figures also indicate that Dome Petroleum has more tangible assets than it is getting an adequate return from to support its assets structure. On operations, it had declining profitability.

In this example, it can be said that the company has ample assets and cash flow to assure its solvency but that the internal cash flow generation will not support the targeted growth rate. Thus the question arises: Will, at some point, the stockholders' equity have to be diluted to bring off the desired growth?

An optimistic stock price can work two ways: first, it limits the appreciation potential of the stock; second, it permits the management to raise money with small dilution of equity. In August 1971, Dome Petroleum stock had a $370 million market capitalization. In the previous year, its capital expenditures were about $26 million more than cash flow. It might therefore be able to raise $26 million through sale of 7 percent more stock and thereby increase book equity by 30 percent.

However, the $370 million market capitalization is greater than the $240 million value at which the company oil and gas reserves and property are appraised, and the appraised value can be raised only by placing a value on nonproductive acreage. In attempting to judge whether this move is sensible, we can look at the record for this stock in the early 1960s. In 1963, Dome Petroleum stock traded for about $15 a share and had a cash flow of $2.32 per share. In August 1971, the price was $110 and the cash flow about $4.80. The price increased 600 percent; the cash flow, 110 percent. Reserves of oil reported by the company had increased about 110 percent.

Thus, the cash flow is limited in proportion to the market capitalization it supports. Dome Petroleum has been altered to the point where we cannot forecast growth based on the record.

Spending Far above Cash Flow

The per-share data in Tables 4-H and 4-I are for the Marriott Corporation, hotel and restaurant operator. The data suggests that Marriott was extending itself.

In four years, the company went from capital programs fully covered by cash flow to triple cash flow in capital expenditures.

TABLE 4–H
MARRIOTT PER-SHARE DATA
(as of July 31)

	1965	1966	1967	1968	1969	1970	1971
Net income	0.40	0.47	0.52	0.62	0.72	0.86	0.99
Cash flow	0.61	0.87	0.95	1.19	1.40	1.69	2.04
Capital expenditure.	0.69	0.74	1.31	2.17	4.60	4.50	3.49

Of course, growth must be based on ability to raise considerable outside capital premised on optimistic projections of future profits from the new investments. The changes in capitalization are shown in Table 4-I. The radical change was that MHS

TABLE 4–I
MARRIOTT
($ millions)

	1965	1966	1967	1968	1969	1970	1971
Funded debt . .	$ 1	$ 31	$ 45	$ 76	$104	$131	$167
Net worth . . .	$ 26	$ 31	$ 41	$ 47	$ 66	$ 76	$127
Percent debt . .	4%	50%	53%	62%	61%	63%	57%
Shares (millions).	10.2	10.9	11.7	12.0	12.4	12.5	13.8

went into the hotel business: the debt includes lease purchase obligations.

There is no question about the growth's being intentionally generated. Because hotels are depreciated over decades, the depreciation rate went from 8 percent in 1964 to 4 percent in 1970. The question is whether we must judge a hotel operation's cash plowback in the same fashion as we judge most of a manufacturing business. Usually, the hotel operator can secure full financing for construction, and the depreciation is projected to pay off the mortgage; the operator is concerned only with getting a good return on operating capital.

Whether MHS succeeded can be seen in the changes in plowback rates between 1966 and 1970. In 1966, MHS had retained cash flow equal to 24 percent of gross assets. In 1970, the plowed-back cash flow was 10 percent of gross assets (including leasehold interests). Return on common equity was 18.5 percent in 1966 and 16.5 percent in 1970. The company might argue, properly, that there has been some growing-pains attrition in return on equity and that it actually speeded up the growth in cash flow per share by its use of capital leverage, but there is little excuse for the decline in cash plowback return; the ratio of cash flow to assets declined drastically.

In the 5 years 1966-70, inclusive, MHS had retained earnings of $38.5 million. Including a financing in the fall of 1970, it raised $59 million through sale of stock and convertible debentures. The number of shares issued or issuable went up 40 percent, but the financings amounted to 235 percent of book equity at the end of 1965. Effectively, book value per share increased 200 percent in 5 years instead of the 150 percent that would have arisen from retained earnings.

Situations like this fascinate security analysts because of the combination of velocity and hazards. No one who can analyze is under the illusion that he is dealing with a Xerox-like exclusivity and self-generating growth. The hotels and restaurants business is highly competitive; perhaps hustlers can play this kind of high-risk operation and carry it off.

The 1970-71 hotel market showed the hazards that had not at first hit the major chains. In February 1971, hotel occupancy was the lowest in percent of rooms rented since 1933. Analysis of trends in public travel showed that name chains had been growing at the expense of the older motels and hotels. In the meantime, a trend toward discount motels was under way. These appealed to regular travelers, who would go off the main road to save $8 to $10. Rate-cutting had not begun in earnest among hotels and motels, whose 1970 profits were sustained by rate increases, but it seemed inevitable that bankruptcies of hotels would see them convert to discounting just to cover mortgage payments and current operations.

Therein lies the real drawback with MHS-type growth. In the first two or three years of a new program, the company stock may rise in P/E ratio. In subsequent years, when the growth effort is fructifying, the trend in the P/E ratio may be downward. The enthusiasts who bid the stock up in the first place recognize that they do have P/E ratio risk and also that the pep-pill-energized growth may decelerate. In the meantime, the real early birds, including managers, peel off some stock whenever it gets strong.

Capital Cities Broadcasting (CCB)

CCB is a good example of high leverage combined with high

cash flow. CCB started as a television station owner, assuming obligations of $24 million in 4 years through 1961. Debt then stood at 85 percent of capitalization. In the 6 years through 1967, it had retained earnings of $23.5 million, raising net worth from $4.3 million to $27.6 million, at which point equity had improved from 15 percent to half of capital. In the same years, it had another $8 million of depreciation and $15 million of capital expenditures.

Profits plowed back averaged over 30 percent on stockholder capital during the years 1961-67. The total cash flow compared to total capital in the period gained from 11 percent in 1962 to 19 percent at the 1966 peak and averaged 14 percent over the 6 years. (Because CCB added a big goodwill factor to its balance sheet with television station purchases, gross fixed assets do not properly express assets at cost; total capital is assumed to have a figure closer to real cost of assets to CCB.)

In the 6-year period, earnings per share increased 29 percent compounded yearly. This company managed to grow almost 30 percent in profits while investing only half of its cash flow in new fixed assets. In a sense, it contracted to pay for assets it could not really afford, and it used the cash flow to pay for them.

CCB was so pleased with this performance that it decided to try again in 1968, when it bought Fairchild Publications, exchanging its convertible preferred stock for Fairchild. This type of transaction always complicates cash flow analysis because there is a goodwill item between the tangible assets pooled with the acquiring company assets and the market price of the stock traded.

CCB paid $10 million cash for 25 percent interest in Fairchild, and then gave Fairchild Publications stockholders preferred stock worth $36 million, based on the conversion value of the preferred stock in 1968. It pooled only about $8 million of net added assets from the exchange of shares. Its book capital at the end of 1969 was $80 million (including $24 million of debt). If one adds $28 million more to adjust for the market value of the stock traded for Fairchild, total assets at cost become $108 million (this figure, of course, does not appear anywhere on the books).

In 1970, the profits of Fairchild were down, and the cash flow of CCB was $12 million after a special charge of $1.9 million. The cash plowback was about 15 percent of assets on the balance sheets but only 11 percent on the $108 million used to adjust for actual cost. Although 1970 had been a grim year, CCB was still in good financial shape. It owed less money than in 1961, when debt was 85 percent of capital.

Unfortunately, the company was less profitable than it would have been without Fairchild Publications. In 1970, CCB contracted a $58 million television and radio station acquisition, Triangle Broadcasting, which would provide CCB with bigger television stations. The acquisition also increased CCB's debt by about $58 million. Quite possibly it was attempting to apply the bootstrap style of growth that had worked in a simple business to a more difficult, diversified operation that takes greater management skills. Its broadcasting operations have been good, but the diversification was unfortunate.

The Capital Cities example shows that although debt can be used successfully in acquisition of valuable franchises, such as broadcasting stations, a company can create problems for itself when it tries to translate the same growth method in acquisition of a production and marketing business, such as periodicals publishing, in which it has little experience.

Use of Capital Debt in Banking

Franklin National Bank (Long Island and New York)

Bank operations statistics show how capital is employed and what results are obtained. Franklin National Bank was the first banking company to raise capital other than common stockholder money. In 1962, it sold $20 million of preferred stock, and in 1963 it sold debentures, raising $30 million. The debentures became about one-fourth of the capital. In 1967, it acquired another bank through exchange of convertible preferred stock. After that, it had about half senior capital.

Franklin Bank had opened New York City branches, and its deposits and loans were growing at the rate of about 15 percent a year. Between 1963 and 1970, Franklin about doubled its net income per share — not quite up to its growth rate in the decade before when it had only common stock equity. Although Franklin made progress that management said was in line with its objectives, the stockholders interests were not well served. The middle price for Franklin in 1962 (bear market year) was $42, and its price at the end of March 1971 was $42.

Growth was accomplished by adding loans that gave a lower profit margin than Franklin had earned before it expanded into New York City. During the period from 1963 to 1970, the major

TABLE 4–J
FRANKLIN NATIONAL BANK
($ millions)

	1963	1970
Gross income (interest, fees, etc.)	$55	$217
Net income from operations	$11	$ 26
Income tax rate	24%	7%
Operating income as percent of gross income . . .	20%	12%

New York banks maintained or increased their operating profits before taxes at a rate in excess of 20 percent of income from loans. The earnings per share of the major banks as a group increased at least as much as did Franklin's earnings. Franklin did have a gain in rate of return on stockholder equity, but the gain was in proportion to the rest of the industry, which was prosperous in 1970.

It seems clear that Franklin used the senior capital as a base for carrying loans that just paid the cost of the senior capital. Its posture as a challenger in the New York City banking market meant that it had to take some marginal loan business. In the long run, its position in New York could prove to be worthwhile, but in the short run it did little for stockholders.

Apparently the market image of the stock suffered because investors assessed the increase in risks relative to common equity as a weakening in quality. Bank stocks usually trade at a consistent ratio of price to book value. While the ratios of price to book value for most bank stocks did not change much in the 1963-70 period, Franklin stock's ratio declined from about three times to one and three-fourths times.

The function of bank capital is to act as protection for depositors in the event that large loan losses might exceed reserves. In the period in question, Franklin doubled the dollars of loans per dollar of common equity from $8 to $18, so that loan losses of 6 percent of loans after exhausting reserves could have wiped out common equity. In the earlier year, it could have withstood 12 percent of losses before loans losses equaled equity capital.

While it is true that Franklin's aggressive program was accomplished with profits and dividend growth as good as the industry's, the combination of lowered profit margins and greater risk exposure must have contributed to the loss in market image for the stock. A 30 percent profits decline in 1971, attributable to loan losses, confirmed the market's skepticism.

Georgia-Pacific Corporation (GP)

Timberland-based companies with acquisition policies operate on a philosophy that part of the return to the owners will arise from a gain in value of the woodlands as a diminishing resource that replaces itself. It is further reasoned that if you borrow long term to purchase timber property, by the time the debt is due the property value will have kept pace with inflation. It is thought that over 20 years the property value should gain by 150 percent from inflation at 4 percent. Improved management of woodlands may help to keep the supply equal with the economy so that shortages do not become much of a factor in price progress. Since Pacific coast forests take 75 years to regrow, we must be reserved in enthusiasm about this theory.

Examination of GP's balance sheet for appraisal of the adequacy of depreciation and depletion reveals the obvious fact that nearly three-fourths of the fixed assets are factories, paper-mills, and distribution facilities. These assets cannot be assumed to increase in value as a result of inflation. Instead, because they are factors in the pollution of waterways they are subject to the requirement for added investment — for pollution control expenditures — to remain in operation.

According to GP's reports, depreciation was 4.5 percent of the gross plant account in 1966. Technically, this amount would recover the cost of the facilities in their lifetime. However, in 22 years it will take over twice as many dollars to replace the earning assets. GP attempts to outrun the problem by doubling its assets every five years, acquiring capital in the marketplace. GP carries off its plans relatively well; the main problem is that the company thereby becomes more vulnerable to the business cycle. In the 1960s, GP made its largest expansion in the paper industry, in which it previously had little experience, on the theory that paper would balance the cycles in wood products. Unfortunately, GP contributed to overexpansion in an industry that already had too much capacity and that proved vulnerable to recessions. Changes in balance sheet ratios between 1961 and 1966 show the inadequacy of the cash flow plowed back by GP to sustain growth.

The doubling of net income between 1961 and 1966 through use of leverage brought few complaints from stockholders.

TABLE 4–K
GEORGIA-PACIFIC
($ millions)

	1961	1966	Percent Change
Timber (net)	$120	$217	+ 80
Plant account (cost)	$263	$665	+155
Debt	$149	$418	+180
Common equity	$219	$378	+ 68
Debt percent of capital	38%	51%	
Sales	$350	$659	+ 85
Cash plowback	$ 44	$ 71	+ 60
Cash plowback return	9.5%	6.75%	
Earnings per share adjusted	$ 0.63	$ 1.31	

However, between 1966 and 1970 growth in earnings per share actually did slow down. In 1970, Georgia-Pacific profits declined about as much as the average of the forest products industry in the recession.

Georgia-Pacific has issued stock dividends at a 4 percent annual rate. The above figures are from the 1966 annual report and are not adjusted for the stock dividends; such adjustment would reduce 1966 EPS to $1.13. My assumption is that the 4 percent stock dividends were sold and treated as current return by stockholders.

TABLE 4–L
GEORGIA-PACIFIC
($ millions)

	1970	Percent increase over 1966
Timber (net)	$ 256	+ 18
Plant account (cost)	$1,332	+100
Working capital	$ 224	+ 49
Debt	$ 640	+ 53
Common equity	$ 659	+ 73
Debt percent of capital	49%	
Cash plowback	$ 155	+118
Cash plowback return	8%	
Earnings per share	$ 1.56	+ 19

In 1970, Georgia-Pacific had its first decline in net income since it emerged from obscurity two decades ago. There has been substantial progress with borrowed capital. When it was small, the debt helped the company bootstrap itself to the big time. Usually, problems crop up when a company continues to use debt aggressively after it has become larger.

Short-Term Debt for Financing Customers

The foregoing examples have been concerned mainly with the use of debt for acquisition of long-term assets. Many companies regularly carry substantial amounts of short-term debt to finance customer purchases. Most of the time the receivables so financed could be sold to banks or finance companies; the assets financed are actually liquid. The companies elect to carry their own accounts because they can make more profit that way. The interest rates are lower than would be charged if they sold the receivables.

Another type of customer financing is the rental and leasing, rather than the sale, of equipment. This practice is common in the office machinery industry, and in many instances the customers have not signed full payout leases; thus, the company uses short-term borrowing to finance long-term receivables. Usually, the supplier is able, if he wants, to sell the equipment to some sort of finance company, but he is often required to do so with recourse.

In examining statements, it is wise to determine the uses of the short-term debt. In working with computer stocks, short-term debt must be watched because frequently the debt will build up when the company is first delivering large numbers of a new model. One should check to see that maturing of the short-term debt declines when the customers have accepted the equipment. Often, a couple of years pass before the rental income begins to offset the debt.

5

Quality of Accounting:
When Should Profits
Be Recognized?

In 1970, the subject of corporate financial reports became a matter of great controversy. The purposes of this chapter are to explain the extremes in points of view about what should be called profits and to explain some of the accounting items that may conceal values or liabilities.

Questions in the Controversy

We could take the position that the only profits are the amounts of money available in the year for distribution as cash dividends. Until a decade ago, European corporations issued year-end statements that did say that the profits were about the same as cash dividends. They stated that reserves had been adjusted as shown on the balance sheets; however, they did not tell you what they had put in or had taken out of reserves.

The American-style corporate report attempts to tell the stockholder what profits were earned in cash from operations but were kept by the company for reinvestment in new plants and working capital. The statement indicates dollars that have been expended on buildings and machines, to increase inventories, and to carry larger accounts receivables for customers. The inventories presumably are valued at what they can be sold for, and the receivables are stated net of reserves for bad debts.

Up until about 1960, this was our understanding of the meaning of figures in financial statements. Sometime in the last couple of decades corporate managers, with some support from accountants, began to say that cash-only profit reporting did not allow for the expenses incurred in creating values that would contribute to future growth. A simple example is the payment of commissions to life insurance salesmen. In the first year of a new policy, the commissions paid in cash are equal to at least half of the premiums, but in later years such commissions are only 5 percent of premiums. Unless such expenses can be spread over the life of the premium payments, a fast-growing company is unduly penalized.

In the 1960s, some computer companies decided that the costs of getting a computer order should be spread over the years when the machinery was expected to be on rental. Then it was decided that if the profits from a new product were to accrue well into the future, costs of invention and design should be spread over the expected product life, and the development costs should be treated as capital investment on the balance sheet.

Oil companies are still another example of a changed accounting approach on development costs. These companies said that the costs of dry holes were really part of the investment in productive wells.

In 1970, some people began to propose a balance sheet item for human resources. Under this item, a company could capitalize training costs and amortize such expense during the years when trained employees would contribute to the company's progress.

The earnings reports of California savings and loan associations have been a long-standing curiosity. These companies report earnings *before* appropriations to reserves. By appropriating most of earnings to reserves, they can go on for years with most of their earnings sheltered from federal income taxes. They argue that their reserves will not be lost through bad debts and are employed to earn more profits for stockholders, but since they do not pay any dividends, the stockholders really have no evidence that the profits belong to them.

Recognition of Profits — Cash or Accruals

It is difficult even for analysts to find out whether the book figures for the assets, and the additions to or subtractions from them, are tangible figures or simply opinions *about* values. Many accounting practices are available simply to make a company look better in terms of reported profits; very few make it look worse than it is. Some reasons for using questionable accounting practices are: (1) the company management wants to enhance the price of its stock; (2) regulatory commissions insist on accounting that seems to justify inadequate rates for utilities and transportation companies; (3) loan provisions require maintenance of minimum working capital, which can be puffed up; (4) management does wishful thinking about bad receivables and slow inventory that should be written off.

Some questions about accounting methods are apparent on examination of a balance sheet. Others may have to be deduced from your own calculations and may even require detective work. A simple item is *capitalized development costs* for products not yet marketed, which appears frequently in reports of technology companies and computer software companies. Costs of developing programs are capitalized. To make anything out of these figures, you need to see the amounts of increase and the amortization. When the asset item grows rapidly, you should question if recent earnings are overstated because the asset may not really be worth its carrying value. If the write-off of capitalized intangible assets is equal to or greater than the new additions, at least current earnings are not overstated. Sometimes companies accumulate such assets for several years and then write them off in one swipe. Sometimes they want stockholders to think the loss was a sudden disaster rather than an accumulation of deferred expenses.

Accounting for Assets

Although book assets once were thought to be equivalent to liquidation values, accountants now argue that liquidation value is not realistic in describing the property, tangible or intangible, of a going concern. Their point is that while a healthy company could be sold as a whole (the buyer pays some amount at least equal to book value), the sale of the assets of an unhealthy company would almost surely realize less than the book value, however defined.

There are two extreme points of view on how the account books are to define the moneys that go into or come out of

fixed assets, and accountants will certify that a variety of
statements from both points of view are accurate. One group,
the conservatives, says that the only asset is the sum paid to
outside suppliers or principals for purchase of property or
equipment. Normally, however, there are makeready and start-up
costs in connection with new assets — such items as engineering
of products for production, trial runs on machinery, and preparation of manuals for use in the factory or sales department or at
customer locations. In the computer field, it is always necessary
to do some systems and program work prior to installation. The
supplier may fund this work, or the user may pay for it.

The items above are often thought of as the true cost of building
a capital asset and are recognized as such by liberal accountants.
Tax collectors recognize most of them as deductible. Certain
companies expense them currently, and some report to stockholders that there were unusual start-up expenses in a year when
earnings might look disappointing. The company that expenses
costs that are on the borderline between tangible and intangible
provides a fixed assets cost that is lower than other companies
might show. Because the inclusion of such items in the assets
cost make the profits greater, in such cases the book figure for
stockholder equity tends to be lower than when optional expense
items are capitalized.

Pooling of Interests

In a great number of mergers, the method that accountants
use to combine the financial statements of the companies
merged is called *pooling of interests*. In this method, the items
on the balance sheets are merged line by line. The separate
identities then disappear in the new statement, except that the
capital accounts will include items that were not on either
balance sheet before the merger.

The capital accounts will include shares of common stock or
preferred stock that were not previously part of the capital of
the larger company that survived the merger. In no case are we
likely to find that the balance sheet value for the newly
issued stock is the same as the market value of this stock at the
time it was accepted by the previous owners of the company that
was merged into the larger company.

In the Capital Cities Broadcasting (CCB) example in Chapter 4,
the preferred stock exchanged for stock of Fairchild Publications
had a market value of $28 million, based on its privilege to

convert into 900,000 shares of CCB common stock, which was worth $28 million at the merger date. The net worth of common stock of Fairchild was about $8 million, and this amount was added to the capital accounts of CCB. The $28 million is not indicated on the balance sheet.

Since CCB delivered $28 million worth of securities that could have been sold for at least 90 percent of the agreed value, why did they not show on the balance sheet that they paid that much? There are at least three reasons they did not.

One reason is that the accountants take the position that Fairchild had only the $8 million of net worth that appeared on its balance sheet. If the acquiring company wants to show the additional $20 million, it must carry it as goodwill, an item considered intangible. Most people think goodwill should be written off over a period of years. However, the Internal Revenue Service refuses to admit such write-offs as deductible expenses before taxes. Even if CCB had paid $28 million in cash, the IRS still would not let it amortize the assets of Fairchild based on a cost higher than the original cost.

Another reason the acquiring company may not want to show the acquisition via stock at market price is that it would create a much higher book value for its common stockholder equity. Since it probably paid a market price equal to perhaps 15 times earnings (equivalent to an earnings yield of 6.666 percent), its rate of return on stockholder equity would be much lower than it previously had been earning on the book value of stockholder equity. It would appear to have made an inferior investment.

When the merger is made through exchange of preferred stock, usually convertible, managements consider that using the market value of the stock exchanged as the book value would cause a distortion. Some analysts, including Value Line (an investment rating service), take the position that the common stockholder equity has been reduced by the amount by which the value of the preferred stock exceeds the book equity of the acquired company. Sometimes the indenture of the preferred stock provides that it shall have a liquidating value about equal to the value it represented in the exchange. In the pooling of interest method, the acquiring company gives the preferred stock a stated book value small enough so that it will not reduce the common stockholder book value before the merger.

For instance, Tenneco issued 4,342,574 shares of $5.50 cumulative convertible preference stock, with a stated value of $25 per share and a liquidating value of $100 a share. It carried the preference stock at $108 million, although it was issued with an asserted value of $434 million for the Kern County Land Company. Tenneco takes the position that the preference stock ultimately will be converted into common and that it would not be realistic to show it at liquidating value.

American Brands has a different view of the goodwill question. In 1970, it made several acquisitions, and its annual report says: "Intangibles resulting from business acquisitions are comprised of brands and trademarks and cost in excess of net assets of businesses acquired, including $347,855,000 related to principal acquisitions in 1970. The intangibles are not being amortized, as they are considered to have continuing value over an indefinite period." Since all the acquisitions were accounted for as purchases, American Brands was compelled to show the goodwill because the accountants would not certify it any other way. If the company proposed to amortize the goodwill, it would be saying that it overpaid for the acquisitions. The company segregates profits by category, and it will be possible for investors to judge the success of the 1970 acquisition program.

Investment analysts are divided in their opinions about pooling of interests accounting. My attitude is that cash profits are the best measure of performance. If the companies can pay more dividends because of acquisitions, they will have proved their worth.

Defective Foreign Earnings

Numerous American companies report profits that are earned in low tax jurisdictions — Puerto Rico, for instance. Offshore drilling platforms operated overseas are usually owned by corporate subsidiaries in countries such as the Bahamas and Panama. The newest gimmick is to assign patent rights and royalties to subsidiaries in low-tax countries. These profits cannot be brought back to the United States without payment of income taxes to bring the total payments up to U. S. rates. The companies argue that as long as they are expanding overseas they can invest the money to promote even greater growth.

In practice, numerous companies find themselves long of cash overseas and short of cash in North America. Their excess cash is usually in dollar deposits at interest, but they often have to borrow at higher interest cost in the United States to fund their requirements. Technically, the profits are not overstated, but if we regard profits as funds available for payment of dividends, the reported earnings are exaggerated, if not overstated.

Earnings on oil production in Arab countries are taxed at higher rates than those in the United States; so there are no restrictions on repatriating such earnings. Curiously enough, American investors have been worried about the profits in the oil countries more than they have been about the eventual tax liabilities of the sheltered earnings.

Drug stocks comprise a group that has used tax shelter gimmicks actively to speed up profits growth, and the market has honored them by raising the P/E ratios as the quality of earnings has gone down. In short, investors should be aware that a lot of profits earned overseas really are not available to American stockholders.

Expense Deferrals

We have already seen that some life insurance companies as well as equipment renting companies consider that the marketing cost in the first year of a policy or rental contract really applies to future years as well as to the first year. Therefore, they set up part of such sales cost as an asset. It may be buried as an investment in the rental equipment account or as a noncurrent receivable. The profits created by these expense deferrals really do not exist in cash that can be invested in new assets.

Large numbers of substantial corporations have fixed assets whose costs are at least as great as the sales of the year. The fixed assets wear out, and some charge against sales must be made to repair or replace the machines, vehicles, and so on. Most companies must spend money on methods and systems to use the machines, and they also have money tied up in equipment that is being prepared to do work but is not yet in use. Most companies are trying to grow; in consequence, every year money is tied up in preparation of new facilities.

Depreciation

Depreciation is a much-debated subject among companies that have a high ratio of fixed assets to sales: electronic data processing firms, electric utilities, oil producers, real estate operators, airlines and railroads, pipelines, telephones, mining, and checmical processing.

Depreciation is a material cost factor when assets and capital are greater than revenues. In typical utilities and transportation companies, $2-4 of capital are required to provide a year of revenues. In the computer business, $1-1.50 of new equipment is needed to generate $1 of revenue. In oil production, the ratio may be $3-4 to $1. The depreciation factor is the reason we spend so much time in examining cash flow of corporations with large assets, particularly the ones with debt.

In theory, depreciation is intended to recover only the cost of assets. However, in an inflationary economy recovery of cost is insufficient. When the purchasing power of a dollar decreases by half every decade, the cost must be recovered very fast so that new assets can be bought with the money, and the new assets must be put to work long before the facilities being depreciated are worn out.

U. S. tax laws permit corporations to depreciate fixed assets on a declining basis; therefore, they can write off larger portions of cost in earlier years and smaller amounts later. Numerous companies use this provision for tax reporting but report to stockholders that the assets are being depreciated in even yearly increments.

Often, the assets to be amortized are development expenses for new products, designs, software, marketing costs, and so on. Occasionally, we find a statement that reads as follows.

Operating profit	$6,497,000
Depreciation and amortization .	987,000
Income taxes credit	189,000
Deferred income taxes	2,719,000
Interest cost	567,000
Net income	2,413,000

In this example, the company reported a loss to the Internal Revenue Service; it elected to capitalize certain expenses that were fully deductible. The balance sheet showed the following increases.

Prepayments	$1,925,000
Deferred charges	1,141,000

This company, Franklin Mint, was growing very rapidly and would not show much profit if it charged off all expenses as incurred. It had a big backlog of orders. There is an argument about whether it would be as misleading to show no profits as it would be to carry on with capitalizing of intangibles. The problem is that investors can be led to place excessive valuations on stocks.

Reports that include large amounts of deferred income taxes should be looked at skeptically. In many cases, the companies are unable to repeat the creative programs that originally may have justified the capitalizing of intangibles. When they repeat the process, they are likely to capitalize projects that do not pay off.

It is not unusual for new stock issues to be sold at prices that are based on earnings created by capitalizing deductible expenses. Companies obtain capital on terms that would be unacceptable to investors if only cash profits were reported.

For most companies, the practice of reporting earnings after straight-line depreciation when assets are written off on an accelerated basis usually increases earnings by no more than 10 percent. Therefore, if the deferred taxes in a year or the deferred tax reserve on the balance sheet is more than 10 percent of earnings or of earned surplus, respectively, the assets side of the balance sheet probably will contain some capitalized expenses that normally would be expensed. More often than not some of these items will have to be written down in a manner that penalizes future earnings.

Advantages of Fast Write-off Policies

The only reliable measure of profitability is return on capital. Therefore, if after decades in business a company, using the fastest practicable expensing of capital additions, enjoys a high rate of return on stockholder book equity, it *is* a moneymaker. Long-established growth companies traditionally have liked to expense as much as possible. A young company that has fast write-off policies and also has a high return on capital is almost always better than a young company that shows high profits as a result of a generous policy of capitalizing intangible additions to assets, even though, in theory, the difference in accounting method should not have much effect since there is just as much justification for one policy as for the other.

The benefit from rapid write-offs is more practical than theoretical. The manager who knows he must recover costs promptly and show profits, too, is more precise in his planning and decisions. The manager who knows he can carry intangibles as assets for years before being called to account tends to spend and build in a more easygoing fashion. The problem is not that the fellow with the long-deferred accounting does not bring along projects of great ultimate value, but that they are not of much value to stockholders who in the short run sacrifice earnings on capital that usually more than offset the long-term benefits.

Inventory Accounting

Extraordinary expenses or write-offs that explain the poor earnings reports more often than not are inventory write-downs of some kind. Inventory consists of new raw materials, parts from suppliers, parts and materials being worked on in the company facilities, and finished goods ready for delivery to customers.

Between the fresh raw materials and the finished goods on the dock and billed to the customer is much material of questionable value. Usually, such inventories are said to be priced at cost or market, whichever is lower. However, they are not given the market price that would be obtained if they were offered for sale in their partly finished condition. Their assigned value is their standard cost as part of finished goods.

Even the value of finished goods in the inventory may be questioned. A simple example is women's apparel: stock only six months old may be almost worthless. The new model turnover of technical products is such that what appear to be current goods really are not, because all sales for future delivery are of a version that has superseded the original model. The work-in-process inventory, usually includes a supply of components and partially worked material for the first model, which is of questionable value.

Because companies differ in their handling of bookkeeping for inventory, the problem is to estimate just how much inventory *actually* is useful and marketable. In theory, to be safe only two items should be carried as inventory: new materials in original packages, priced according to the supplier's current price list and carried as regular catalog items by the supplier; and items that are finished goods on vehicles ready to go to the customer. In practice, most companies cannot value those items simply, because the Internal Revenue Service will not stand for it (nor would stockholders, because they would not understand the long-run advantages); accountants argue that work in process should be carried at the cost that will be absorbed in finished goods.

Companies report total inventories, and we may have to measure the total as a number of days' sales. For manufacturing, inventories usually equal from 30 to 90 days' sales. Smaller relative inventories are normal for foods, chemicals, petroleum, drugs, and cosmetics; inventories tend to be large in machinery and tobacco. It is best to take an industry sample and see how a company compares with the sample. Changes in the ratio of sales to inventory are important, particularly where products are price-sensitive, as in electronics or metals.

Such is the nature of the U. S. economy that business cannot afford to hold goods very long. The money cost alone eats up annually about 8 percent of the value of anything in stock. Everything rusts, fades, evaporates, or gets stolen if on hand too long. Thus, inventory *should* be exactly the amount needed to fill customer orders and provide for smooth flow of production and distribution, but such accuracy, of course, is beyond the bounds of possibility. However, the most successful companies control inventories to the point where they have minimum inventory losses and write-downs. Nobody completely avoids inventory losses, but most organizations find that a clean inventory is favorable for active merchandising and that a slow-moving inventory is associated with a bogged-down sales effort. Efforts must be diverted from selling new products because of the need to get rid of the dogs.

Inventory obsolescence is a real problem. Manufacturing companies commonly make the bulk of profits on items that will be superseded by more advanced products within a year or so. Usually, the company personnel and customers are cognizant of the timing of product displacement by new models. The company sales department has mixed demands; it wants stock of the mature products so that it has something to sell, but it also wants to have the right to talk about the new line before it is really ready.

When a product line is going out of production, a company commonly builds a supply of spare parts. The transition between old and new models can cause inventory accumulation; auto makers, for example, always try to get a few more cars from the tools and dies that are written off.

A company management can specify quantities of inventory based on current sales volume by having the accounting department make monthly write-offs of the quantities of parts and finished goods that exceed some number of days' selling rate.

Department managers thus are forced to obtain good forecasts of catalog item sales rates and to control purchasing and production, which stops the practice of making a "few more items" because the machinery is set up.

This type of accounting control gets faster action because the manager is influenced to cut down supply as soon as sales decline; he does not wait to see if the decline is temporary. It is possibly the best way to force instant adjustment of stocks to sales. Texas Instruments uses this method, and in 1970 its inventory decrease was greater than the sales decrease for the year, even though sales for the first 6 months were higher by 14 percent.

Use of this method stops or restricts production of items for which orders are slumping but permits continuation of supplies of hot selling items as long as they stay hot. In some cases, of course, the method entails write-off of excess goods already bought or made, but managers make extra efforts to assure that they do not have to absorb such costs.

Well-controlled retailers use a similar control procedure. For instance, a fast-moving women's apparel retailer will attempt to turn over its stock about once a month.

Builders of large units of equipment, such as computers, nuclear plants, underground mines, and process plants, have an inventory problem in that their new models or projects encounter start-up problems, and a lot of money gets tied up in plant and materials. Analysis in the computer industry gives us some special accounting factors. For instance, IBM has a long history as a rental equipment firm. Sales of data processing equipment are almost exceptions. When it builds data products for rental, IBM charges all the costs directly to its assets account; so these items affect inventory only at the raw materials level. IBM has a small inventory for a business its size.

Competing companies, such as Burroughs and Honeywell, traditionally have been sellers of products, and rental sales are a modern development for them. Burroughs rentals were under a fourth of gross revenues, while IBM had over two-thirds of rental income. With big orders for large computers to be sold rather than leased, Burroughs built computers into inventory. During 1969 and 1970, Burroughs was to build about 40 of its Model 6500 super computers, which had an average value per system of about $3 million. This was a big shift in commercial product emphasis, and Burroughs was slow in completing the software programs that make the computers function. Its inventory account about doubled in two years, partly because it did not book sales until computers were accepted by customers. A further cause of inventory increase was the faster than expected buildup in production in new plants.

For a while, Burroughs' inventory account was a burden to it and a worry to investors. It was suspected that the company had a large increase in goods in stock that either were not in demand or contained serious defects. During the period until the inventory cleared up, the stock was in some disfavor.

Accrued Profits

Life Insurance

At the start of this accounting discussion, the recognition of profits was discussed. In general, it is correct to recognize a profit before it is available in cash if the company has an ironclad commitment to be paid specific cash receivables. In practice, most profits that are recognized before the cash comes in are based on experience rather than on contract.

In 1970, many life insurance companies began to report probable profits. The change followed years of discussion among security analysts, accountants, and companies in quest of a reporting method that would reflect the anticipated profits on policies sold in the year subject to report. In the late 1960s, the three groups agreed on methods that would be acceptable to accountants and the SEC.

Life insurance, annuties, and most other policies bear the expense of agents' commissions mainly against the first premium paid by the policyholder. Insurance regulators require statutory operations reports that show commission payments fully charged against current operations. Since life insurance companies grow, the first-year commissions tend to depress profits year after year. Security analysts and some companies argued over the years that the first-year balloon payment to the agents should be spread over the years when the policyholders would be paying premiums. For instance, if policyholders normally pay premiums for an average of seven years before the policies lapse, one can say that the sales expense should be prorated over the seven years or at least a major part of the period. By capitalizing and then amortizing sales commissions, the reported life insurance profits can be 200 percent higher; earnings might be $6 million instead of $2 million.

Twenty years ago most life insurance companies wrote only life policies, and investors understood that growth suppressed profits. Today, however, most companies combine life insurance with other insurance and financial activities, and their reported profits would dwarf life insurance profits unless the companies reported as described here.

Computers

The growth of business equipment rental has meant a big increase in sale of machines to leasing companies for the purpose of recovering cash. One problem in making such sales has been that the manufacturers do not have full payout lease contracts from the customers. Some companies, wanting to show profits on the equipment at the time it is first rented to customers, set up affiliated leasing companies to which they would sell machines. The leasing companies raised capital as separate corporations, although in some cases the manufacturer provided some form of guarantee of the leasing company's debt.

In 1970, accountants took a more conservative view of profits that could be booked on sales when the vendor did not have iron-clad contracts to be paid the full sales price of goods or services. In one prominent case, auditors refused to certify Memorex Corporation profits that were based on sales to an affiliated leasing company.

For decades, automobile companies have financed sales of cars and trucks through captive credit companies, but these companies extend credit on only part of the purchase price when the buyer assumes obligation to pay off the loan. This is the difference between the contract to pay out the price and the lease contract that does not provide for 100 percent payout. Cash profits are better than profits based on assumptions that customers will lease equipment long enough to pay at least as much as the sales price, or will continue to pay premiums on policies for a number of years equal to past experience — or that dry holes are part of investment in good wells. We can say that we have a paper profit, but if we do not realize it in cash, there is no real profit.

Financial statements *should* show how much cash profits were realized in cash. If a company has spent a lot of money in favor of future growth, analysts can project a high growth rate and offer a premium in terms of stock price ratio to allow for the investment. The companies should not *pretend* to have achieved future goals by exaggerating recent expenditures to reach the goals.

Profits

Doubtless the stockholders and managements will feel happier to see $2 instead of $1 per share of reported profits. But unless these profits are real, managements still do not have the money in the form of cash profit to invest in new assets or to pay dividends — the acid tests. The numbers make us feel good, but we cannot *use* the value for anything constructive. Analysts used to adjust earnings upward; now they question whether accounting is too generous.

Regulated Industry Profits — Utilities, Telephone, Airlines, Railroads

The industrial entrepreneur who believes in expensing any kind of intangible cost would be hard put to show profits in regulated industries. In general, product development-type businesses try to price their up-to-date goods high enough to get fast returns of previous expenditures. Later they let prices go down at a pace that permits about the same return on written-down net assets.

In the regulated industry, the commissioners make the companies handle their accounts in a way to make current costs as low as they can in order to justify minimum rates to customers. For instance, even the interest on capital tied up plants under construction is added to fixed assets. Then they allow 40 years or more to write off plants. The management of a regulated business is inhibited from making risky expenditures for the future because they may not be allowed as costs of providing the service.

In the long run, though, the regulators must approve rates for service that permit sufficient revenues for the company to pay for its capital. Some regulated businesses are cyclical (airlines and railroads) and are in competition with other companies. While the approved rates may be sufficient when each company has all of the business on certain routes and can supply the exact amount of service required (in practice, transportation companies are in competition over most of their route structures and must offer more service than is needed because of competitive factors) often these rates will not be sufficient.

How does one assess profitability, then?

Most investors will not have time to puzzle out all of the intricacies of accounting practices; so some shortcuts must be used to help us see whether the companies being studied are prudent in their accounting practices. Here are two truisms.

1. The company that wants us to believe that it has put together a structure of high value in terms of assets bought with capital, and retained earnings will show maximum dollars on its balance sheet for assets owned.

2. The company that believes in showing low carrying values on its balance sheet, for assets owned will have low numbers.

The data in Table 5-A relates plowback of earnings and depreciation to assets growth. "Retained cash flow as percent of net assets" is the easiest measure to get from an annual report. The purpose of this sample is to show that regulated companies are less profitable in terms of retained cash flow than are standard industrial companies. I prefer to work with fixed assets at cost, but these data give a good comparison. Low rates of depreciation result in higher numbers for net plant (depreciated value of fixed assets). What we really want to

TABLE 5—A
APPARENT EFFECTS OF PLOWBACK ON ASSETS GROWTH

	Retained Cash Flow as % Net Assets	Depreciation Rate as % Gross Assets	Net Fixed Assets per Share		% Change 1958–68
			1958	1968	
American Tel. & Tel. . .	9%	4.7%	$38.00	$63.00	66%
American Electric Power.	5	2.8	25.60	36.90	44
Merck	16	7	24.30	44.40	83
Dow Chemical	18	8	20.10	37.60	88
Mobil Oil	13	5	17.87	33.55	90
IBM	29	13	9.10	32.20	212
Burroughs	24	10	7.60	16.20	114
General Electric	13	8.7	8.12	18.20	125
Westinghouse	11	3	9.90	16.50	65
Southern Railway	7	7	23.85	30.25	36
American Airlines	8	2.8	13.05	52.10	298
Columbia Gas System . .	6	3	34.00	49.60	45

know is whether the profit rates and depreciation rates make much difference for long-term growth and stockholder benefits.

The gain in net fixed assets per share was in proportion to the depreciation rate. The correspondence was not exact, but you can see that IBM, with the highest rate, had the biggest gain, while American Electric Power (AEP) increased net fixed assets only 4 percent a year. By 1968, IBM had scrapped most of its 1958 net fixed assets, while AEP was still writing off most of its 1958 plants and would continue to do so for 20 to 30 years. American Airlines financed its asset growth by borrowing and convertible debenture financing.

Detail in Study of Cash Plowback

Table 5-B shows various aspects of accounting.

TABLE 5—B
TENNECO, INC., DEPRECIATION VERSUS RETIREMENT
($ millions)

	Dec. 1969	Dec. 1968
Plant a/c at cost	$4,189	$4,071
Capital expenditures 1969		317
Assets purchased in acquisition 1969		49
		$ 366
Total 1968 plant plus 1969 capital expenditures		$4,437
Less Dec. 1969 plant a/c		4,189
Apparent retirements		$ 248
1969 Depreciation		$ 170

From these data, there were $78 million more retirements than were provided from depreciation. An itemized plant account (Table 5-C) supplies clues about adjustments in accounts. Note "Producing leasehold," which declined $97 million. On the liabilities side of the balance sheet, we find the following decreases: "Non-interest-bearing purchase obligations, . . . subject to redetermination," down $48 million. "Outside stockholders' interest in subsidiaries," down $40 million. The notes in the report do not explain this last item. It appears to have been an imaginary asset on the 1968 statements. Excluding $97 million, December 1968 plants was $3,974 million. There was a $45

TABLE 5–C
TENNECO, INC.
($ millions)

	1969	1968
Plant, property, and equipment at cost		
Gas transmission	$1,913	$1,809
Producing and undeveloped oil and gas	894	783
Producing leasehold interests, subject		
to redetermination	159	256
Refining and marketing	211	218
Machinery, equipment, and shipbuilding	386	355
Packaging	272	259
Chemicals	252	245
Land use and other	98	143
	$4,188	$4,071
Less: Reserves for depreciation, depletion,		
and amortization	$1,288	$1,203
	$2,899	$2,868
Deferred Charges		
Investment in consolidated subsidiaries		
in excess of net assets at date of		
acquisition, less amortization	$ 40	$ 37
Issue expense on preferred stock and		
long-term debt	41	25
Other	20	20
	$ 102	$ 83
	$4,054	$3,897

million decrease in land in 1969. Retirements, therefore, appear to have been about $105 million.

Depreciation was only $65 million more than retirements of worn-out plant or obsolete plant. The information is an accurate description of Tenneco financial operations; the question is whether it is realistic in an inflationary world. Tenneco reported that it had $165 million of net income but allowed only $28 million for income taxes ($2 million deferred).

Should the stockholders be skeptical about the earnings as reported? Half of the fixed assets are pipelines, which will be useful as long as natural gas is available at costs that permit it to be marketed in the northeast quarter of the United States. Based on prices paid for leases in the Gulf of Mexico in December 1970, Tenneco appears to think that the supply will be enough to keep the pipelines in business. In the years since the main pipelines were placed in the ground, costs of construction have at least doubled. If the gas supply runs out, as it well may, in the next quarter-century, Tenneco obviously will not have generated enough cash flow to replace earnings that would cease.

Full-Cost Accounting

Note 2 in the report says Tenneco capitalizes all productive and nonproductive well-drilling costs of oil and gas exploration. Amortization of producing and nonproducing property is provided on the unit-of-production basis. Unrecovered book cost divided by the quantity of remaining reserves gives unit cost.

The Financial Analysts Society Accounting Committee is strongly opposed to full-cost accounting and would like accountants to reject it as acceptable reporting. The argument is that it avoids prompt expensing of dry holes, but companies that use full-cost accounting argue that dry holes are part of the cost of developed oil and gas reserves. In practice, a pipeline utility is forced to use full-cost accounting to puff up its rate base for rate determination.

Capitalizing of costs that are deductible for tax purposes leads to more generous current reporting of net income than would be possible in other companies. Most of the companies that use full-cost accounting are among the smaller oil exploration and producing companies in the United States or Canada.

6

Growth Forecasts

A random sampling of data on stock prices, earnings, and reinvestment can be used to show that forecasts of growth are risky. Many observers say it is impossible to forecast growth with enough accuracy for it to be any help to investors. This chapter will show what can be done about forecasting company growth.

Growth forecasts can be right within certain restrictive parameters. One cannot at all times make useful forecasts for every stock on the list. The following statements are what I will seek to demonstrate as useful hypotheses.

1. Grades I and II stocks (rated by my method, Chapter 3) will live up to their growth projections and will deviate less from the trend than will lower grade stocks. Therefore, only few stocks are really susceptible to statistical growth forecasting.

2. In any 10-year period, most stocks are much more likely to

grow at rates consistent with the rate at which they reinvest earnings than at higher or lower rates.

3. When the plowback of earnings is at a high rate — 10 percent or more — cyclical interruptions in growth will be overcome within two or three years and the growth reasserted with few exceptions.

4. When the plowback is high, the company is unlikely to experience a cyclical interruption in growth of profits that is as severe as the cyclical experience of its industry.

5. When the plowback is as low as that of the U. S. economy, fluctuations in earnings around the trend of long-term growth are likely to be random, and therefore growth forecasts, even if accurate, will be of little value to investors. When the plowback is low but earnings do not vary much from trend, the dynamics of growth will be insufficient to override the more or less unpredictable changes in valuations of stocks in general.

6. Growth rates in sales, dividends, and stockholder equity capital follow the company's long-term growth trend more closely than do profits and are better guides to short-term growth than are profits.

7. Statistical analysis is helpful in forecasting changes in growth rates. It is easier to foresee a slowdown than an increase in growth, and it is possible to project changes before the stock market recognizes them.

8. Only a few investors believe that accurate growth forecasts can be made, and stock prices are not very precise in discounting growth. Skill in growth forecasting should give the investor more advantage over the crowd.

Definition of Growth

Growth is defined in terms of *the decades-long progress of the matrix of data in a company record*. It more closely resembles the trend in Gross National Product than the changes of the three- or four-year cycles that affect the economy. The rate of long-term growth in most companies alters its trend value quite slowly. The short-run changes are due to success with new models or slumps when business is slow.

Often you will hear that a company has a major change in its growth trend as evidenced by a recent quarterly report. In the summer of 1970, I met a man who told me he was short of Avon Products. When I asked his reasons, he said that the June quarter report showed that it had slowed down. Had he studied the March quarter report, which showed a 27 percent gain? No, he had not. Did he know about Avon Products accounting methods? No, he did not. Avon is on a current cash basis; each year it has major new product or market promotions that hit the quarter when they occur. In 1970, there were no new promotions in the first quarter but a big one in the second quarter. By December, Avon chalked up another in its multi-decade history of 17 percent profit gains.

Items that should be measured when making long-term growth forecasts include the following:

1. Cash plowback return
2. Sales per share
3. Retained earnings/book value
4. Profits on added assets and sales
5. Capital structure factors
6. Industry trends and company penetration of markets
7. Product development effects

Quality measurement suggests how confident to be about any forecast. Earnings per share should be studied last. Earnings are more variable than other statistical components.

Cash Plowback Return

Cash plowback return (CPR) is helpful because it shows the various accounting factors used by corporations. To derive CPR, we add up retained earnings, depreciation, and other reserve strengthening, including intangibles, amortization, and deferred taxes; then we combine the fixed assets at cost plus the working capital. The cash plowback is a percent of the assets, which indicates the rate at which the company increased its potential earnings assets through internal sources.

DERIVATION OF CASH PLOWBACK RETURN (CPR)

Company Assets ($ millions)
1. Fixed assets at cost $100
2. Working capital 50
3. Investments and other assets * 10
     Gross Operating Assets $160

Company Cash Plowback
1. Net income $15
   Minus dividends   5
             .... $10

2. Depreciation and amortization 10
3. Foreign operations reserves,
   Increase in deferred taxes, etc. 1
   Cash Plowback in Dollars $21

To calculate percent cash plowback return, divide $21 (CP) by $160:

$$\frac{21}{160} = 13.1 \text{ percent}$$

* Including intangible assets on the theory that most of them cost the company market value of securities exchanged in acquisition or that cash was expended for the intangibles.

This example shows a fairly high cash plowback return. U. S. industry as a whole has CPR of 5 percent. The best large companies, such as IBM, Coca-Cola, Avon Products, Eastman Kodak, and 3M, have CPRs of 11 to 17 percent. Large growth companies, such as AMP Inc., Polaroid, Xerox, and Emerson Electric, have similar CPRs. Other large progressive companies, such as Procter & Gamble, Sears, Roebuck, and J. C. Penney have CPRs at about 8 percent.

When a management has a long record, its tracks are not hard to follow. Its policies and methods are developed so that it seeks about the same rate of return on capital in new facilities as in old, and its policies include reinvestment of a given proportion of profits. For decades, the Du Pont Company has included rate of return calculations in annual reports. Management comments on the recent performance against standards, but it takes a little arithmetic to figure out how well they perform against these standards. Most companies have such rate of return goals.

In any case, one may conclude: (1) if CPR is 10 percent or higher, the long-term growth is fairly certain to agree with this percentage rate; (2) if CPR is about 8 percent, growth will probably conform to a trend that agrees with CPR; (3) if the CPR is below 8 percent, the forecasting value becomes marginal.

Some adjustments may have to be made. For example, use of plowback to replace old assets may have the effect of offsetting plowback by a significant amount. Why? Because if a company grows at 5 percent a year, in 20 years 40 percent of its assets are 20 years old. If a company grows at 10 percent a year, in 20 years 15 percent of its assets are 20 years old.

Most company annual reports do not state how many dollars of fixed assets were retired in the last year, but they do state how much was invested in new fixed assets. The balance sheet shows the amount of fixed assets at cost for the last year and the previous years.

BOOK RETIREMENTS EXAMPLE
($ millions)

	Dec. 1970	Dec. 1969
Fixed assets at cost $100		$94
Increase		$ 6
Expended on fixed assets in 1970		12
Difference		6

An investigation of SEC reports and statistical reports probably would reveal that this company scrapped plant and equipment that cost $6 million. If the company plowed back earnings and depreciation of $21 million, the $6 million of retirements would reduce to $15 million the funds that provided for growth. The $6 million was almost 30 percent of plowback that had to be used for replacement.

If the annual report showed that the fixed assets increased $10 million on $12 million of expenditures, the retirements used $2 million of the cash plowback. In this case, retirements were only 9 percent of plowback.

When the plowback is high, especially from 10 percent up, the retirements take such a small portion of plowback that over 90 percent of the cash flow is left for growth. In such cases, one may disregard retirements. If the cash plowback is 4 to 6 percent, one may assume one-third of it is used up in replacements of workout assets.

Retained Earnings/Book Value

Earned growth is what I call the measurement of retained earnings compared to stockholders' book equity. In this measure, net income for the year after subtracting dividends — earnings plowback — is divided by the book equity at the beginning of the year to obtain the figure for earned growth as a percent. For a quick measure, you can use the book value per share, which is published in most statistical services. Subtract the dividends from the earnings per share and divide the result by the January 1 book value.

Always check to see if there are convertible preferred stocks outstanding. When the book value of convertible preferred issues is a major fraction of total stockholder equity, take this amount into the calculation. Subtract preferred and common dividends from net income, and then measure the earnings plowback against the combined book value of preferred and common issues. The preferred stockholders' investment partly finances the common stock and ultimately will be converted to common stock.

For most companies, this measure of earned growth will prove to have a percentage value fairly close to cash plowback. It is actually the simplest measure of growth one can get from assets analysis.

Sales per Share Trends

Sales per share for most companies grow at about the same rates as earnings and assets. To obtain sales per share, simply divide the company's sales by the number of shares. Usually, the sales growth is more regular than the earnings trend, since profit margins are more sensitive to the business cycle. Several behavior patterns show up. Plotting of sales per share should show: improvements in profits not confirmed by sales growth; continued sales growth in the face of lagging profits; sales changes from acquisitions that alter the mix; growth in new type of activity that changes the ratio of sales to assets; effects of decline in high turnover business and growth in slower turnover operations.

Texas Instruments (Earned Growth Less than Cash Plowback)

The Texas Instruments chart (Figure 6-1) shows a lot of movement, which makes it worth studying with some care. Measuring either peaks or troughs, one finds that sales increased at nearly 15 percent a year in the 1960-70 period. Earning per share grew at 12 percent compounded, indicating that the profit margin on sales was declining somewhat. The earned growth trend (EG on chart) was about 12 percent, which is in line with EPS. In 1966, T.I. raised capital by sale of common stock, and that explains the bulge in the book value line on the chart. The effect of this financing was to push the book value trend up to 15 percent, although retained earnings would have supported only an 8 percent trend in the years from 1966 through 1971.

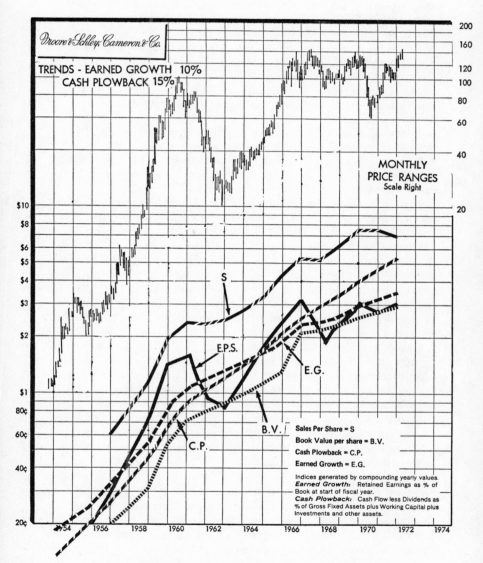

Figure 6-1. Texas Instruments (TXN)

The cash plowback trend (CP on the chart) averaged 18 percent and was still at 16 percent late in the decade. Rapid obsolescence means that fixed assets can become nonproductive at an unusually rapid pace for such a dynamic company; therefore, the high plowback can be misleading as a guide to growth. T.I. operates in a business that has an extraordinary rate of decline in prices and cost of products. The functions of integrated circuits had price declines of 90 percent in the 3 years through 1970. Not everyone was using the complex circuits that had the full-cost decline, but the simpler circuits had drastic price declines for competitive reasons. At the same time, the oil industry demand for seismic exploration service, a higher margined business for T.I., stopped growing after 1966. In sum, T.I. was generating a good deal of cash flow, which was supporting the sales growth at a time when profit margins were under pressure.

Just looking at the zigzag lines can make one wonder about the chances for making a sensible forecast of profits. As I write, T.I. has just experienced nine months of recession. The sharpness of the sales decline naturally makes one wonder if the dynamic growth is over. However, in the 24 months of 1968 and 1969 sales went up 50 percent, which was more than was expected; the sales for all of 1970 were even with 1969. By the end of 1971, the company had built up its cash account out of plowback and assets control to $180 million, which exceeded all its debt.

I have given this much attention to T.I. as an illustration of earned growth and plowback trends because this kind of stock is quite useful for capital gains trading. The company is innovative in a volatile business; it is determined to grow, as it regularly tells its stockholders; its financial policies are conservative; and it favors a strong cash balance. In 1971, T.I. began to challenge the computer industry with a very large computer for engineering problem-solving and a line of minicomputers that incorporate advanced microelectronic circuitry.

Cenco Instruments (Cash Plowback Less than Earned Growth)

Cenco has been built through acquisition and the use of leverage. The cash plowback trend had a value of about 12 percent, while the earned growth was about 15 percent. First glance at Cenco's chart (Figure 6-2) indicates that earnings per share (EPS) have kept up to the index of earned growth. But

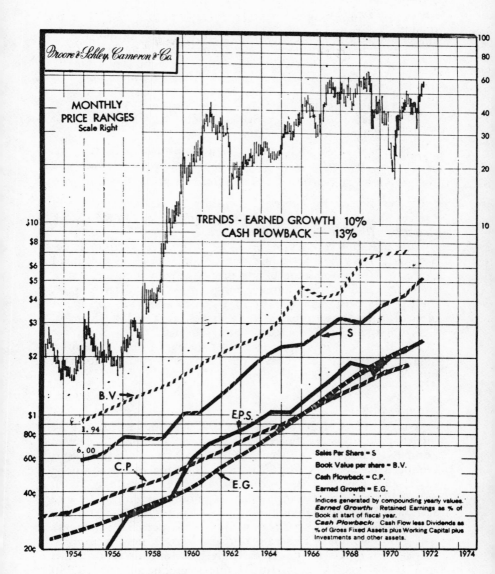

Figure 6-2. Cenco Instruments (CNC)

before reaching any conclusion, we should look at the capitalization.

Total Capitalization (October, 1971, estimated)

Long-term debt, $95 million, including: $20 million of 5 percent subordinated notes, convertible into 365,000 shares at $53 per share; $10 million of 5 percent convertible notes, convertible into 153,840 shares at $65 per share; $7 million of 4.5 percent notes, convertible into 115,000 shares at $60 per share; a new issue of $35 million convertible debentures, which would be convertible into 750,000 shares at $46.50.

Preferred stock, $9.7 million value, represented by two issues, convertible into 340,000 shares of common stock.

Common stock equity, $84 million (4.3 million shares).

Conversion of the notes, debentures, preferred stock, and exercise of option would increase the number of common stock shares by 1,750,000 shares, or 45 percent.

Although the conversion prices of several convertible issues were well above the market price for the common stock, additional shares will preempt some of the profits growth in future years. In order to have per share earnings grow 10 percent a year, total profits must grow 16 percent a year to allow for conversion of debentures and preferred stock issues. In the last 15 years, Cenco had about 12 percent annual growth in earnings per share. If it continues to use leverage with new debenture offerings after the old ones have been converted, Cenco will be able to grow this fast in the future.

Avon Products

Avon's trends of growth in terms of sales and earnings have etched a steady steep but parallel pattern of about 16 percent annually. The return on shareholders' equity in the past 5 years has been between 35 and 38 percent. The big question among investors is how long this record of growth can continue. When will the law of diminishing return set in on an organization with sales of $950 million annually?

Foreign business constitutes about 30 percent of Avon's worldwide volume. The rate of gain in this new sector was increasing 27 percent a year through 1970, and the end of this trail is not yet in sight. Initial sales were begun in 1969 in

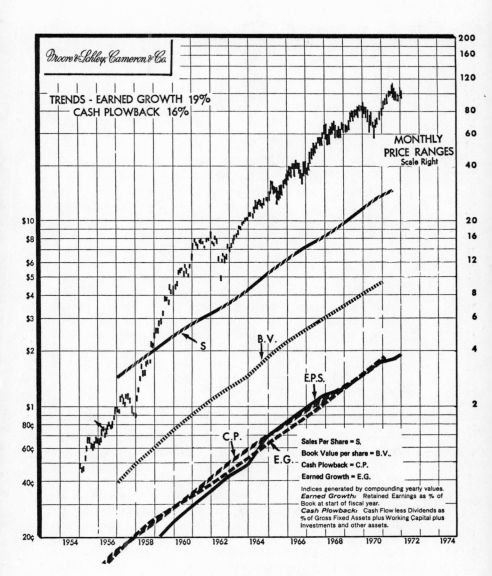

Figure 6-3. Avon Products

Ireland and Japan, and plans call for entry in Argentina, Sweden, and Holland. These newer ventures, along with the company's established position in England, France, Spain, Germany, and Italy, already give Avon the largest foreign business in the world among cosmetics manufacturers. The superb merchandising job that has been executed for its quality products in the United States has been readily applied with few revisions in foreign regions. In part, the highly attractive packaging and the quality of Avon cosmetics and toiletries have contributed to the success. Faster growing foreign sales are likely to contribute about 50 percent of the company's overall volume within the next 5 to 10 years.

The breadth of Avon's products is impressive. No member of the household is left out — infant, growing child, teen-ager, parent. While a high quality product has been one of the cornerstones of Avon's success, attractive, eye-appealing packaging similarly has been a company hallmark.

The topping to Avon's many successes in this business is its management group. By the same ease that the company's product leadership exceeds all competition in the field on a worldwide basis, Avon management similarly stands as the best staffed and most professionally organized in the field. A host of domestic and foreign cosmetics operations are the creation of a central figure whose creative talents may be emotional whims in directing the business, and such a management structure may encounter transition pains when the control passes from a one-man show to a typical corporate structure. However, Avon is staffed by a well-lubricated management team, functioning on a systematic scheme of a group effort.

Pfizer, Inc. (Coordinated Growth)

The record of Pfizer shows what can be done with a balanced pharmaceutical operation that is diversified among ethical and proprietary drugs, chemicals, and cosmetics. In the last two decades, the company has grown in sales at between 9 and 10 percent, with only mild deviations. Profit margins have remained between 8.5 and 9.5 percent (post-tax). Earnings cycles are internal, relating more to product success than to the general economy. Profit margins in 1970 were the best in four years.

A management transition occurred in the mid-1960s, and that partly explains the earnings plateau for a couple of years. There is a good deal of difference in the style of management

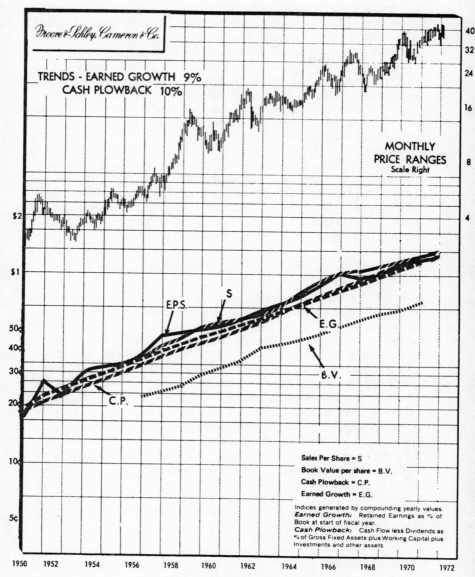

Figure 6-4. Pfizer, Inc.

under John Powers, the current chief executive, and that under his predecessor. Powers believed that the research effort could be stimulated, and a series of new drugs brought to market had a lot to do with the reasserted growth.

Plowback growth shaded off to about 8 percent in recent years. However, this is an interesting example of how stock-option exercise supplements plowback growth. In 1969 and 1970, the premiums over book value paid by exercise of options were about 1 percent of gross assets each year. When a stock follows an even growth path, premiums from stock-option exercise can be depended on to finance part of growth.

Almost half of Pfizer's sales have been overseas, which has helped to balance cycle problems. It has maintained its human health business at about half of sales, has had success with animal medication, and has become a factor in cosmetics. Such a statistical record is evidence of well-controlled as well as creative management. Pfizer is a good example of the first three statements at the beginning of this chapter.

Aluminum Company of America (Earnings Growth Not Confirmed by Sales)

In 1960, an analyst working with me projected that the earnings per share of Alcoa should grow at 13 percent a year during the 1960s, as it did. It is also true that Alcoa's sales grew at 6 percent a year in the same period. The book value of the common stock grew a little more slowly, a fact confirmed by the plowback trends, which were about 5 percent compounded.

During the 1960s, investors came to recognize that the basic growth of Alcoa was more like a 5-6 percent rate than the higher rate of gain for the earnings per share. The stock price pattern, which is also shown on the Alcoa chart (Figure 6-5) traces a history of no net gain in stock price over a 10-year period. The explanation is that the stock in 1960 was selling at a price that discounted growth at the 13 percent rate, but, further, the valuation basis was the 1960 stock market, when all stocks were valued more highly than in 1970. This example is presented to show how the stock market does, in the long run, look through the earnings to the matrix of growth indexes.

J. C. Penney and F. W. Woolworth (Sales per Share Prefigure Resumption of Earning Growth)

The large retail chains carry on store expansion programs that

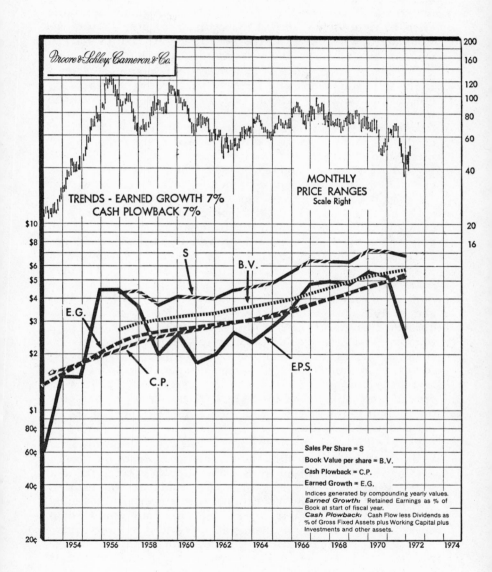

Figure 6-5. Aluminum Company of America

are laid out on definite schedules. Penney and Woolworth both undertook more vigorous store-building programs after the discount trend of the 1950s had begun to mature. You can see from the upward curves in the sales trends in Figures 6-6 and 6-7 that there was a speedup in sales growth after 1960.

Our analytical problem is to foresee the response of earnings to the sales volume growth. Penney's sales growth through 1961 occurred at only a 5 percent rate. In the next five years, the pace went up to almost 10 percent a year and hewed pretty close to a 10 percent trend through 1970. In the first three years of the speeded-up growth, profits showed little response and profit margins declined. In 1964, profits took off on a 15 percent trend, which stopped in 1969. The surtax was a partial explanation, but the continuation of the arrested growth in 1970 was an effect of the recession.

During the period of more vigorous growth, the indexes of plowback and earned growth turned up and gained at the same pace as the more vigorous sales growth. In this case, there was correlation of the data series, and the investor is encouraged to project that the profits will catch up to the sales trend. The only cloud here is that after funding the previous growth surge internally, Penney needed to raise money in the market in 1968 and in 1970. Assets turnover was not so good with the more diversified inventory now required. Nevertheless, analysts were confident that profits would catch up to sales and capital growth.

On the surface, the Woolworth record looks disappointing compared to Penney's growth. The sales per share trend shows that after growing at 5 percent in the years up to 1963 its sales grew 10 percent or better for 8 years. There was an encouraging profit spurt through 1965, and then nothing happened. Profit margins did not decline.

During the 1960s, the profits of Woolworth's British subsidiary went downward, and this slump was aggravated further by devaluation. From the analysts' point of view, the larger new stores, particularly the Woolco stores, would be the basis of earnings growth. The Woolco program began in 1962, and the company said that it expected the program would be in operation 10 years before there was a payoff. The store square footage and sales gains had been made with no increase in the rental obligations; the problem was to make the new stores grow up to the rental costs.

This type of situation is well worth investigating as a mild

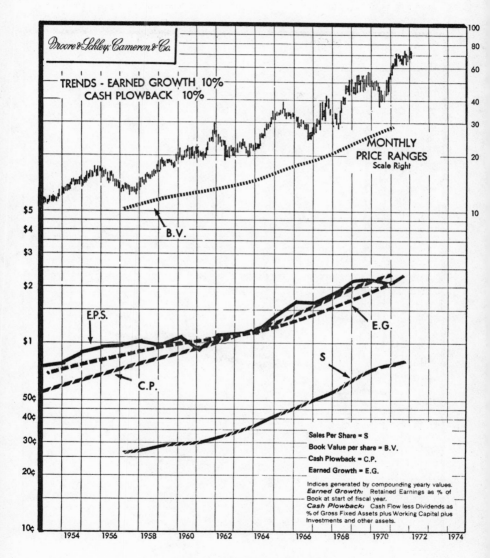

Figure 6-6. J. C. Penney

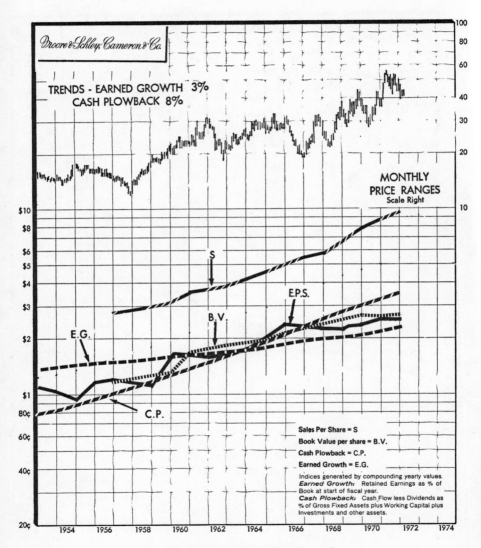

Figure 6-7. F. W. Woolworth

form of speculation. When the profit on capital has not shown any real sign of an upturn and is low to begin with, and when sales have been going up for five years with no profit response, the prospects are good that if the company is going to respond in profits it often will get a big spurt in a business boom.

Smith, Kline & French (Slower Sales Growth and Level Earnings)

The Smith, Kline & French example is somewhat unusual in that the sales slowdown was mild and the profits slowdown involved no severe setback. Through 1965, sales grew at a regular 10 percent pace, and profits kept right up. Figure 6-8 shows that there had been other years of flat earnings; stock had dipped but recovered. When earnings went flat in 1966, the stock went down with a bear market by a larger-than-usual amount and kept drifting down thereafter. This was more than the usual cyclical problem.

In 1965-66, professional investors became vocally concerned about the future of SKF tranquilizing drugs. The company was nearing the end of the patent protection period for Thorazine, which SKF marketed under license, and there was grave concern about its amphetamine drugs, which were suspect as drug abuse potentials. Although these drugs accounted for less than 20 percent of SKF sales, they were known to be more important to profits. A palace revolution ensued and a new president was elected. The new goals were vigorous pursuit of proprietary drug and cosmetic sales and a violent shakeup of the research department, which had been ineffectual for years.

Although the profits were level for five years, the plowback indexes declined moderately but still averaged about 9 percent, which is about double the plowback rate of the economy. SKF was accumulating cash and had no debts. While the stock was the subject of debate among analysts, it continued to be of interest to investors because of basic strength and vigor of new management. It was able to pay a liberal dividend with no visible strain. In 1970, quarterly earnings showed consecutive gains, and the stock began to come back in favor on the theory that it would start to improve its still respectable sales growth and have earnings gains in proportion to sales growth.

Hercules, Inc. (Sales per Share Progress in a Lagging Industry)

Hercules continued to increase sales on a 7.5 percent trend in the 1960s, when the chemical industry was having a hard time.

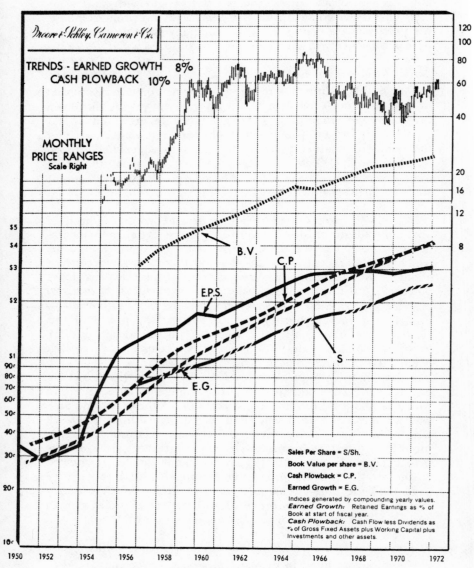

Figure 6-8. Smith, Kline & French Laboratories (SKF)

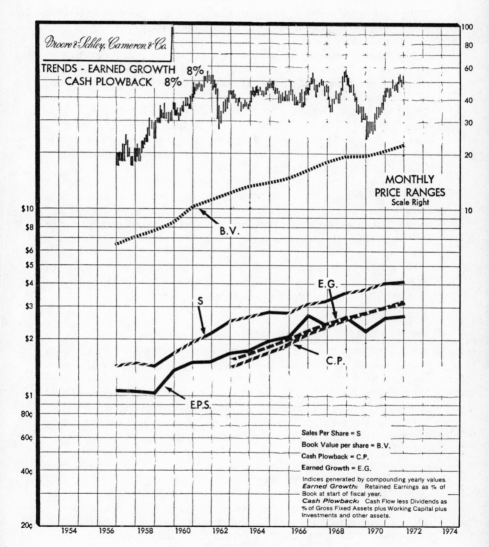

Figure 6-9. Hercules, Inc.

This example fits my specification for good quality stocks that, over a decade, growth will cycle around a trend but possibly not in a precisely predictable way. Hercules sales kept up to the rates of reinvestment as measured by earned growth and cash plowback after allowance for retirements that offset about one-fifth of cash plowback.

My technique does not allow for the rate of overexpansion by Hercules and its competitors in the 1960s, but this problem was reviewed in Chapter 4. The chemical industry tripled its debt in the years 1962-70 and built capacity much faster than its plowback rate. Hercules increased plant at 17 percent a year from 1962 to 1970 to attain capacity all out of proportion to its market share. Apparently, Hercules and the industry generate enough cash flow to keep up with their market opportunities, and borrowed capital just pays for overexpansion.

A period of price pressure would be necessary to force scrapping of obsolete plants, followed by a boom in business to pull profits back to the sales trend. This type of stock had sales and profits growth of one and one-fourth to one and one-half times that of the Dow-Jones Industrials index, and it probably will fluctuate with the averages.

Hercules stock continues to maintain a P/E ratio premium of 20 percent compared to the averages. Investors pay for the prospect that profits will resume a growth trend nearer 8 percent.

Sperry Rand (SY) (Sales per Share Not Confirming Growth)

This example looks similar in some respects to the Alcoa example, and yet the stock price behavior was altogether different. During the 1960s, the chief executive of SY made it plain that dependence on defense contract business would be lessened, and investors expected that sales volume would not grow very fast, particularly since it was expected that the most important growth would be in lease rental for Univac brand computers.

In 1961, the Univac Division wrote off all its obsolete computers, and there were doubts about whether the division had much future. Top management acted as though it had doubts about Univac, but in the mid-1960s it was evident that Univac would have a place in the computer market. Profits began to rise for the whole company, due in part to the overcoming of losses in defense products. The debt ratio improved with actual reduction of debt by 40 percent between 1962 and 1967. The

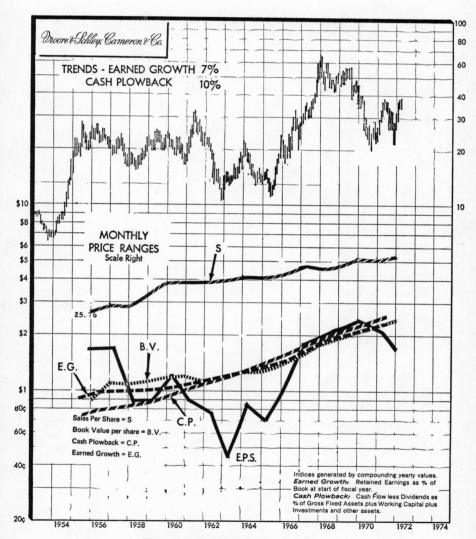

Figure 6-10. *Sperry Rand (SY)*

gain in book value came largely from the exercise of warrants. By 1967, common stock equity was over 75 percent of capital.

In 1969, investors began to look at the growth in sales from a more critical point of view. By then, Univac was earning a profit margin about as good as anyone expected. If sales growth was to be 4 percent at a time when cyclical divisions were enjoying prosperity, was it realistic to hold the stock on a basis that discounted future growth at 10 to 12 percent? When the stock traded around 50 in 1968 and 1969, selling was by those who simply felt that the stock lacked promise. In the summer of 1969, earnings reports showed that profit margins had begun to decline. Stages in the 1969-70 bear market found the stock vulnerable because the long-term growth expectation had come down and investors foresaw cyclical vulnerability.

In the winter of 1970-71, investors who studied SY appeared to come to the conclusion that the stock would be about as good as the averages. It was a large, diversified industrial manufacturer, in satisfactory financial condition, and it was expected to about hold its position in the industries it served. Buyers of the stock expected that it would adjust itself to a market rating about in line with the averages.

Raytheon (Sales per Share Needing Explanation)

Raytheon's record is one in which only the plowback trends give indication of the long-term ability to grow. In the late 1950s and early 1960s, the fortunes of Raytheon shifted with the tides of military missile developments. Stock action shows that this was a popular speculative vehicle, and the stock became popular again after 1965, when Raytheon acted as though it was going to become a more active acquisition company. It made modest acquisitions that suggested it would be a factor in the glamor industries of the period. After the stock had risen on a basis of anticipation, Raytheon made larger acquisitions in consumer appliances and process plant construction to almost double the company sales. Having made these moves, it disbanded the acquisitions teams.

Raytheon no longer seemed glamorous. Then, as the bear market set in, investors concluded that its defense business might collapse and that its commercial business was not very interesting. By halfway through 1970, Raytheon's younger management had shown that it had good operating control with no setback in profits; so investors took a closer look at the company. In

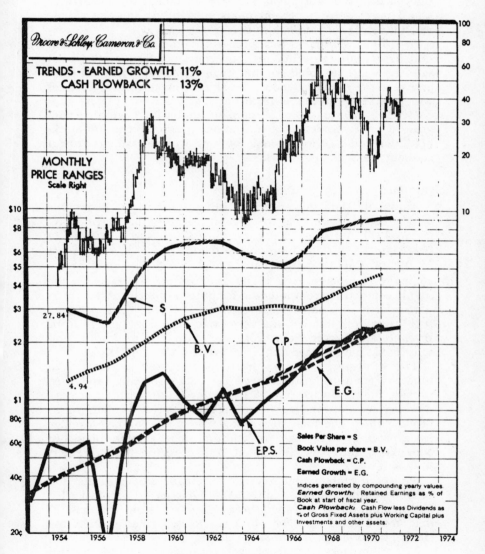

Figure 6-11. Raytheon

this case, the sales trend did not suggest dynamism, and it was more useful to look at the solid balance sheet and the good plowback record. Raytheon was robust enough in mid-1970 to afford purchase of 5 percent of its outstanding stock at a time when the stock sold at book value.

In 1970-71, Raytheon was successful bidder on a solid amount of defense contracts. While investors could not foresee substantial sales growth, they could see that financial performance was good and that the company should be able to make further progress with profit margins that were only about 2.5 percent of sales.

Here is an example of a company that with negligible sales growth for a decade made continuous progress in use of stock-holder capital. We would look for it to achieve earnings growth at about the rate of plowback.

Automatic Data Processing (AUD)

Automatic Data Processing is distinguished in the glamorous field of computer services by its good margins (16.7 percent pre-tax in 1970 and over 18 percent in 1967-69) and good quality (see Figure 6-12). Both of these characteristics directly reflect Automatic Data's capable management, which has enabled the company to emerge as a strong and prosperous leader in the highly competitive computer service bureau industry. AUD caters particularly to smaller companies and mainly sells packages such as payroll and accounts receivable. About 20 percent of its revenues are derived from brokerage office data processing, and some banks have farmed out their payroll work to AUD.

The strategic philosophy practiced by Automatic Data is to isolate a genuine business need for data processing and then provide the means to serve it. Its tactics are to create or acquire new services that can be sold profitably, thus slowly enlarging its product line. The final step is to broaden the market coverage by expanding nationally; in addition to the main plants in New York and New Jersey, AUD had regional data centers in 18 cities.

One of the observable keys to Automatic Data's success has been its ability to attract, train, and hold the clerical people needed for preparation, processing, checking, and routing the mass of data accumulated each day. In a real sense, it has assumed the clerical personnel problems of the client.

The company's record of fast earnings per share growth correlates with its cash plowback and earned growth trend. With

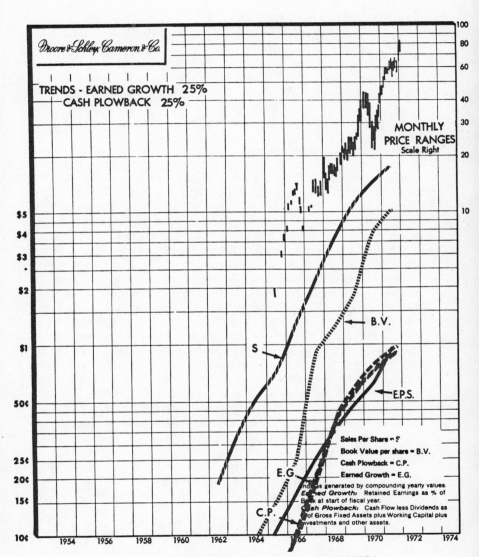

Figure 6-12. Automatic Data Processing (AUD)

earned growth of 48 percent and cash plowback of 45 percent, AUD had one of the best records in industry. As the company grows, its cash plowback and earned growth is likely to drop back below 30 percent.

Growth Stock List for 1970

The list in Table 6-A was prepared in the summer of 1970 for a study of growth. The basis of this list was one made in 1960. Of 48 stocks chosen, 28 were hardly settled growth stocks in 1960; 9 were distinct turnarounds since then; and including a couple that were not public, 19 were not large enough to be called growth stocks in 1960.

My standards were that the companies concentrate in congeneric businesses and that growth mainly be financed internally through plowback. The growth rate forecast has to tie in with plowback and sales growth as well as profits growth. Although I made an exception, I wanted sales of $100 million and profits comfortably above $5 million, preferably $10 million. Cyclicality of earnings must be accepted among the durable equipment firms.

When you maintain such a list, you must review it regularly. In 1971, I had some reservations about a few of my 1970 forecasts because of doubts about whether some would live up to the projections. Motorola was bogged down with electronic industry stagnation. Diversification into paper-making definitely had slowed the growth of Georgia-Pacific. Delta Airlines was a good company in a bad industry. Parker Hannifin proved more vulnerable to the capital goods cycle than I had forecast and made the long-term projection questionable. Tektronix was a problem because it seemed that its prodigious technical effort was in giving more sensitive instruments to a market that had stopped growing. Memorex's problem was that its emphasis had switched from the better quality products that it had sold to the me-too products that it rented as discounted substitutes for IBM equipment.

Digital Equipment's recession setback did not seem too serious, although the 20 percent growth might be too high. Coca-Cola, Kresge, and Melville Shoe looked as though they would outperform my forecasts.

Price Performance

Using a method described in Chapter 11, I rated the list of stocks in Table 6-A according to the growth rates that were

TABLE 6–A
SUPPLEMENTAL GROWTH STOCK LIST FOR 1970
(stocks not on 1960 lists)

Stock	Grade	Growth Discounted	Forecast Growth	Discounted Growth ÷ Forecast Growth	P/E Used for Discounted Growth, Aug. 24
Automatic Data	III	28	25	1.12	47
American Hospital Supply	II	21	12	1.75	36
AMP Inc.	I	13	13	1.00	22
ARA	II	17	12	1.42	26
Avery	III	23	15	1.53	32
Baxter	I	22	16	1.35	39
Becton-Dickinson ...	II	18	13	1.40	28
Black & Decker	II	15	11	1.35	25
Bristol-Myers	II	13	11	1.18	22
Burroughs	II	18	15	1.20	26
Chesebrough.......	II	12	10	1.20	19
Carnation	II	11	10	1.10	17
Cenco	IV	12	11	1.09	14
Clark Equipment	IV	4	9	.44	9
Coca-Cola	I	16	10	1.60	31
Crown Cork	II	7	11	.64	11
Delta Airlines	III	8	10	.80	12
Digital Equipment ...	I	24	20+	1.20	40
Diebold	IV	15	11	1.36	20
Emerson Electric	I	13	11	1.18	23
Max Factor	II	13	10	1.30	20
Georgia-Pacific	III	20	11	1.82	30
W. T. Grant	III	8	10	.80	14
International Flavors & Fragrances	II	22	11	2.00	40
Kerr-McGee	III	14	10	1.40	19
Kresge	III	18	13	1.38	25
Lubrizol	II	18	13	1.38	28
Marlennan	II	15	12	1.25	26
Manpower	III	7	12	.58	12
Marriott	III	20	15	1.33	26
McDonald's	III	19	15	1.27	23
Melville Shoe	III	14	12	1.17	19
Memorex	III	16	15	1.07	25
Moore Corp.	II	14	11	1.27	22
Motorola	IV	12	12	1.00	16
Nalco...........	I	14	13	1.07	24
Pacific Petroleum	IV	25	15	1.66	35
Parker Hannifin	III	3	10	.30	9
Perkin-Elmer	III	13	12	1.08	15
Planning Research ...	III	23	15	1.53	23
Plough	II	18	10	1.80	28

(Continued on next page)

TABLE 6–A *(Continued)*

Stock	Grade	Growth Discounted	Forecast Growth	Discounted Growth ÷ Forecast Growth	P/E Used for Discounted Growth, Aug. 24
Prentice-Hall.	II	13	10	1.30	23
Purolator.	III	10	10	1.00	14
Robins	III	14	13	1.08	19
Schlumberger	II	11	11	1.00	17
Simplicity Patterns . . .	II	19	13	1.46	32
Sterling Drug	I	13	10	1.30	23
Tektronix	II	11	12	.92	14
Warner-Lambert.	I	13	11	1.18	23

discounted by the then market prices. The whole list gained 35 percent in price from August 1970 to May 1971, during a period when the market gained 25 percent, showing that price progress was greater by about the difference in growth rates between the stocks and the market averages.

The ratio Discounted Growth divided by Forecast Growth meant that at 1.0 the stocks were in line with the August 1970 market level. Those with ratios above 1.0 were more expensive than those with the lower ratios. Half of the stocks with the lowest ratios gained 43 percent, while half of the stocks with higher ratios gained 22 percent.

Quality grades shown in Table 6-A differ in some cases from those shown in the appendix. Quality rates are revised yearly, and there are changes and corrections.

In 1970, selections were made in a bear market, and the subsequent price gains were made from the bull market. The following lists reflect some changes that I made in growth estimates during the fall of 1971.

Table 6-C includes a group of companies long recognized for growth. Even these have had interruptions in their progress, but I reasoned that they still had the creativity and drive to reassert growth. I added another batch of companies that I believe will prove important growth stocks in the 1970s. Several of them have some cyclicality, and others have been growth companies for less than a decade.

TABLE 6–B
SUPPLEMENTAL GROWTH STOCK LIST FOR 1970 – PRICE CHANGES

	August 1970	May 1971
Automatic Data*	35	58
American Hospital Supply	32	33
AMP Inc.	51	66
ARA	99	132
Avery	29	32
Baxter*	25	32
Becton-Dickinson	37	38
Black & Decker	46	71
Bristol-Myers*	57	64
Burroughs	108	130
Chesebrough	35	52
Carnation	61	84
Cenco*	34	47
Clark Equipment	31	45
Coca-Cola	72	101
Crown Cork*	15	21
Delta Airlines*	30	44
Digital Equipment*	70	80
Diebold	56	68
Emerson Electric	53	72
Max Factor	35	38
Georgia-Pacific	52	51
W. T. Grant*	43	65
International Flavors & Fragrances	56	69
Kerr-McGee	90	132
Kresge*	45	85
Lubrizol	55	93
Marlennan	44	68
Manpower*	28	39
Marriott	28	45
McDonald's	36	79
Melville Shoe	34	53
Memorex*	70	47
Moore Corp.	32	36
Motorola*	47	83
Nalco*	43	54
Pacific Petroleum	26	28
Parker Hannifin*	34	43
Perkin-Elmer	25	43
Planning Research	20	21
Plough	merged with Schering	
Prentice-Hall	36	46
Purolator*	57	88
Robins	27	31
Schlumberger	77	120

(Continued on next page)

TABLE 6—B *(Continued)*

	August 1970	May 1971
Simplicity Patterns	74	119
Sterling Drug	35	44
Tektronix*	28	40
Warner-Lambert	59	73

*More attractive stocks in August 1970.

Valuation Hypotheses

The relative P/E ratios given in Tables 6-C and 6-D are based on the method described in Chapter 11. The only change was the addition of one-tenth of a multiple to stocks that actually scored higher in quality than Grade I.

The relative P/E ratios are most sensitive to the growth rate forecasts, particularly from 10 percent up. All the forecasts shown are supported by plowback of earnings. With cyclical and phased growth stocks such as Polaroid, Digital Equipment, AMP, and Capital Cities, we are dependent on analysis of statistics other than reported earnings.

TABLE 6—C
REVISED 1971 GROWTH STOCK LIST

Stock	Quality	Projected Growth	Dividend Payout	Hypothetical Relative P/E
American Express	II	15%	35%	1.95
American Home Products	I	9	60	1.60
Avon Products.	I*	13	70	2.20
Coca-Cola	I*	12	60	2.00
Eastman Kodak	I*	10	50	1.75
International Business Machines.	I*	11	50	1.85
Johnson & Johnson	I	15	30	2.05
Eli Lilly	II	11	50	1.65
Merck.	I*	10	60	1.80
Minnesota Mining & Manufacturing	I*	10	50	1.75
J. C. Penney.	I	9	45	1.50
Pfizer.	I	10	50	1.60
Procter & Gamble.	I	9	45	1.50
Schering-Plough.	I	14	40	2.00
Sears, Roebuck	I	9	45	1.50
Xerox	I	13	30	1.80

* One extra quality grade measured.

TABLE 6–D
STOCKS CONTINUED FROM 1970 GROWTH LIST

Stock	Quality	Projected Growth	Dividend Payout	Hypothetical Relative P/E
Automatic Data Processing . . .	II	20%	0%	2.60
AMP, Inc.^c	I	10	30	1.45
ARA Services	II	12	30	1.55
Avery Products^c	III	12	30	1.45
Baxter Laboratories	II	15	20	1.90
Black & Decker	II	10	50	1.55
Burroughs	II	13	15	1.60
Carnation	II	10	30	1.40
Cenco Instruments	III	12	15	1.35
Crown Cork & Seal^u	III	10	0	1.05
Digital Equipment^c	III	15	0	1.65
Diebold^u	IV	10	20	1.10
W. T. Grant	III	12	50	1.60
Emerson Electric^c	I	12	50	1.80
International Flavors & Fragrances	I	12	40	1.75
Kerr-McGee	III	10	30	1.25
S. S. Kresge	II	15	20	1.90
Lubrizol	I	12	30	1.65
Marlennan	II	10	55	1.55
Marriott	III	17	0	1.90
McDonald's	III	17	0	1.90
Melville Shoe	III	13	45	1.70
Moore Corp.	I	10	40	1.55
Nalco Chemical ^{c u}	II	15	45	2.05
Pacific Petroleum	III	15	35	2.00
Perkin-Elmer^c	III	11	30	1.35
Polaroid^c	II	13	15	1.60
Prentice-Hall	II	10	50	1.50
Purolator^c	III	10	35	1.30
A. H. Robins	II	12	30	1.55
Schlumberger	II	10	30	1.35
Simplicity Patterns	I	13	35	1.85
Sterling Drug	I	12	50	1.80
Warner-Lambert	I	10	40	1.55

^c Cyclicality has been material factor in earnings.
^u Unions have hurt company or customer operations.

The relative P/E ratios are quite sensitive to the dividend payout. In that the new money for the stock market is almost entirely the cash inflow of tax-sheltered investors, the dividends will become increasingly important for stock valuation.

The relative P/E ratios shown here are based on 5 percent as normal growth. They will therefore work better if compared to the S&P 425 than to the Dow Jones Industrials Average, which grows 4 percent.

We use a discount calculation that leans toward the bear market side. Real growth stocks sell below these at times. For Eastman Kodak, it would have helped in 1971. Based on trailing earnings, the S&P 425 traded around 19 times earnings through the third quarter. When EK was at 34 times, the relative P/E was above 1.75; but in midsummer its P/E at 29 times clocked a relative P/E of just over 1.5, and then it did gain on the market.

The relative P/E ratios used are those that should result in price progress at the same rate as the earnings progress. In the long run, if the growth forecasts are correct it is projected that

TABLE 6–E
OVER $5 MILLION NET INCOME STOCKS
FOR A 10-PLUS PERCENT GROWTH LIST

Stock	Quality	Projected Growth	Dividend Payout	Hypothetical Relative P/E
Anheuser-Busch...........	II	12%	30%	1.60
C. R. Bard..............	II	12	20	1.55
Capital Cities Broadcasting[c]...	IV	12	0	1.15
Citizens & Southern	II	10	50	1.50
Walt Disney[c]	III	15	10	1.90
Fedders Corp.[c]	IV	11	25	1.20
Gannett Co..............	IV	15	30	1.70
Gardner-Denver[c]	III	10	45	1.35
Genuine Parts	III	10	40	1.35
Hewlett-Packard[c].........	III	10	25	1.25
Hudson's Bay Oil & Gas	III	11	45	1.50
Levitz Furniture[c].........	V	15	0	1.40
Louisiana Land & Exploration .	II	10	55	1.55
Masco Corp.[c]	III	15	20	1.75
Mercantile Stores	II	10	25	1.35
New Process.............	II	15	55	2.00
Pepsico Inc.	II	11	40	1.55
Petrie Stores............	III	15	30	1.80
Roadway Express[c]	II	14	15	1.70
Ryan Homes [c]	IV	15	0	1.50
Skyline Corp.[c]	III	15	15	1.70
Tampax Inc..............	I	13	60	2.00
Wachovia Corp.	II	10	25	1.35

[c]Cyclicality should be expected.

the relative P/E ratios shown would agree with behavior of the stocks. The most dynamic stocks may lead their statistics. When investors are confident that high growth will persist, they often discount the next year's earnings, which will give them extrapolated relative P/E ratios closer to the hypothetical numbers shown.

Old reliables, I believed, would continue or reassert growth. On the very highest grade stocks, I included a few that might grow slightly less than 10 percent.

Stiffer standards and some changes in forecasts led to removal of a dozen stocks from the 1970 list.

Bull Market Relative P/E Ratios

Once or twice in a decade the overall stock market reflects enthusiasm, and the relative P/E ratios of stock with projected growth of 10 percent plus tend to expand by 25 to 50 percent above the hypothetical relative P/E ratios listed. In other words, 1.60 might rise to 2.00, and 2.00 can expand to 3.00. At such times, purchases expose the buyer to extra price risk.

Based on their records, the stocks in Table 6-F would not qualify as growth stocks in terms of consistent EPS gains of 10 percent, internal cash generation, or sales growth. My judgment is that they will prove themselves in the 1970s.

TABLE 6–F
STOCKS EXPECTED TO BECOME 10 PERCENT GROWTH STOCKS

Stock	Quality	Projected Growth	Dividend Payout	Normal Relative P/E
Brunswick Corp.	V	13%	15%	1.3
First National City	III	10	50	1.4
Walter Heller International	III	10	40	1.3
Honeywell	III	12	35	1.6
Norton Simon	IV	13	0	1.25
Texas Instruments	III	12	25	1.5

These companies were targeting growth at rates of 10 percent or better in most cases. The majority were still plowing back cash earnings at rates that would support their growth objectives. For a variety of reasons, I thought that they would not quite live up to the goals. For example, the hospital supply business was no longer the bonanza it had been. Electronic equipment

TABLE 6–G
STOCKS FROM 1970 LIST ESTIMATED TO HAVE GROWTH
LOWER THAN 10 PERCENT

	Projected Growth Revised
American Hospital Supply	8%
Becton-Dickinson	9
Bristol-Myers	8
Chesebrough-Pond's	8
Delta Airlines	8
Max Factor	8
Georgia-Pacific	7
Manpower	6
Memorex	?
Motorola	7
Parker Hannifin	7
Planning Research	?
Tektronix	8

and components had become brutally competitive. The cosmetics business was changing with a new generation of consumers. Industrial equipment faced years of lower capital spending.

7

Cyclical Industries

CYCLICAL industries are those in which profits go up and down as much or more than do profits of American industry as a whole. Included are: industrial materials (chemicals, metals, textiles, fibers, minerals, forest products); cars and trucks; machines and machinery; electric-electronic (consumer products, industrial equipment, components, aerospace, medical, civil, environmental); transportation (air, rail, highway).

Industrial Materials

Industrial materials are natural and synthetic products that in the aggregate maintain constant shares of world economies. Because services grow faster than do world economies, products made of industrial materials are not strong growth prospects. The volume of materials used varies with the business cycle. Materials used in soft goods seem to be as cyclical as those used in durable equipment. In the second quarter of the 20th century, synthetic chemicals had a lively growth era, but in the

1970s demand settled back to the growth rates of the industries that use them — for example, autos, building, apparel, and furnishings. The quantities of metals and wood products consumed maintain growth trends in line with world economies.

Capital Intensiveness

Industrial materials are produced from plants and mines with large capital investments relative to sales. This factor limits their flexibility in adapting to changes in demand or to needs for supplying materials with different specifications. Company managers must have skill in design and operation of big physical assets. They live with the need to build new, bigger, and better plants to correct the deficiencies of plants that were once big. This type of manager takes pride in his ability to forecast markets and prices five years in advance, when the new plant facilities will be operating with new processes and product specifications. As a group, the managers are committed to the concept that if they do not build new plants they will be bypassed as other companies outdistance them in the efficiency contest.

Product Development

We live in a talent-intensive economy. Communications between suppliers of goods and their customers have been speeded up by electronics. Suppliers of industrial materials must adapt to change and must respond to new customer requirements and to the impact of new competitive offerings in terms of either price or product qualities.

The engineering abilities of materials suppliers tend to be stronger in the product origination and process areas than at the customer service end. The companies and their researchers see their job as invention of new basic materials or discovery of mineral deposits and producing commodities. Most of them assume minor roles in the conversion of materials to end products. Many of the companies spend a lot of money on research and engineering and think they are doing as much as they can.

One of the largest companies, E. I. Du Pont de Nemours, spent about $270 million on research in 1971, which equals 7 percent of sales. In the late 1960s, it got about $1 of sales increase per $2 of research. New product sales were better than this ratio indicates. Du Pont had declining prices in major products and had to overcome product obsolescence. It continued to have gross profits before depreciation of between 25 and 30 percent of sales, which is good, and its profits on capital averaged 3 percent better than the Dow Jones Industrials. The problem is that the strong companies in industrial materials are large and are hard put to grow very fast or to shelter themselves from the business cycle.

Product Prices

The maturity of the industrial materials suppliers make them subject to price pressures most of the time. In many years, demand is below capacity, and in a year when operations are as low as two-thirds of capacity some suppliers will cut prices to

TABLE 7–A
PRICE SENSITIVITY OF INDUSTRIAL MATERIALS IN RECESSIONS AND BOOMS
(Declines: mild, 10%; typical, 10–20%; severe, over 20%)

Material	*Cyclical Price Declines*
Aluminum	Mild
Copper	Severe
Steel	Mild
Sulfur	Severe
Potash	Typical
Petrochemicals	Typical
Synthetic fibers	Typical
Molding plastics	Typical
Plastic films	Mild
Synthetic rubbers	Mild
Alloying metals	Typical
Solvents and acids	Typical
Industrial gases	Mild
Tool metals	Severe
Antipollution chemicals	None
Adhesives and coatings	Mild
Pigments and binders	Mild
Detergent chemicals	Mild
Papers	Typical
Lumber and plywood	Severe
Oil field chemicals	Typical
Cement	Typical
Plumbing and pipe	Typical
Glass	Typical
Wallboard and siding	Typical
Fiber glass	Severe

hold volume needed to meet expenses. The lower cost suppliers usually meet price competition. The companies operate world-wide and are impacted by all the economic and political factors that cause oscillations in raw materials prices. Investment analysis in this category calls for sharp sensitivity to the effects of price change on earnings.

Chemicals

Since 1957-1959, chemicals prices have had a level price trend, whereas industrial commodity prices have gone up. In 1969 and 1970, industrial chemicals had softer prices than most commodities,

TABLE 7–B
CHEMICAL PRICES, 1968–1970
(wholesale price indexes—1957-59 = 100)

	1968		1969		1970	
	High	Low	High	Low	High	Low
Chemicals and allied products .	99	98	99	98	102	99
Industrial chemicals	99	98	98	97	99	97
Industrial commodities.	110	108	115	111	119	115

and in 1970 price recovery was less than that for industrial commodities. This behavior is partly attributable to excess capacity as well as lower costs from modern plants. The price trends were mitigated by the higher growth in chemical sales, as shown in Table 7-C. During the recession, chemical sales were better than sales of all industrials.

TABLE 7–C
GROWTH COMPARISON, CHEMICALS VERSUS ALL COMMODITIES
(production indexes—1957-59 = 100)

	All Industrial	Industrial Chemicals	Chemicals and Allied Products
1970 index . . .	170	285	243
Annual growth. .	4.5%	9%	7.75%
1969 index . . .	172	280	237
1970 change. . .	–1%	+2%	+2%

Chemicals in World Markets. Chemical exports from the United States are a very important factor in our trade balance.

The fact that exports are about two and one-half times imports shows that the United States is an efficient producer.

	Chemicals			U.S. Trade Balance*	
Year	Exports	Imports	Trade Balance	Total	Excl. Chem.
1970 . . .	3,826	1,450	2,376	3,263	887
1969 . . .	3,383	1,228	2,155	1,963	192d
1968 . . .	3,287	1,129	2,158	1,410	748d
1967 . . .	2,802	958	1,844	4,733	2,889
1966 . . .	2,675	955	1,720	4,812	3,092
1965 . . .	2,402	769	1,633	6,101	4,468
1964 . . .	2,364	702	1,662	7,901	6,239
1963 . . .	2,009	701	1,285	6,180	4,895
1962 . . .	1,862	772	1,090	5,249	4,159
1961 . . .	1,804	738	1,066	6,275	5,209

($ millions)

*Including military grant aid.
d—deficit.
Source: U.S. Department of Commerce.

Profits. Table 7-D shows how profits have lagged behind sales growth since the mid-1960s. Overexpansion was a major culprit, causing operating rates to decline from 85 percent to 74 percent in June 1971. The optimum operating rate is 90 percent. Probably not until the mid-1970s will the desired plant utilization be achieved and profits be restored to the rate earned in the early 1960s. The profit gains for the industry between 1970 and 1975 could be around 80 percent.

Recommendations. The investor should first look for companies that have fairly high average profits on capital and have had sales and profits growth at least one and one-half times the growth of the economy. By high average profits, I mean 3 to 6 percent more than the Dow Jones Industrials. The DJI earnings have been about 10.5 percent of the composite book values. The better companies show earnings equal to 13 to 17 percent on book; a few firms in industries earn 20 percent or more. In chemicals, Dow and Hercules are above average; Lubrizol, 3M Company, and Nalco have been very profitable. (3M Company is discussed in Chapter 9.)

TABLE 7–D
COMPOSITE CHEMICAL INDUSTRY*
(per share data based on Standard & Poor's group stock price indexes)

1963	1964	1965	1966	1967	1968	1969	1970	
26.69	31.88	34.52	38.18	38.63	43.96	47.18	47.51	Sales
6.60	7.99	8.59	8.97	8.12	9.37	9.55	8.89	Operating income
24.73	25.06	24.88	23.49	21.02	21.31	20.24	18.71	Profit margins %
2.10	2.41	2.64	2.88	3.15	3.51	3.70	3.90	Depreciation
2.22	2.58	2.55	2.58	1.99	2.56	2.52	1.95	Taxes
2.75	3.34	3.41	3.50	2.84	3.16	3.17	2.69	Earnings
1.83	1.99	1.89	1.94	1.87	2.00	1.94	1.90	Dividends
10.30	10.48	9.88	9.17	7.35	7.19	6.72	5.66	Earnings as a % of sales
66.55	59.58	55.43	55.43	65.85	63.29	61.20	70.63	Dividends as a % of earnings
62.36	72.87	76.78	75.38	60.53	61.43	57.95	47.11	Price High
52.50	62.96	68.78	49.82	50.87	50.20	40.08	36.93	(1941-43 = 10) Low
22.68	21.82	22.52	21.54	21.31	19.44	18.28	17.51	Price/ High
19.09	18.25	20.17	14.23	17.91	15.89	12.64	13.73	earnings ratios Low
3.49	3.16	2.75	3.89	3.68	3.98	4.84	5.14	Dividend High
2.93	2.73	2.46	2.57	3.09	3.26	3.35	4.03	yield % Low
18.61	20.09	21.94	23.51	24.40	26.25	27.17	27.77	Book value
14.78	16.63	15.54	14.89	11.64	12.04	11.67	9.69	Return on book value %
7.77	8.99	9.90	9.93	10.21	11.21	11.79	11.75	Working capital
2.71	3.85	4.88	5.41	5.07	4.59	5.40	5.93	Capital expenditures

* The companies used for this series of per share data are: Airco, Inc. (formerly Air Reduction); Allied Chemical; American Cyanamid; Chemetron; Dow Chemical; Du Pont; GAF Corp; Hercules Inc.; Monsanto Chemical; Olin Corp.; and Union Carbide.

Metals

The rate of return and growth rates of big metals companies are shown in Table 7-E.

Alcoa profits were very depressed a decade ago, and in 1970 it had just recovered to average performance. Asarco benefited from higher metal prices and from investments in Australia and Peru; in 1971 Asarco had a sharp profits decline that cast doubt on the future of its high profits growth. Inco had growth more from prices of nickel and copper than from tonnage but in 1971 had an earnings setback. Kennecott growth came from copper prices as much as from growth in quantities of copper sold. In the 1960s, Kennecott had about the same earnings growth as Motorola, and in 1960 it had a generous dividend policy. However, in 1970-71 it had become more cautious and cut its dividend,

TABLE 7—E
BIG METALS' RATE OF RETURN AND GROWTH, 1966–1970

Company	Average Earned on Book Value	Average Growth Profits	Sales
ALCOA (Aluminum Company of America	11%	8%	5%
ASARCO (American Smelting & Refining)	15	12	4
INCO (International Nickel)	16	8	8
Kennecott.	14	10	10
Bethlehem Steel	8	0	4
National Steel.	9	0	4
Englehard	16	20	20
Brush Wellman	8	5	4
Phelps Dodge	15	11	11

even though earnings seemed ample to cover the previous rate. Phelps Dodge, an entirely North American copper producer, has favorable costs. Between 1960 and 1970, profits almost tripled. In 1971, its setback of 35 percent was caused largely by a strike. Dividends were a little over 40 percent of profits and unusually safe. Phelps Dodge is possibly the safest metals investment in the world. Englehard was aggressive in acquisitions and development of operating properties in addition to its main role as the world's largest dealer in metals and minerals.

Metals stock prices tend to rise after almost all other stocks. This tendency seems particularly true for copper company stocks. Among metals producers, copper companies have had the best average earnings growth. Unlike other industrial raw materials, copper is really scarce, and its long-term price trend approximately compensates for inflation. Since the late 1940s, copper has about doubled in price. Although high grade copper deposits in Africa and South America could produce at costs low enough to threaten the 50-cent average price per pound, the enormous capital required simply is not available because of the political risks. The large U. S. producers, Phelps Dodge and Kennecott, are not threatened by foreign supply. The only large secure foreign copper mines are in Australia and South Africa.

Figure 7-1 compares the earnings and dividend records of Phelps Dodge and Kennecott to two electronics stocks. All four have had profits cycles at about the same timing, but the P/E ratios of the copper stocks were one-third the P/E ratios of the electronics stocks. Dividend yields were about triple the yields on the electronics stocks.

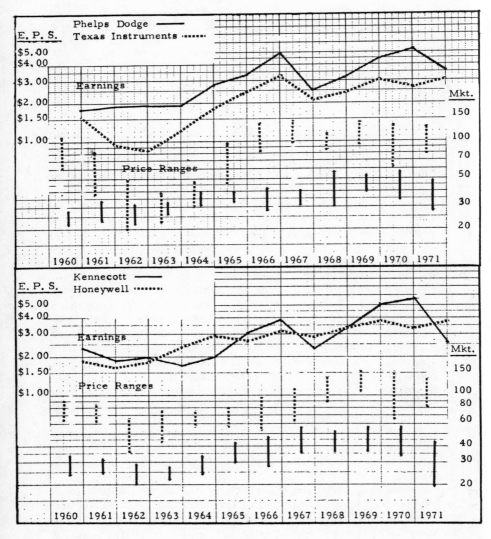

Figure 7-1.

Building Products

Table 7-F shows the rate of return and growth data for building industry companies.

TABLE 7—F
BUILDING INDUSTRY'S RATE OF RETURN AND GROWTH, 1960–1970

Company	Average Earned on Book Value	Average Growth Profits	Sales
Armstrong Cork	9%	0%	3%
Carrier Corp.	11	5	7
Georgia-Pacific	14	8	12
Johns Manville.	10	2	5
Lone Star Industries	8	0	4
NL Industries	13	0	4
Owens-Corning Fiberglas	8	0	7
PPG Industries	7	0	5
U. S. Gypsum	7	neg.	4

There are explanations for the poor performance, but the main point is that this is a tough business. In the late 1960s and early 1970s, the total volume of construction was strong relative to the U. S. economy, but building companies were not able to obtain much profit from the alternating strength of commercial and residential building.

Few people have the skills needed to invest successfully in a slow-moving, cyclical type of business. Good profits on building stocks were obtained in the second half of 1970 and early 1971, but it was largely a professional market play.

Building Growth Stocks. Construction is an enormous area in which specialists develop. In Chapter 6, five stocks were added to my growth stock group (see Table 7-G). For example, Masco, which pioneered single-handle faucets, is one of the 40 most profitable larger companies in America, with 10 percent post-tax profits on sales. The two national builders, Kaufmann & Broad and Ryan Homes, have been 20 percent growth stocks and bid fair to continue. Skyline Corporation is the number-one mobile homes firm with earnings of $15 million and growing above 20 percent.

Air conditioning offers two growth candidates. Tecumseh Products is the principal supplier of compressors for the industry. It is somewhat cyclical but had an average growth above 10 percent. Fedders Corporation was a turnaround in the mid-1960s. I do not foresee continuation of 30 percent gain in sales per share, but it is capable of growth as high as 12 percent a year.

Numerous financial service companies also are related to the building field; for example, savings and loan firms, real estate investment trusts, and mobile homes financing.

TABLE 7–G
BUILDING INDUSTRY GROWTH STOCKS, 1960–1970

Company	Average Earned on Book Value	Average Growth Profits	Sales
Masco Corp.	23%	13%	15%
Kaufmann & Broad..............	20	25	25
Ryan Homes..................	25	25	12
Skyline Corp.	50	42	27
Fedders Corp.	20	15	12
Tecumseh Products	18	10	11

Cars and Trucks

American investors who know Ford and GM have 80 percent of the information about the car and truck manufacturing business and almost all of the figures on the profits. Motor vehicles do not have sales growth faster than that of the economy, and yet these two companies often generate 5 percent of the profits earned by all corporations. Ford originated production line manufacture, and GM wrote the book on management. Numerous other companies have participated in the production of cars and trucks, all know what is in the book, and yet the lessons have been hard to apply.

Truck manufacturing is mainly in subsidiaries of the car makers and of multidivision companies such as International Harvester, Signal Companies, and Consolidated Freightways. Automotive manufacturing stocks are useful mainly for income when they are cheap. In a bull market, stronger gains usually may be had in growth stocks.

Other Automotive Companies

The most successful automotive manufacturers, other than GM and Ford, in the main provide replacement supplies and parts. The largest companies make car, truck, and machine tires, which have milder cycles than do vehicles. It is a tough, competitive business with militant labor unions. Firestone and Goodyear are the more consistent companies. As a group, they grow 2 percent faster than the Dow Jones Industrials, although usually their dividend yields are lower. Investor experience with them is similar to the overall market.

There are growth companies in the replacement parts field. Purolator, Inc., filter maker, has the longest record of growth in sales over 10 percent a year; profits on common equity average about 25 percent. Genuine Parts Company, a distributor of replacement parts to independent repair shops, has had a growth rate that consistently topped 10 percent. Monroe Auto Equipment has been growing over 15 percent a year thanks to smart promotion of replacement shock absorbers.

In summary, the automotive field does give some investment opportunities, although intermediate capital gains are what we may look for.

Machines and Machinery

From the investor's viewpoint, industrial equipment manufacture is a complex group of cyclical industries. Since these industries are involved with the automation of manufacturing — which is essentially application of electricity to increase productivity — we can reason that they should grow faster than the national economy. We think that fact can be demonstrated.

Long-term plots of earnings per share can help to show the rhythms of industry leaders such as General Electric, Caterpillar Tractor, Clark Equipment, Cincinnati Milacron, Ex-Cell-O, and Warner & Swasey. The amount of fluctuation in earnings per share (see Figure 7-2) is obvious; the difficult thing to foresee is when the cycle moves will occur. In general, their ups and downs are greater than those for the market averages, and different timing often is involved. In a period of a rising economy, profits of equipment suppliers most often tend to move up later than do those of the majority of other companies. Capital goods booms usually come late in a period of business expansion.

Problems

Most capital equipment makers employ workers who belong to relatively militant unions. Serious, long strikes have been common for the companies; therefore, it has been necessary for some equipment makers to provide labor cost escalation in sales contracts.

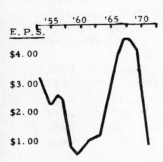

Cincinnati Milacron

Machine builder suffers over 50 percent setbacks in profits in downcycles.

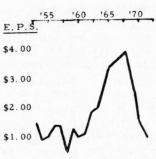

Warner & Swasey

The metal working machine industry is subject to severe cyclical declines.

Caterpillar Tractor

Because it grows at almost 10 percent, Caterpillar profit cycles have been moderate.

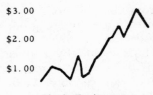

Clark Equipment

Average growth of 10 percent has had softened profits declines. Strikes have been a factor in earnings setbacks.

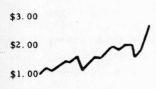

General Electric

Strikes have caused profits setbacks for GE whose sales mix tends to avert downturns.

'55   '60   '65   '70

Ex-Cell-O

When precision machine tool work slumps, Ex-Cell-O has had profits setbacks of 50 percent or worse.

'55   60   '65   '70

Figure 7-2.

Because of erratic new order patterns, it is fairly common for business to be booked at discounts from list prices or profitable prices, list or other. In the past, during a slump suppliers of electric power apparatus have contracted for a couple of years' output; then they have endured a profitless prosperity.

Stocks

At some stage in a bull market, machines and machinery stocks will have a large percent price change. It is not usual for them to top out right at the time a bear market starts its decline. Often they do not begin to rise until months after the averages have turned up. The question is how to judge when to own them or sell them short; price moves do not often coordinate with sales and profits.

Book Value or Dividend Ratios

Not many investors pay much attention to book value as a guide to stock price trends; however, the book value is a more stable statistic than are the oscillating earnings. Dividends are also consistent, although not immune to cuts. Some machine stocks sell at book value in bear markets, and the higher grade stocks usually sustain some amount of premium compared to book value.

As a rule, the highest price relative to book value has been about double the lowest. For example, if in past years the stock usually had a low at one and one-half times book value and it is now at three times book, it won't go up in response to further profit gains. If in a bear market its price is near the low historic ratio of price to book value, it will stop its decline even in the face of collapsing earnings.

Electric-Electronic

Although their growth is above the rate of the world economies, most electric and electronic businesses are cyclical in sales and severely cyclical in profits. Only a few of the companies have avoided organization of workers by militant unions. Although engineering and product design are important in electric-electronic industries, most companies have failed to translate technical effort into regular profits growth for stockholders. Disorderly price competition is prevalent in the industry groups.

Overpricing of Stocks

Because the industries are engaged in a number of interesting technologies, investors have long been likely to overrate the stocks in terms of prices paid in proportion to dividends and profits. Speculators tend to be gullible when they hear and read the language of press releases. There is a tendency to confuse the sales department praise of new products with analytical evaluations.

Consumer Products

Most American homes are equipped with a dozen household electric-electronic items; such products represent mainly a replacement market, some sectors of which are subject to Japanese competition. Very high profits earned in the last quarter-century left companies such as Zenith, Whirlpool, Magnavox, and Corning Glassworks with strength for future efforts; however, numerous other companies lost their shirts. In 1971, the stocks participated fully in the bull market, confirming their usefulness as capital gains vehicles.

Growth in factory sales of consumer electronic products ceased after 1966. The early 1960s was the era of color television and stereophonic music. As far as is known, no new products of such importance are now ready for a big growth phase. Cyclical recovery can be foreseen in color television set sales, but prospects did not look terribly strong in mid-1971.

In the consumer electrical category, more has been occurring. Air conditioning grew firmly in 1970 and 1971, and new types of appliances continued to hit the market. Electric hair curlers were hot items, although most sales were made by cosmetics firms. In summary, new electric appliances tend to be fad devices, and it is hard for investors to profit from them.

Industrial Equipment

Although diversified, the industrial electric-electronic group has a common purpose. It helps its customers to automate their facilities for greater productivity. Most of the equipment manufacture requires a great deal of skilled labor and is not susceptible to automatic production. Employment costs are high relative to sales volume. As a consequence, labor relations tend to be difficult, and strikes are frequent, although workers are relatively productive.

Product engineering is often a source of problems. The companies are expected to provide advanced performance and minimum prices to customers, and competitive bidding is usual. Equipment must be made to perform at customer locations; so supplier personnel normally is absorbed in the field, servicing equipment until it works.

Products are paid for with capital funds that must be appropriated by the buyers. Decisions to buy are often major ones for the customers, arrived at quite differently from purchase of materials or supplies to be consumed in day-to-day operations. Decisions on orders are subject to cycles in capital spending; the order placement seldom occurs at times most satisfactory for suppliers.

Demands on management are relatively complex. In these industries, the assortment of managements includes a range of competence that is about the same as in American industry as a whole. Most managers have had to make changes in their companies to adapt them to product and market changes not foreseen by the men who built the companies. They have had to decide when to phase out old business divisions as they create new operations on a pioneering basis.

It is most difficult for people on the outside to appraise correctly all the variables in the industrial electric-electronic industry. Security analysts have difficulty in making accurate forecasts for industrial electronic company earnings because of the variables mentioned.

Emerson Electric Company stands out in this group of stocks. As a manufacturer of electric motors, lighting products, controls, and systems, Emerson achieved consistent growth at 14 percent a year from 1953 through 1970.

Electric. The major electrical companies, General Electric and Westinghouse, dominate the industrial electric markets. They make most of the electric utility apparatus, and they manufacture electric equipment for factories that use electric motors, drives, controls, and power distribution equipment. In 1971, GE and Westinghouse were more prosperous than they had been in a long time. They grow about 2 percent faster than the U. S. economy. Neither was able to establish profitable foreign operations in the era when most American companies created big foreign operations; so their growth is essentially tied to the growth in American electric power consumption.

Electronics. Over half of industrial electronics is in computing, a subject covered in Chapter 9. Communication and broadcasting equipment are manufactured by such companies as A. T. & T., General Telephone, RCA, I. T. & T., and some aerospace firms. It is hard to find a direct investment in this category. Most of the growth is in telephone equipment.

Components and Supplies

The main factor in electronic components is volatility of sales and product prices. The stocks tend to have bigger price swings than do the stock market averages. Although new inventions are characteristic, competitive forces and cycles in customer businesses make it hard to sustain high profit margins.

In Chapter 6, I explained the variable growth of Texas Instruments, which has been a creative supplier of components for modern electronics. To keep ahead, Texas Instruments has had to reduce product prices 30 percent a year. It is hard to imagine a business with sales growing at 10 percent a year in the face of 30 percent yearly price cuts, but T. I. does it. Growth attracts competition, but the pace of change in products and prices plus the cycles in customer demand make this a bloody business.

One company that has stood out for steady growth in electronic components is AMP, Inc. This company is a supplier of connecting devices for electronics, but its success is based more on the supply of machinery and tools that automate application of its products in customer plants.

It is difficult to forecast the future of these stocks. Knowledge of AMP, Texas Instruments, and Motorola may be all that is needed. One should be wary of most stocks in the electronics components area. The time for small companies is past, and the, also-ran companies do not have the appeal.

Aerospace

There can be profit opportunities in aerospace stocks, but it is difficult for most investors to make good judgments. The electronic part of Defense budgets has a tendency to gain relative to overall budget.

Medical, Civil, Environmental

Almost every investor is aware that there should be growth in medical electronics and civil affairs and also that there must be environmental testing electronics. Therefore, stocks of such manufacturers have high market prices.

For many years, medical electronics was a struggling small business. However, by 1970 it had become fairly large and had begun to attract giant corporations. Du Pont Company entered the body-fluid analysis field. Hewlett-Packard, a major electronic instruments firm, broadened its line of medical instruments. H-P was one of many companies questing for hospital computer automation. It seemed that the resources of big companies would subsidize their medical electronics efforts in a fashion that would make things difficult for small specialty firms. However, SCAM Instrument, a company with success in hospital electronics monitoring, had changed its business by acquisition of Riley Stoker. By upgrading Riley, it more than doubled earnings, and steam generating became more important than hospital systems.

In civil electronics, the most profitable products were Motorola's two-way radios for police and industrial guards. Motorola earns about half its profits from mobile radios and dominates the field.

When we examine environmental electronic-electric gadgetry, it becomes clear that direct investment is impractical. The instruments used to measure pollutants are largely cheap versions of laboratory instruments. The electrostatic precipitation equipment used in smokestacks are minor products for large companies and even for a pollution specialist such as Research-Cottrell.

Investment in this whole area is a matter of stock price guesswork. There is no opportunity to buy value in terms of earnings and dividends; so the investor must make an optimistic projection about future earnings and then forecast what the stock market evaluation of the projected profit will be and when earnings might be realized, if they are.

Transportation

Airlines

Many years ago one of my predecessors, a Wall Street pundit, commented that everyone engaged in the transport of people in vehicles eventually went broke. The implication of this forecast is that the airline industry is on an inexorable course toward bankruptcy. In the past, when people carriers went bust, or almost ruined their associated freight haulage departments their passengers were on the surface. The prospect of having bankruptcy hit while thousands of passengers are in the air is more disquieting. If bankruptcy is averted, the airline industry will have enjoyed the most remarkable combination of rejuvenated management, intelligent behavior on the part of federal bureaucrats, and enlightened self-interest on the part of the U.S. public.

The airline industry is a victim of managerial concern for volume rather than profits, regulatory conceptual confusion, irresponsible public demands for service, and investment industry emphasis on raising too much capital. The industry has unrealistic ideas about the service that can be supplied economically. They offer to move every businessman who has a whim to go from his location at 5:00 P.M. on Friday to some other city. They provide extravagant schedule availability, flying empty airplanes all over the landscape under the guise of service. They have bought quantities of airplanes on the assumption that each airline would get all the business. They have completely disregarded the sensitivity of people on the ground, whose former tranquility is disturbed by noisy aircraft.

Federal regulators destroyed a reasonably sensible allocation of route assignments to airlines with a crazy policy of increased competition or access to the profitable routes of other airlines. For some reason, they forgot that a regulated monopoly is provided to assure enforced supply of adequate and economic service. For example, in a schizophrenic fit federal regulators in one year tripled the number of airlines servicing Hawaii. Some years earlier they forgot that Eastern Airlines' profitable New York to Miami service was paying for much desired but marginal airline service in the eastern United States.

Americans are impatient with transportation facilities and, for the most part, expect airlines to haul them about promptly whenever they are in a mood to go. Neither the public nor the airlines seem to have much interest in the different rates for hours or days when people fly. As a consequence, airlines must operate more aircraft than are needed for the people who travel. Weather delays are hardly tolerated. Americans are spoiled by the quality of service provided.

In raising capital for airlines, the investment banking industry was more concerned with the amount of commissions for sales of bonds and stocks than with the economic sense of the equipment purchase schedules. (Bond underwriters really do not look at the merits of their issues the way stock analysts do.) In the mid-1960s, when first fully equipped with jet aircraft, airlines enjoyed marvelous profit rates. For a couple of years, they earned

10 to 13 percent on total capital. While this may not seem like an excessive rate, there is no precedent for a federally regulated industry's sustaining such a rate of return for long. The regulators always create conditions that depress the return on assets below 10 percent. For the airlines, the prescription was more competition and pressure for lower rates.

When deals were being made for financing fleet additions, the companies and bankers assumed that they could increase their capacity and maintain the high rates of return. There was hot debate among stock analysts at the time over the probability that the airline profit rates should come under pressure. The smartest specialists switched to investment management or other specialties. In the meantime, astronomical amounts of bond capital were being raised for airlines. For the next decade, the airlines will be preoccupied with paying off the debt and will not be in condition to pay dividends to stockholders. Until the market catches up to the equipment, there probably will be pressure on rates.

Airline Stocks. Skilled speculators have done well with airline stocks because of their ability to judge the tides of market enthusiasm or skepticism. The ups and downs in airline stocks do not coordinate very well with the profits of the companies. At the end of 1971, the airline group of stocks was trading at over 20 times the earnings they were projected to achieve in 1972 if their earnings recovery should come up to optimistic estimates. In a less glamorous industry, the stocks would be unlikely to discount so far ahead.

Railroads

Most people are conscious of railroads from the financial horror stories in the press or from their frustrations with railroad service for shippers or receivers of commodities. Yet in view of the unobstructed rights of way in and out of cities and towns, the automatic switches and signals, the enormous locomotives, and the hordes of experienced workers, it seems that the railroads should be as adept at moving goods as the telephone system is in connecting voices via intricate routes in seconds.

Some argue that the trucking industry is given advantage by highway systems created with tax money, while railroads pay taxes. A generation ago similar complaints were voiced about government subsidy of barge operations. In another complaint area is criticism of ICC practices, particularly with respect to rate making. Insistence on maintaining competing routes and organizations comes up for a few brickbats, and the feather-bedding and other restrictive practices of railroad labor brother-hoods are given a share of the blame.

All these factors had something to do with the problems of the railroad industry. Books have been written about the plight of railroads and how they got where they are. Actually, they have been in trouble for decades, largely because they have let them-selves be ruled by the past and have never made any effort to attract talent or given scope to the young people who came along in each generation. The railroad industry never seems to have thought of itself as a system that could introduce new technology into the industrial environment. It took a car and truck manufacturer, General Motors, to perfect the diesel-electric locomotive for the railroads. After the railroads had diesels, they really did not look at them as advanced, flexible machines that would result in improved service; they just used them to reduce locomotive costs and to haul longer trains.

Only a few railroads are good at customer services; the industry as a whole hardly understands what the word *service* means. When you hire a trucker to move some merchandise from supplier to customer, the trucker concentrates on that one chore. Railroads always seem to look at cars as links in a chain and never seem to associate a particular car with the immediate needs of a customer. Railroad organizations have proven ill-equipped to cope with business opportunities such as shipping hot metal or tar to arrive at destinations before the materials harden. Users of asphalt tar had to buy highway tankers because railroads simply did not deliver on time. It should be simpler to organize a fully controlled, automated railway system to move the tar a few hundred miles than it is to ship it over a highway that encompasses an enormous variety of road conditions.

Railroad people cannot conceive of a railroad line populated with hundreds or thousands of cargo containers hauled by separated tractors. They cannot seem to imagine columns of cargo carriers rushing along their tracks without each unit's being hooked to another and pulled chain-style by a great big engine. Thousands of trucks rush at a mile a minute along highways parallel to railroads without climbing up each other's backs, and they stop at traffic lights without incident. Moreover, the practical problems of designing vehicles to switch from rail to road cannot possibly be so difficult of solution as the railroads want everyone to think.

Major railroad companies have profits of between $20 and $80 million — large, but not really big. For comparison, E. I. Du Pont de Nemours has profits equal to the 10 largest railroad companies. Railroad balance sheets offer some fantastic numbers. The net fixed assets listed for the railroads are larger than Du Pont's net fixed assets. Half a dozen railroads list $1 *billion plus* of fixed assets. One need not be a business expert to be skeptical about billion-dollar balance sheets when the average profits are about $40 million.

Railroads do not depreciate their roadbeds, although they do expense track repairs and materials. Accounting practices have resulted in fixed assets figures that are much too high for the income-producing capacity of the rails.

Only a handful of railroad stocks have had dividend growth as good as the industrial averages, which means about 4 to 5 percent average annual increase. Southern Pacific is unique in having raised its dividend 12 times in the 13 years through 1971. Its price performance has been similar to the whole market, but its yield was usually 1.5 to 2 percent higher than the yields of industrial stocks. It made its highs and lows with the whole market.

Illinois Central, Gulf, Mobile & Ohio, St. Louis-San Francisco, and Canadian Pacific have had dividend growth equal to or better than the averages. In 1971, it did appear that railroads as a group were improving their profits relative to the economy.

Highway Transport

The highway cargo hauling industry is possibly the most sensible group of transportation companies. Unfortunately, they are the most labor-intensive companies, and drivers are represented by the aggressive Teamsters Union. Ease of entry by almost anyone who so desires makes competition severe, and the common carriers also compete with shipper-operated trucks. The highway carrier industry is difficult for investors to analyze. Most of them have had series of mergers, which were difficult to integrate. The industry as a whole has had limited access to the equity market for capital, and most companies operate with high ratios of borrowed capital, as shown in Table 7-H.

Retained cash flow of 20 percent of capital would be good in an

TABLE 7–H
CAPITAL RATIOS AND CASH FLOWS
(1970; $ millions)

	Debt	Equity	Retained Cash Flow	Capital Spending
Associated Transport. . .	$ 31	$19	$ 4.5	$ 6
Consolidated Freightways	84	73	22.5	25
Leasway Transport	157	42	48	80

industry whose equipment lasted longer than do trucks. In practice, financing trucks with debt is less risky than debt financing for stationary machines, since trucks are marketable. The availability of credit, of course, makes it easier for competition to get equipment.

Trucker Stocks and Qualities. The stock market rates truck company stocks in a normal manner for the qualities and growth. The quality ratings are fairly low because of the irregular profits. Trucking stocks are a small group in terms of shares and market capitalization and are a kind investor specialty.

Earnings Records. The better records of Roadway Express and McLean Trucking are given in Chapter 4. Roadway has hardly any debt capital. Figure 7-3 shows the earnings per share history of four stocks. The only one free of cyclical setbacks was Roadway Express.

Equipment for Transportation. Managements of transportation equipment and materials have had a hard life in the last decade. The companies buy:

airplanes	radios and radars	signals
locomotives	buses	freight loaders
freight cars	rails and ties	containers
truck trailers	large diameter pipe	tires
truck tractors	pumps and valves	

Suppliers for the industries exist in enormous quantities, particularly those for jet engine and diesel fuel. Earnings of the equipment makers are possibly the most severely cyclical of any group one can name.

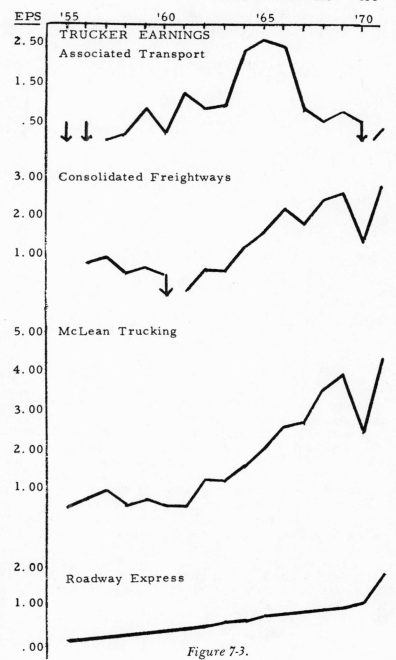

Figure 7-3.

8

Staples Industries

A staples industry is one that supplies products or services that are used up in a short time and have a relatively steady market demand. Staples industries are diversified and include: consumable products (food, beverages, household supplies, tobacco); financial institutions (banks, credit companies, insurance, and others); retail trade (general merchandise, department stores); fuel-energy industries (oil, gas, coal); regulated utilities (electric power, natural gas pipelines, telephones).

One of the themes of this book is that we should want to invest in the stocks of companies whose managements can make major decisions that when implemented can distinguish a company from rivals. Such opportunities are found in these industries, except in the utilities. In developing my concepts, I have stressed the possibility for application of entrepreneurial talents, internally generated growth, product development, high profit rates, and ability to adapt to changes in our economic society. In modern times, utilities have not been entrepreneurial industries.

Consumables

Growth and Competition

Companies that supply foods, beverages, and household products are sheltered from most business cycle effects. They are bothered to some degree by price and supply cycles in agricultural products, including coffee, cattle feed, chickens, fats and oils, and others. Some problems concern the environmental effects of their products and process wastes. Marketing factors are major determinants of their success or lack thereof.

We have to differentiate between items whose intrinsic components are of high value compared to selling prices and those in which raw materials are small parts of the total cost. For instance, soft drink formulators have insignificant raw materials costs because the bottlers buy their own sugar, the main commodity used. Meat suppliers deal with expensive commodities whose qualities can be evaluated by consumers. Raw materials are of middling importance in soaps and detergents which are affected by commodity supply and prices only to the degree that they use tallow. Bakers have substantial raw material costs and perishability to cope with.

Prices of Consumables Stocks

These stocks are somewhat less volatile than most stocks. The good ones seldom become very cheap in terms of price ratios as measured relative to earnings or dividends. Table 8-A gives some data to help judge the probable timing of price changes for the stocks. Growth rates are approximations of growth in recent years and probable growth in the early 1970s. The methods described in Chapter 6 were used.

Relative Yield

The historic relative yield will be described in Chapter 11, which covers methods for valuing stocks. The relative yield is a ratio of the cash dividend yield of a stock to the concurrent cash dividend yield of the Dow Jones Industrials Average. For example: A stock has a dividend of $1. At market price of 25, its yield is 4 percent. On the same date, the DJI dividend may be

$36, with the index at 900; its yield also would be 4 percent. At that point, the relative yield would be 1.0 (4 percent on the stock divided by 4 percent on the averages). Again, if yield on stock is 3 percent, the relative yield would be 0.75 (3 percent on stock divided by 4 percent yield of the averages); for a stock with current yield of 5 percent, the relative yield is 1.25.

TABLE 8–A
GROWTH RATES AND RELATIVE YIELDS–CONSUMABLES STOCKS

	Average Growth	Historic Relative Yield	Dividends as % of Reported Earnings
Beatrice Foods	9%	0.75	45%
Borden Co.	4	1.10	65
Campbell Soup	4	0.90	60
Carnation Co.	9	0.50	30
Consolidated Foods	9	0.65	50
General Foods	5	0.90	60
General Mills	8	0.65	45
Kellogg Co.	8	1.10	65
Kraftco	7	1.15	60
Standard Brands	8	0.90	60
Ralston Purina	8	0.65	40
Colgate-Palmolive.	6	0.70	50
Procter & Gamble	8	0.70	55
Coca-Cola	13	0.50	60
Pepsico, Inc.	10	0.60	45
R. J. Reynolds	7	1.40	55
Philip Morris	15	0.90	40
Norton Simon	13	No div.	0

Staples stocks are a good group of stocks for the application of relative yield in judging whether the stocks are cheap or expensive. Although the stocks do alter their growth rates, such change happens gradually. More common is for a company to alternate between strong and slower phases in growth, which usually are related to product changes and may include acquisitions.

Fluctuations in Relative Yield. A stock with a relative yield of 0.8 might fluctuate from 0.6 to 1.0. Sometimes, the variation may occur when the averages have large moves and the individual stocks do not move in pace with the market. At times, the company may be having excellent success when the cyclical sectors of the economy are in recession.

Relative Yield, Growth, and Payout. From Table 8-A, we can see that relative yields tend to be low compared to the Dow Jones Industrials when long-term growth is higher than the averages. Some of the differences between the yield of a stock and the yield of the averages can be explained by quality considerations. The growth of this group has been around 8 percent compared to about 4.5 percent for the Dow Jones Industrials. The relative yield has been about 0.8 compared to the DJI. Over the years, their yield has been about 0.75 percent less than the DJI and growth has been 3 percent better, so that investors have had a return of about 2 percent more than on the averages.

Assuming the Dow Jones Industrials are in the middle of their range of fluctuation as measured by dividend yield that has been around 4 percent much of the time, purchase of this group of stocks when their relative yields are about in line with historic experience should result in a return to the investor that is about 2 percent better than would be obtained from random stock purchases. If the yield on the averages was below 4 percent, we would have to buy these stocks at relative yields that were higher than usual in order to get a better than average return on our money. In bear markets, when the Dow Jones Industrials yield is over 4.5 percent, you may be able to buy the stocks at relative yields that are lower than normal. These stocks normally move up as promptly as does the general market in years when prices are rising, and they are often more stable in the bear markets.

TABLE 8–B
FOODS–COMPOSITE

	Sales per Share	Earnings per Share	Dividends per Share	Price/Earnings Ratio High	Low	Book Value % Return
1961 ..	92.75	2.60	1.48	27.80	19.33	11.11
1962 ..	95.87	2.71	1.58	24.63	17.53	11.24
1963 ..	98.47	2.92	1.69	22.54	19.19	11.50
1964 ..	103.66	3.31	1.79	21.46	19.95	12.34
1965 ..	108.79	3.44	1.94	21.34	19.59	12.22
1966 ..	119.93	3.81	2.05	18.08	13.23	13.23
1967 ..	120.78	3.95	2.18	17.03	14.49	12.98
1968 ..	127.40	3.91	2.25	19.42	15.17	12.36
R1969 ..	133.71	3.80	2.29	19.17	16.52	12.36
P 1970 ..	141.13	4.24	2.33	16.44	12.81	13.35

Food

The progress and profits of the food industries are shown in Tables 8-B. 8-C, and 8-D; data is based on Standard & Poor's indexes. As shown in the composite, Table 8-B, all companies have grown 4 percent a year in sales, which is less than the growth of the majority of industrial stocks. However, earnings overall have been less cyclical than those for other industrials, and profits on book value have been slightly higher.

Packaged foods (General Foods, General Mills, Gerber Products, Kellogg Company, Quaker Oats, and Standard Brands), with a sales growth at about 6.5 percent, were the most profitable of the 7 categories in the composite, while meat packing companies had the lowest profit rate.

TABLE 8—C
PACKAGED INDUSTRIES RECORDS, 1961—1970

	Sales per Share	Earnings per Share	Dividends per Share	Price 1941—43 = 10		Price/Earnings Ratio		Book Value % Return
				High	Low	High	Low	
1961	54.63	3.05	1.68	100.00	64.28	32.79	21.08	16.64
1962	56.37	3.30	1.87	90.78	61.72	27.51	18.70	16.80
1963	60.26	3.55	2.07	89.37	74.17	25.17	20.89	16.68
1964	66.41	3.84	2.19	95.06	88.04	24.76	22.93	16.74
1965	70.66	4.13	2.36	98.57	88.16	23.87	21.35	16.80
1966	77.73	4.42	2.48	88.89	66.68	20.11	15.09	17.80
1967	84.11	4.75	2.67	86.13	74.88	18.13	15.76	18.13
1968	91.52	4.81	2.84	97.90	75.39	20.35	15.67	16.37
1969	102.75	5.20	2.90	99.40	84.44	19.12	16.24	18.64
P1970	107.89	5.55	3.03	101.55	78.21	18.30	14.09	18.85

Stocks in these indexes at the present time are preceded by an asterisk.
*General Foods (12—31—25)   *Quaker Oats (12—31—25)
*General Mills (2—19—69)   *Standard Brands (12—31—25)
*Gerber Products (1—4—61)   Beechnut—Life Saver (1—18—56 to 1—17—68)
*Kellogg Co. (5—3—61)   Best Foods (2—20—46 to 9—24—58)
                                 Cream of Wheat (1—16—35 to 8—9—61)

In general, the most profitable companies have established strong consumer brand identification, and they are not much affected by commodity supply and price problems. They have know-how in packaging, and they cater to consumer interest in convenience and to impulse eating. Many companies have above-average growth, and several have done well with simultaneous acquisition programs and profit improvement.

TABLE 8–D
MEAT PACKING INDUSTRIES GROWTH RECORD 1961–1970

	Sales Per Share	Earnings Per Share	Dividends Per Share	Price/Earnings Ratio		Value Percent Return
				High	Low	
1961	246.49	1.47	1.04	21.39	18.52	4.62
1962	250.72	1.71	0.97	20.04	12.50	5.30
1963	245.22	1.73	0.97	16.92	14.30	5.29
1964	255.78	2.79	1.00	12.92	10.13	8.15
1965	250.37	1.85	1.19	20.95	14.96	5.44
1966	275.01	2.25	1.21	15.65	10.09	6.93
1967	325.05	2.99	1.47	14.71	9.57	6.97
1968	323.38	2.52	1.18	21.44	14.33	7.32
1969	345.12	2.77	0.95	21.68	13.82	7.77
P1970	339.83	3.22	0.98	13.50	10.03	8.99

Among the New York Stock Exchange listed stocks, almost half of the packaged brand name food stocks are in Grades I and II. Perishable foods stocks as well as grain millers are in lower grades. It is easy to differentiate between the high grade and low grade stocks in this category. The sample of food and beverage stocks in Chapter 3 was selected for quality.

The Turnaround Record. Over half a dozen substantial branded food product marketers have been successfully upgraded in terms of profits on capital in the last decade. That these are billion dollar sales companies with long histories indicates that this industry area is particularly susceptible to application of good marketing and acquisition talent, which tells us a bit about the nature of managerial talent in this country. Not many managers are good at redirecting cyclical materials-producing companies, but a lot of executives have the flair for stimulating consumer goods marketing companies. The measure I used for judging turnarounds was simply profit on stockholder capital. The turnaround companies had improvements on capital from about 10 percent to around 15 to 17 percent on equity capital. No turnarounds have occurred when the companies have been in commodity businesses, with profits of 5 percent on capital.

Beverages

Beverage stocks normally move up as promptly as the general market in years of rising prices, and they are often more stable in bear markets. They have grown more rapidly than other staples industries and are an exceptionally profitable group. The below-average profits growth in 1970 was caused by the U. S. Food and Drug Administration's ban on cyclamates.

TABLE 8–E
BEVERAGE INDUSTRIES' GROWTH RECORD 1961–1970

| | Sales | Earnings per Share | Dividends per Share | Price/Earnings Ratio | | Book Value % Return |
				High	Low	
1961	16.22	1.19	0.87	30.18	23.24	15.20
1962	17.31	1.30	0.88	26.16	19.32	15.64
1963	19.10	1.40	0.96	27.45	21.02	15.77
1964	23.40	1.71	1.04	27.27	22.40	17.57
1965	26.34	1.98	1.17	29.41	23.35	18.68
1966	30.25	2.26	1.26	25.75	20.62	19.37
1967	32.70	2.47	1.38	32.57	22.44	21.69
1968	35.61	2.73	1.51	35.75	27.39	21.96
1969	40.41	2.96	1.69	34.42	27.83	21.85
1970	46.09	3.41	1.82	30.55	23.48	23.58

Tobacco

In the early 1960s, arguments over the relationships between cigarettes and health slowed down tobacco industry stocks. Tobacco companies acquired food, beverage, office equipment, transport, and other subsidiaries, whose profits tended to depress their incomes as percent of sales. However, by the late 1960s tobacco profits showed an upturn. Investors might observe that health warnings and taxes do not stop smoking.

TABLE 8–F
TOBACCO INDUSTRIES' GROWTH RECORD 1946–1970

| | Earnings | | Dividends per Share | Book Value | |
	Per Share	% of Sales		Per Share	Percent Return
1951	1.02	6.40	0.79	9.38	10.87
1954	1.18	7.54	0.86	10.18	11.59
1957	1.63	8.61	0.98	12.00	13.58
1960	2.22	9.63	1.24	14.88	14.92
1963	2.48	10.16	1.46	17.67	14.04
1965	2.68	10.32	1.57	18.76	14.29
1967	3.10	9.61	1.70	19.31	16.05
1969	3.52	7.93	1.96	20.75	16.96
1970	4.17	8.37	2.07	17.72	23.36

Financial Institutions

Financial institutions, include banks, credit companies, savings institutions, life insurance, property insurance, mortgage insurance and banking, mutual fund management, securities brokerage and underwriting, and leasing.

Average Profit Rates

Over the last 15 years, banks' profits on stockholder capital have been comparable to profits of the Dow Jones Industrials Average. In 1970, the profit rates were superior to earnings of industrial stocks. Bank stocks have dividends equal to 45 percent of profits, while other stock averages have had 55 to 65 percent dividend payout records. The lower dividend payments of bank stocks have been compensated for by the difference in growth rates.

During the 1960s, banks had a rising trend in return on capital because of inflationary demand for loans. For a number of years, bank earnings on capital had been lower than industrial company earnings. The 1970s began at the peak for banks in terms of profit rates. By early 1971, loan demand had declined with lower interest rates. It seemed unlikely that bank profits would outperform industrial profits for a couple of years, but at the same time banks appeared capable of earning at profit rates at least as good as industry in general.

During the period of rising interest rates in the later 1960s, bank deposits were not growing so fast as profits or stockholder book value, and this lag may have been a factor in the modest stock market appraisal of bank stocks when they were in their best profits growth period. In the meantime, bank loans were increasing at a clip as fast or faster than book value and even profits. The bank makes its profits mainly on loans and secondarily on sale of services. When money demand is high, depositors draw down deposits. In 1969 and 1970, we saw the phenomenon of time deposits being reduced while the public switched to short-term Treasury issues that yielded as much as 7 percent. Meanwhile, banks borrowed enormous sums on high-rate Certificates of Deposit and Eurodollars and from the Federal Reserve, and profits went up. To the extent that they could, depositors held smaller amounts of demand deposits.

About a dozen major banks had growth at 8 percent or better during recent decades. Some of them plowed back a higher portion of earnings or had higher returns on capital, and some were improving operations. Very dynamic large companies are not found among banks, but quite a few speeded up growth in the last half of the 1960s. When you compare banking to other staples industries such as utilities, retailers, petroleum, and foods, the number that grew 8 percent a year in profits is impressive.

Variations in Growth

The banking business experienced big changes in the 1960s, the most important being the need to pay much more for deposits. There was a time when interest rates in the short-term money market were so low that corporate treasurers did not bother to invest cash at interest. They just left their money in the bank. In the late 1940s, Treasury Notes in one year paid 1.125 percent. Banks in those times had lots of demand deposits for which they paid nothing but on which they could earn only a pittance.

In 1971, the trend had reversed, and money in unprecedented quantities was flowing into time and savings deposits in face of declining interest rates. By February 1971, Treasury bills yielded under 4 percent where for the 2 prior years they had yielded more than bank interest accounts. Demand deposits did not go up right away because business was paying down bank loans and reducing the compensating balances that had been demanded by banks along with the loans. However, the total quantity of funds available to banks went up, and they experienced some amount of profit squeeze.

Over any money market cycle phase, banks have numerous opportunities to supply funds to business profitably, even when the borrowers' profits are poor. The supply of bond and stock market funds is likely to have timing different from bank money. Most bond market money flow comes from flow of money into pension funds and life insurance reserves, creating a rather even stream that has a slight tendency to slower growth in recessions. Much stock market new money also comes from institutional sources, and a smaller new money flow that varies by large percentages comes from individual decisions to make new stock investments. In general, individuals add to their stock investments with new money when they feel and really are prosperous. Most of this money comes from people in the top tenth of the personal income brackets.

The effect of public interest in buying or liquidating stocks is to facilitate equity financing for industry in the bull market years and inhibit it in down years. Thus, in down years the long-pull institutional investors are nearly overwhelmed with opportunities to buy long-term bonds or stocks. In such years as 1970 and early 1971, institutions were offered fabulous bond buys and also bargains in stocks. Industries such as utilities needed their billions of new money as usual, and the public was not buying much stock. At the start of 1971, a flurry of up prices in bonds occurred, followed by a flop in February when bond price declines were as much as 6 percent in a couple of weeks.

In this kind of situation, the bond market flop sends the would-be borrowers back to the banks until bonds perk up again. In many cases, banks get commitment fees for holding themselves ready to make such loans.

About five dozen bank issues have adequate trading markets for most investor purposes, although only about one-third of these have capitalizations big enough for major institutional investors. As a group, banks' rates have been 1 to 3 percent stronger than the averages of most large stock groups. Valuations of the stocks are usually about in line with other stocks as measured by yields and P/E ratios.

Essentially, the bank stock investor should be looking for 10 percent long-term return and possibly interim gains from purchases at below-average prices. If growth is proportionate to earnings plowback, the banks will continue to grow faster than most staples industries. Cash dividend yields are competitive with most other stock groups.

Selection comes down to quality plus better profit and plowback rates. Bank stocks are from average to somewhat above average in quality. In Table 8-G a few bank stocks are arranged according to profit on capital and earnings plowback in the six years through 1970. The right-hand column is the price divided by the book value at high and low market prices. In most cases, the stocks with higher plowback of earnings merit higher ratios of price/book value.

Table 8-H shows that many banks pay dividends at about the same percent of book value year after year. Therefore, their dividends grow at the same rate as plowback of earnings.

Debate about Book Values

Some bank analysts consider that stockholder equity should

TABLE 8–G
BANK STOCK EARNINGS PLOWBACK

Bank	E/Bk 1970	E/Bk 1965–69	% Plowback 1970	% Plowback 1965–69	Price Range 1970	Price/ Book Value
Citizens & Southern	18%	14%	9.5%	8.5%	37–27	3.90–2.95
Valley National Bank	16	14	9.1	9.0	28–20	2.57–1.85
Wachovia Bank	14	14	9.3	9.5	58–45	2.22–1.72
Bank of New York	17	14	10.7	8.0	54–39	2.04–1.47
National Bank Detroit	14.5	11.5	10.2	7.0	50–37	1.13–0.83
Cleveland Trust	13.5	11.5	9.2	8.0	121–83	1.41–0.97
J. P. Morgan	14	11	8.3	5.0	71–50	1.85–1.30
Republic, Dallas	15	12	7.6	5.0	30–21	2.27–1.57
Bank America	14.5	14	7.5	7.5	67–49	2.05–1.50
Chase Manhattan	13	11	7.4	6.5	56–38	1.75–1.18
Northwest Bancorp	13	12.5	7.4	6.5	37–27	1.53–1.15
Mellon Bank	11	9	6.2	5.0	58–49	1.27–1.07
Wells Fargo	10.5	11	6.0	6.0	43–29	1.28–0.84

TABLE 8–H
DIVIDEND PAYMENTS AS PERCENT OF BOOK VALUE

	61	62	63	64	65	66	67	68	69	70
Bank America	7.3	7.3	7.1	6.9	6.6	6.4	6.7	6.1	6.9	6.6
Citizens & Southern	4.2	4.0	4.1	3.9	3.8	4.6	5.1	5.9	6.0	7.7
Cleveland Trust	2.4	2.2	2.3	2.3	2.5	2.8	3.3	3.6	3.9	3.8
CONILL	4.2	4.2	4.2	4.5	4.7	4.8	4.9	5.1	5.3	5.4
First National Bank of Boston	5.2	5.5	6.0	5.9	5.4	5.4	5.4	5.2	5.3	5.2
National Bank Detroit	4.2	4.2	4.0	4.1	4.0	3.8	4.3	4.3	4.2	4.4
J. P. Morgan	5.5	5.3	5.5	5.4	5.8	5.7	5.8	6.0	6.2	6.4
Republic Bank	6.2	6.1	6.0	5.9	6.3	6.9	6.9	6.7	6.9	7.2
Valley National Bank	4.6	4.5	4.4	4.4	4.9	5.0	5.3	6.0	6.5	6.7
Security Pacific	4.5	4.2	4.2	4.6	4.6	4.3	4.5	4.5	4.7	4.7

include general reserves and 50 percent of loan loss reserves. The argument is that the book equity would be insufficient to carry the deposit and loan structure without the reserves. From this it would follow that the returns on equity calculated are higher than they would be if they were taken as percent of the equity capital plus reserves. To make such a calculation, we would combine the yearly reserve appropriations with the operating earnings. Since reserves increase at about the same rate as book value or even more slowly, the return on equity capital computed in such fashion would be a little lower.

My theory is that the most readily available statistic is more influential than adjusted statistics. Investors will find bank stock book values updated quarterly. When you see that every year the stock price has ranged from one and one-fourth to one and three-fourths times book value, it looks like a helpful guide. Table 8-G shows a good correlation between rate of profit on equity capital and the premium over book value at which the stock trades. Dividend payout percents also look important to investor evaluation.

Earnings of banks are subject to dispute among management, accountants, and investor analysts. The accountants say that real earnings are those figured after losses or gains on the bond portfolios of banks. Banks say that over the years the portfolio gains and losses always balance out. Prior to the 1960s, no one disputed this assertion because it was correct. However, in the 1960s the near doubling of interest rates caused a series of bond portfolio losses that seemed too large to be recovered. In late 1970 and early 1971, the rapid easing of loan demand put banks in position for big bond portfolio additions and it seemed that they might recover the prior losses.

In practice, I think investors pay more attention to dividends than to earnings. Whenever a statistic is in dispute, investors tend to downgrade its importance.

Book Value Ratio

S&P stock reports carry the entry "Ratio of Price to Book Value for Banks." Since 1963, when bank stocks sold at the same P/E ratio as the S&P 425, the price/book ratios changed little.

TABLE 8–I
PRICE/BOOK VALUE RATIOS OF BANK STOCKS

	1963 Mid Price/Book	April 1971 Price/Book
Chase Manhattan	1.5	1.8
CONILL	1.7	1.4
First National City	1.7	1.7
J. P. Morgan	1.7	1.7
Bank America	2.3	1.9
Citizens & Southern	2.3	2.9
Cleveland Trust	1.4	1.1
Northwest Bancorp	1.5	1.5

Relative Earnings

Bank stock EPS gained substantially compared to industrial stocks. In 1963, banks were underearning, and the market accorded a P/E ratio above 18 times in recognition of the latent earning power. In 1971, some investors thought banks had had maximum earnings, while industrials were underearning. The relative P/E for bank stocks was 1.0 in 1963 and about 0.8 in April 1971 compared to the DJI.

As stated earlier, relative yield compares yield of stock to yield of Dow Jones Industrials. The relative yields changed less than the relative P/E. Dividend payout as a percent of operating earnings was somewhat lower. The April 1971 yield on bank stocks at 3.4 percent was about the same as the DJI yield. Some studies we are making suggest a tendency for bank stocks to outperform the DJI when relative yield is at parity. Our relative yield studies show that individual bank stocks that were over-priced in 1963 corrected their relative yields. By August 1971, the rise in industrial stock prices had left banks behind, and they had become relatively undervalued.

TABLE 8–J
BANK STOCK RELATIVE YIELDS VERSUS DJI

	1963	1970	Aug. 1971
Cleveland Trust	.50	.75	1.12
First National City	.85	.90	1.08
Franklin N.Y. Corp.	.60	1.10	1.36
J. P. Morgan	1.00	.90	1.20
Marine Midland	1.00	1.05	1.52
DJI yield	3.3%	4.2%	3.6

Retail Trade

For investors, general merchandise retailing stocks are possibly the easiest group to use as a mirror of the U. S. economy. Their sales grow at about the same rate as consumer income, and the better managed companies sustain their superiority over decades. The stock prices fluctuate almost exactly with the general stock market, while profits cycles are about the same as total corporate profits. The best companies are a bit more recession resistant; the middle grade retail stocks have earnings that vary with the business cycle; and the lower grade stocks may have more severe cycles, but only the most marginal companies ever go in the red.

Sales Mix

General merchandise retailers have ability to adjust their wares to changing consumer preferences and can expand or contract departments with relative ease. When skiing, camping, or boating is popular, the merchandise mix is adjusted in proportion. Paintings are offered by Sears, Roebuck. The effect is to keep general merchandise in tune with the economy.

Food retailers are not in such flexible postures as is general merchandise. The public spends somewhat more on convenience foods, but food does not have growth equal to the economy. The importance of national brands and directly comparable food items subjects grocers to direct comparison shopping and price comparisons. From time to time, consumers blame inflation and rising food costs on grocery chains. The 1960s were a difficult period for the grocery retailers, who had to cope with the premium stamp craze at a time when food costs were rising quite fast. Future prospects are to grow with the economy.

TABLE 8–K
RETAIL FOOD CHAINS GROWTH RECORD – S & P INDEX*

	Sales	Earnings		Book Value % Return	Capital Expenditures
		Per Share	% of Sales		
1956	239.09	3.12	1.30	14.71	6.15
1957	255.70	3.62	1.42	15.50	6.64
1958	277.44	3.57	1.29	14.24	5.29
1959	286.32	3.63	1.27	13.24	4.59
1960	293.76	3.78	1.29	12.89	4.47
1961	302.82	3.78	1.25	12.07	4.67
1962	311.17	3.83	1.23	11.63	4.55
1963	318.81	3.79	1.19	11.06	3.93
1964	331.89	4.13	1.24	11.39	4.62
1965	339.20	4.16	1.23	11.11	5.23
1966	367.21	4.39	1.20	11.10	6.16
1967	377.07	4.13	1.10	10.05	5.48
1968	399.19	4.29	1.07	9.96	5.77
1969	439.97	4.70	1.07	10.19	7.94
1970	464.69	5.08	1.09	10.57	8.36

* Per share data adjusted to stock price index level. Average of stock price indexes 1941–43 equals 10.

Table 8-K shows how food chain earnings growth slowed down in the 1960s. The capital expenditures data shows the heavy expenditures in the 1950s that caused the industry to become overexpanded.

Age and Market Domination

Market domination is essential to long-run success in a retail business; retail chains are very dependent on great depth of management. The importance of depth was demonstrated in the 1960s.

From the late 1940s through the 1950s, new retail companies dominated the field with discounting and new stores in suburban areas. Stores of new retailers were thrown up on open fields, often near groceries, and for a while they outflanked the major established chains that had stores in downtown areas. However, in the 1960s older companies recovered the initiative, using more methodical planning and relying on established distribution facilities. The most spectacular example was the conversion of Kresge from a downtown variety chain to a major mass merchandiser, a feat accomplished with the aid of its corps of experienced store and department managers, who were adaptable to the retraining for larger stores. J. C. Penney, which has been consistently the most profitable large, low-priced soft goods merchandiser, rebuilt and reimaged its whole company. Sears, Roebuck carried out a stupendous growth program and upgraded its stores so that each was almost a total shopping center. Sears, with its tremendous resources of talent, created new departments that were as big as chains in themselves. It became one of the largest apparel merchandisers, and its program in automotive supplies made it the largest marketer of tires, batteries, and other accessories.

The theory in market domination is that the major store is a magnet for the area's trade. People always like to see what the biggest store has to offer. When they seek goods not readily available in other stores, they gravitate to the big store. Normally, specialty stores try to cluster near the big store, and their pulling power usually helps the big store.

Although a store looks like a unit, it is composed of numerous departments, each of which functions with autonomy in coping with distinct merchandise that has seasonal and style problems. The store departments are backed up by specialty departments in the company, which explains why organization depth helped the strongest chains to take back the initiative in the 1960s. These chains had the people to follow through on the details

of managing expanded operations, while the younger organizations
bogged down when their less competent staffs were unable to
control inventory problems and cope with the more vigorous
competition from the big fellows.

TABLE 8–L
DEPARTMENT STORES' GROWTH RECORD

	Sales	Earnings Per Share	% of Sales	Price/Earnings Ratio High	Low	Book Value % Return	Capital Expenditures
1961....	145.45	4.40	3.03	22.89	15.59	11.29	3.25
1962....	153.32	4.46	2.91	20.92	15.77	10.84	3.78
1963....	162.47	4.86	2.99	19.02	15.94	11.12	3.73
1964....	174.12	6.19	3.56	21.86	14.60	13.22	3.95
1965....	189.10	7.15	3.78	19.94	17.65	13.97	5.03
1966....	203.84	7.26	3.56	17.56	13.84	13.33	6.65
1967....	220.03	7.86	3.57	17.49	12.77	13.23	8.18
1968....	239.06	8.13	3.40	20.06	15.69	12.77	8.60
1969....	258.91	8.22	3.17	20.11	17.25	12.13	11.26
1970....	269.60	7.64	2.83	20.80	14.54	10.63	12.57
1971....	272.31	7.88	2.89				

*Allied Stores (9-17-30) *Macy (R. H.) (12-31-25)
*Associated Dry Goods (1-2-18) *Marshall Field & Co. (9-17-30)
*Federated Dept. Stores (3-26-41) *May Department Stores (1-2-18)
*Gimbel Brothers (10-7-23) *Mercantile Stores (7-30-47)

The resilience of dominant retailers is suggested by the
department store record (Table 8-L). Ability to improve profit
margins in the 1960s was more impressive than sales growth.
This index does not include Sears, Roebuck or S. S. Kresge,
which had stronger growth than the department stores. The
department store group has had growth at about 6 percent a
year. The main concern is that heavier capital expenditures in
the late 1960s and through 1971 may have led to overstoring.

Table 8-M lists a sample of retail stocks according to the
quality as measured in Chapter 3 and according to the growth
rates suggested by earnings plowback. My estimate is that the
higher quality stocks will fluctuate less in earnings than the
lower grade stocks.

Ideas on Trading Retail Stocks

These stocks maintain consistent relative P/E ratios compared
to the DJI and their earnings are cyclical with about the same

TABLE 8—M
RETAIL CHAINS' PLOWBACK GROWTH

Stock	Quality Grade	Plowback Growth
J. C. Penney	I	10%
Sears, Roebuck & Co.	I	8
Federated Dept. Store	II	7
S. S. Kresge	II	13
Merchantile Stores	II	10
Lane Bryant	III	8
W. T. Grant	III	8
Assoc. Dry Goods	III	7
Broadway Hale	III	6
Woolworth	III	4
Marshall Field	III	5
R. H. Macy	III	7
Gimbel Bros.	IV	6
Hart, Schaffner & Marx	IV	6
G. C. Murphy	IV	4
Marcor	IV	5
Allied Stores	V	4
Zayre	V	15

timing. The relative P/E, explained in Chapter 11, is simply the ratio of a stock's P/E to the P/E of the DJI or other average, such as the Standard & Poor's. When you can buy a retail stock for a lower than usual relative P/E, and the market is not at a bull market peak, you are likely to have an above-average price gain. The retail stock group seldom reaches relative P/E ratios more than 20 percent above the usual ratio of relative P/E.

The particular exception among large retailers has been S. S. Kresge, which was converted into a growth company. A plodding variety chain until 1963, Kresge in a brilliant re-development created a whole new chain of discount retail stores (K Marts), drawing on the resources of trained store management. Its sales went from $500 million to $3 billion in 8 years. Because it had no hesitation in growth, the stock in 1972 rose to a P/E ratio about two and one-half times the P/E ratio of the industrial averages, and it was worth the premium.

Fuel Energy Industries

Fuel supply industries are the largest group of industries in terms of total earnings, dividends, and market value. Products of fuel energy industries are: motor fuels, heating oils for power

TABLE 8—N
APRIL 1971 APPRAISAL OF DEPARTMENT STORE STOCKS

Company	Estimated 1971 EPS	April 1971 Price	P/E	Current Rel. P/E	Historic Median Rel. P/E
Allied Stores	2.35	24	10	.6	.66
Associated Dry Goods* . .	2.40	36	15	.9	1.02
Broadway Hale*	2.20	27	12	.75	.91
Federated Dept. Stores . .	2.05	35	17	1.03	1.09
Gimbel Bros.	2.40	30	12.5	.75	.75
W. T. Grant+	3.25	45	14	.85	.71
Hart, Schaffner & Marx* .	1.75	23	12	.8	.97
Hughes & Hatcher*	1.20	11	9	.54	.66
Interstate Stores*	1.40	17	11.5	.7	.89
S. S. Kresge+	2.10	48	23	1.40	1.11
Lane Bryant	1.70	16	10	.6	.62
R. H. Macy	2.35	28	12	.75	.85
Marcor+	1.80	27	15	.9	.83
Marshall Field*	1.90	24	12.5	.75	.81
May Dept. Stores*	1.80	23	13	.8	1.03
Mercantile Stores	5.00	65	13	.8	.75
G. C. Murphy*	2.25	24	11	.66	.74
J. C. Penney+	2.25	48	21	1.26	1.17
Sears, Roebuck*	3.25	67	21	1.26	1.43
Woolworth+	2.55	34	13	.8	.73
Zayre	1.95	27	14	.85	.85

*Below historic Relative P/E on this date.
+Above historic Relative P/E on this date.

and comfort, natural gas, power plant steam coal, metallurgical coal, uranium, petrochemicals, and asphalts.

Almost all companies have a combination of activities in the fuel supply industries. Most of them are classified as assets-intensive in that they require $1 or more of assets per $1 of revenue. This being so, the investor can measure their performance statistically with good results. The following descriptions cover the majority.

International oil producer-marketers. The six "international" companies are very large, and their profit sources are divided about in proportion to world markets: they control most of the tanker fleets, they refine oil products, and they sell to final consuming customers.

North American Integrated Companies. These companies are

marketers of fuels in the United States and Canada, and most of them produce less crude oil than they process and sell. Several have foreign concessions and some sales systems, mainly in Europe. Most profits arise from oil and gas production.

North American Oil and Gas Producers. Very few companies are involved mainly in oil and gas production in the United States. Louisiana Land & Exploration Company and Superior Oil are the only large ones still independent. Most of the oil and gas production companies are Canadian.

Coal Producers. Most of the coal production in the United States is now controlled by large oil or mining companies as well as by utility companies.

Uranium Mining. Uranium production is mainly by divisions of oil and diversified companies, and it has been volatile in terms of profits.

The companies as a group have had profits growth slightly faster than the U. S. economy, partly because of foreign operations. I will try to explain the rising and falling factors that blend into overall progress, and the more dynamic divisions.

Oil

Long Lead Time. Looking at stock price fluctuations, an investor could wonder if the industry were not subject to some violent fluctuations in sales and profits. The determinants of earnings progress are almost always projects that the companies have under development for from 5 to 10 years. When oil is discovered in Alaska or under some body of water, the excitement in Wall Street often creates the illusion that a money tree in full bloom has been acquired. In 1970, speculative buying of oil stocks was based on how much money the companies might succeed in paying for leases in Alaska's North Slope. In study of these stocks, remember that everything takes a long time to pay off.

By the same token, it takes a long time to lose the earning power of established petroleum assets. At times, certain countries have taken the economic benefits out of oil concessions, but sooner or later the companies have been able to restore profits through control of distribution as well as ownership of diversified sources of supply.

Profit Rates and Cash Flow Plowback. As a group, the profits on capital for large oil companies are about in line with American industry as a whole. The companies have average profits equal to about 11 percent on stockholder equity, and most of them earn between 9 and 13 percent. A small handful earn over 15 percent, and, of course, some are quite poor in terms of profits. During the 1960s, most of the larger companies with low profit rates were combined with more profitable companies.

The plowback of cash flow is sufficient to support growth in the 5 to 7 percent range for most of the companies. Few of the companies experience growth at rates different from plowback. Even when acquisitions have been made with exchange of convertible preferreds or debentures, the performance of combined companies has not tended to change much from the growth trend supported by cash plowback of the component companies.

Investment Return and Valuation.   Over the years, investors in large oil company stocks usually have secured investment return superior to that obtained on investments in the averages. Measured in terms of yield or P/E ratios, most of the time the prices of large oil company stocks have been cheaper than the averages. The yields usually have been at least 1 percent more than yields on the averages, while P/E ratios have been 10 to 40 percent lower. Thus, the stocks provided more dividends and earnings per dollar of market value than the majority of stocks.

There has been no sustained tendency for the stocks to change their relative valuation in the market. When the Dow Jones Industrials as a group yielded about 4 percent in the 1960s, the large international oils provided yields of about 5 percent. The dividends were increased most years by 5 to 6 percent.

Growth in earnings and dividends has been more regular than for the industrial stocks as a whole. In spite of sharply higher tax rates applied under the 1969 Internal Revenue Act, the oil companies had relative earnings gains versus the DJI in the five years through 1970.

The smaller oil companies that engage mainly in oil and gas production are rated by investors on a basis similar to speculative stocks in general. Although the majority of such firms are quite well settled in their business situations, there is willingness to discount new prospects.

Earnings.   Atlantic Richfield also incorporates Sinclair Oil. The group was weak in petroleum reserves, but discoveries can

TABLE 8-O
OIL COMPANY EARNING SOURCES

Company	Importance of N.A. Oil Production	Foreign Oil Operations	Marketing, Refining and Chemicals	Percentage Profits on Stockholder Equity		Stock Price High-Low P/E Ratio 1970-71
				1970	5-year Average	
Atlantic Richfield	Most production has been in U.S. and Canada. Has big reserve in Alaska that could double N.A. oil production	Discoveries in Java Sea and Timor Sea will supply 1/5 income by 1975.	Sells about 1½ times as much oil products as come from its wells. This has been a weakness.	8%	9%	23-12
Louisiana Land & Exploration	Most of income from oil and gas is produced in property owned and leased on Gulf Coast and offshore.	None	None	38%	35%	30-13
Mobil Oil	1/3 of oil is from U.S. and Canada.	Over half of oil is produced in Persian Gulf and Africa.	Refines and sells 30% more petroleum products than come from its wells. Foreign marketing is important.	11%	10.5%	13-8
Pacific Petroleums	Bulk of profits are from Canadian crude oil and gas sales.	None	Sells about half its oil products at retail	6.5%	5.5%	38-20
Texaco Inc.	About 1/3 of petroleum is produced in N.A.	Over half of oil is produced in Eastern Hemisphere.	Markets everywhere. Refines 85% of its oil worldwide, about 100% in U.S.	14%	15%	13-8

correct this deficiency. The companies were marginal marketers, which explains its profit history. The high stock price in 1971 discounted promise from oil discoveries on Alaska's North Slope and in offshore Indonesia.

Louisiana Land & Exploration owns a fabulous mineral acreage position in southern Louisiana. It simply exploits its bountiful reserves. Usually, stock price discounts quality.

Mobil Oil is a greatly improved company that is still at a disadvantage because of its relative crude oil shortage compared to its refining capacity. The stock receives a low market rating because of foreign operations.

Pacific Petroleums' low profits on capital occur because it has made enormous investments in the search for oil and gas and had only begun to get its payoff in the late 1960s. Almost $200 million was invested before the first dollar of profits was realized. The stock price is high in recognition of oil and gas reserves.

Texaco Inc. has long stressed the need to discover oil reserves before trying to market them. Emphasis on production and domination by strong top executives have been the key factors. Because overseas growth has been a big factor, the stock is accorded a low price-to-earnings ratio.

North American Oil and Gas Production. The main problem in North America for oil and gas companies is to foresee future oil discovery trends and to purchase the acreage, with favorable cost and supply factors, under which oil and gas may be produced. In the United States, this has meant anticipation of discovery in the Gulf of Mexico and timing of pipeline extensions into the productive areas of the Gulf. Other new underwater oil fields are in the Cook Inlet of Alaska and the Santa Barbara Channel. The North Slope of Alaska has been important for the major companies.

Natural gas production has been a big factor in earnings growth. By and large, the major companies had the gas reserves before the market developed through the 1950s, and gas was important for growth trends of most companies. Until 1970, the Federal Power Commission and the gas suppliers have virtually had a tug-of-war over prices, which has caused distortions in the timing of exploitation of gas prospects. However, in 1970 the FPC began to tolerate the need for higher prices if plans called for enough drilling for new gas reserves.

In about 25 years, our proven supply of gas went from surplus to barely enough. In 1970, the prices approved for new gas sales to pipelines were between 30 and 50 percent higher than they had been a couple of years earlier. It was forecast that 30 cents per thousand cubic feet would be the price in a year or two, whereas 15 to 18 cents was the price in the 1960s.

Petroleum engineers argue that the new prices are barely enough. They search for gas that is five to seven miles below the surface, and it seems miraculous that a string of steel tubes rotating through rock, driving a drill down six miles, actually can find the mineral sought. Nevertheless, the odds are fairly good that the companies with long experience in natural gas exploration will expand their producing capacities.

It is difficult for most of us to estimate the costs and potentials of large company developments in natural gas exploration. Much gas is produced in combination with oil. Usually, the companies argue that in figuring costs gas should be lumped with oil and the whole refining and product delivery process. I suspect that in the past gasoline sales covered most of the costs and that gas was an extra that could be sold cheap for extra profit. In the last couple of decades, the cost of finding and delivering petroleum products has gone up faster than prices, and natural gas has had to carry more of the burden. The effect of this trend has been that the price of gas has been prodded upward so that its price in terms of heat value when burned, is now about the same as oil fuel.

This trend is interesting for the North American petroleum company that has better than average success in finding gas. The industry needs higher gas prices to support the total petroleum operation; however, a lot of gas is found without oil. The market for gas is really tremendous in North America, and in time its price in terms of heat value is likely to be higher than that for other fuels because of its superiority in terms of total combustion and ease of use. For the investor, the natural gas capacities of large oil companies are worth studying. In recent years, even giant Standard Oil of New Jersey and Texaco probably got their profit growth from natural gas.

Gas exploration in Canada has been fortunate, and the Alberta Conservation Commission, which regulates petroleum operations in Canada's main producing province, has insisted that the gas be sold for high prices. Alberta is in the position of an oil-producing country whose revenues are based on royalties. Although Alberta has high reserves compared to current consumption, the province estimates that the supply will not last forever. The

Alberta Conservation Commission gives permits for gas to be exported from the province to eastern Canada or to the United States. The dominion government does not apply pressure for low gas prices for eastern Canada; almost half of Canadian gas is sold to the United States, and eastern Canada has imported gas from the United States.

For the investor, the easiest way to identify investments in natural gas is to study the Canadian companies, because it is easier to calculate how much revenue they obtain from gas sales and what reserves they own. Much of the Canadian gas is wet. The wet gas contains sulfur and has natural gas liquids that are practically gasoline, and the liquids and sulfur are worth almost as much as the dry gas. Growth in sales of oil and gas in Canada is at about one and one-half times the U. S. growth rate.

Tropical Country Oil Production. Investors who followed oil industry news in 1970 remember that stock prices of oil companies were very low in the first half of the year when it became apparent that the oil-producing and oil-exporting countries would make astronomical demands on international oil companies. Late in 1970 and early in 1971, when the OPEC countries were enforcing their demands and in some cases expropriating company facilities, the oil company stock prices were about 50 percent above their lows — price recoveries that were greater than the overall market rise through February 1971.

In effect, investors had discounted not only loss of profits on foreign oil production but big losses to boot. Over the years, international oil companies have been most cautious about their projections of profits from oil production in tropical countries. From time to time, the top officers have been quoted as saying that profits must recover the investment in three years to justify the political risks in these countries. Political officials look at the profits and hardly ever give credit for the capital investment. They also look at the taxes levied by governments in oil-consuming countries and make no allowance for the use of the tax money in road building and maintenance that fosters the demand for petroleum.

Over about half a century, the concept of investment payback in three years has proven correct for the oil companies. Creole Petroleum, the Venezuelan subsidiary of Standard Oil of New Jersey, paid level dividends in the 1960s, but the annual dividends were about 25 percent of the parent's net investment in Creole.

The net investment was revalued up by $400 million in 1961; on Jersey's actual net investment the 1970 dividend was 43 percent. Aramco has paid back its investors at about the same rate.

The Libyan government, however, has changed the terms of oil company contracts for concessions, with the first revision in the second year of production. While the return on net investment was not niggardly through 1971, the companies were threatened with loss of the investment. Newer oil company projects in Nigeria, Indonesia, and the Trucial States seemed less vulnerable to expropriation. When you average the whole experience of oil companies in tropical countries, the good ones more than paid for the bad ones and also paid for unprofitable marketing and refining operations in Europe.

International oil company overseas projects paid off for the companies because they accurately evaluated the risks and appropriate rate of return requirements. Over the decades, the companies managed their stockholder capital at risk in faraway places with strange sounding names better than Wall Street has given them credit for. Either Wall Street underrated their skills or overrated the skills of other industry managements that either concentrated capital in North America or did a poor job overseas.

During the 1950s and much of the 1960s, American corporations, including the oil companies, had unsatisfactory profit experience in Europe. The oil companies compensated for too poor profits in Europe with high profits on production of oil in tropical countries for supply to Europe. American electric and chemical companies simply suffered poor profits in Europe without compensating raw materials profits.

In 1970, the international oil companies seemed at a crossroads; the profits on assets in oil-producing tropical countries might decline, forcing them to obtain a return from operating assets in Europe. Early in 1971, their highest profit assets were probably tanker ships for hauling the oil around Africa or in the Mediterranean Sea. By 1972, they should have found some way to shift costs and prices around to maintain adequate profits on capital.

International Oil Stocks. Table 8-P shows the records of international oil stocks, including Gulf, Mobil, Royal Dutch, Standard Oil of California, Standard Oil of New Jersey, and Texaco. In periods when the yields were below 4 percent, it was likely that in the next 2 or 3 years the stocks would sell lower. Yields have to be near 5 percent before one can be confident of making a profit. The yield in 1970 was the highest since 1953; if history repeats, the stocks should gain firmly in price in the 1970s. Dividend growth at 7.5 percent has been about 1½ times as fast as that of all industrial stocks.

In Table 8-P the two columns on the right show the yield history of the Standard & Poor's 425 Industrials Index. You can see that the tendency for yields of the oil stocks to be higher became more prominent in the 1960s. The curious thing is that the dividend of the oil stock index doubled between 1960 and 1970, a decade when the dividend of the index increased 60 percent. The yields range of the index tended to be lower, while the ups and downs of the yields on the oils ended up in about the same place. The index, in my estimate, was overpriced much of the time.

TABLE 8–P

INTERNATIONAL OIL COMPANY DIVIDEND YIELDS (S&P INDEX)

	International Oil Stocks					S&P Industrial Index		
	Price 1941–43 = 10		Dividends per Share	Dividend Yields percent		Dividend Yields percent		Dividends per Share
Year	High	Low		High	Low	High	Low	
1952	37.88	33.13	1.88	5.67	4.96	5.84	5.05	1.36
1953	35.84	31.45	2.01	6.39	5.61	5.90	4.96	1.34
1954	52.02	34.75	2.06	5.93	3.96	5.84	3.89	1.45
1955	70.17	50.39	2.34	4.64	3.33	4.88	3.51	1.74
1956	85.78	68.19	2.72	3.99	3.17	4.03	3.45	1.84
1957	96.78	71.19	2.97	4.17	3.07	4.62	3.64	1.94
1958	89.75	69.66	2.86	4.11	3.19	4.31	3.15	1.86
1959	88.00	72.41	2.97	4.10	3.38	3.42	2.99	1.95
1960	78.21	62.79	3.08	4.91	3.94	3.61	3.08	2.00
1961	88.54	70.66	3.23	4.57	3.65	3.40	2.70	2.07
1962	99.58	79.83	3.62	4.53	3.64	4.01	2.92	2.20
1963	117.31	98.27	4.01	4.08	3.42	3.60	2.98	2.36
1964	146.69	118.35	4.38	3.70	2.99	3.24	2.83	2.58
1965	144.49	126.33	4.73	3.74	3.27	3.26	2.86	2.82
1966	139.76	108.20	4.94	4.57	3.53	3.79	2.93	2.95
1967	131.95	114.54	5.30	4.63	4.02	3.48	2.80	2.97
1968	160.43	125.87	5.72	4.54	3.57	3.32	2.68	3.16
1969	164.36	110.83	6.02	5.43	3.66	3.32	2.80	3.25
1970	132.13	95.01	6.18	6.50	4.68	4.23	3.11	3.20

Coal

In theory, a growth in coal consumption should be favorable for a growth in profits. The coal industry has a lot going for it; growth in electric power consumption depends mainly on coal. Although nuclear power grows at a more rapid rate, growth in coal production quantities is greater. The world's steel industries rely largely on United States metallurgical coal. Coal reserves are known to be ample for 1,000 years.

Industry problems are environment, labor, safety, and customers. Where coal has been surface-mined by stripping, the public more and more objects to the resulting landscape spoliation and stream pollution.

Coal is so badly needed for electric power fuel as well as for metal refining that the cost of minimizing environmental degradation will have to be absorbed by consumers. The prices of other fuels have been rising faster than that for coal. In the next half-century, coal may come back as a chemical raw material, although as long as natural gas and liquids have been available at cheap prices coal has not been competitive for chemical manufacture.

The two remaining large independent coal producers, Eastern Gas and Fuel and Pittston Company, have had high profits growth since the mid-1960s. The three largest coal producers are Kennecott Corporation, Continental Oil, and Occidental Petroleum. Standard Oil of New Jersey has bought enormous coal acreage in the United States, and plans to become a supplier.

The slowdown in demand for metallurgical coal began to depress earnings of the industry in 1971; labor problems were also severe. Control of sulfur emissions from burning also was an increasing problem. It is not practical at this time to generalize about investment prospects for coal.

Utilities

Electric power, telephone, and gas pipelines are a tremendous industry group, comprising a large fraction of the securities available for investors and the largest group for higher dividend yields. The services they provide are absolutely essential to the functioning of our society.

Utility companies have exclusive access to markets served and are regulated by state and federal commissions, which determine the rates that may be charged to customers. These commissions also monitor the quality of service provided. The regulators are political people who tend to be sensitive to consumers' wishes to pay minimum rates. Policies of regulatory commissions vary greatly in different states. Some regulators have more generous concepts of a reasonable return on investment than do others. Certain commissions demand accounting policies that result in overstatement of earnings by the standards of some investors.

Rate of Return Record

Table 8-Q shows the history of return on electric power company net property, which is approximately the same as net invested capital. Note that the percent earned on net property varied in a narrow range until 1962. The dip from 1951 to 1953 was caused by excess profits taxes. The rise beginning in 1962 came from prosperity and rates allowed to cover the higher interest rates as well as from more liberal reporting of earnings. Inability to absorb higher interest costs and fuel cost hikes were factors in the lower returns on capital after 1967. Although the recent record looked unfavorable, it was better than the experience of industrial companies from 1967 through 1970.

Table 8-R indicates that regulators responded to the need for higher rates which basically recognized the higher cost of money. Most regulatory commissions also recognized that, as well as allowing for interest rate increases, the return on common equity should be permitted to rise. Table 8-S shows that the returns on equity capital remained level in most cases for eight major utilities. Public Service got rate increases in 1971 to compensate for its low return on equity.

TABLE 8–Q
ELECTRIC POWER COMPANIES' RETURN ON NET PROPERTY

Year	Net Property % Earned	Year	Net Property % Earned
1946	5.97	1958	5.61
1947	5.73	1959	5.76
1948	5.29	1960	5.80
1949	5.58	1961	5.78
1950	5.71	1962	6.25
1951	5.30	1963	6.38
1952	5.35	1964	6.46
1953	5.36	1965	6.56
1954	5.51	1966	6.53
1955	5.65	1967	6.50
1956	5.72	1968	6.21
1957	5.60	1969	6.11

TABLE 8–R
REGULATORY COMMISSION ACTIONS ON SERVICE RATES
($ millions, on annualized basis)

Year	Amount of Increases Granted	Amount of Decreases	Net Increase or Decrease
1970	452.2	6.4	+445.8
1969	145.1	5.8	+139.3
1968	20.7	13.9	+ 6.8
1967	0.7	37.7	- 27.0
1966	33.4	56.9	- 23.5
1965	....	113.4	-113.4
1964	27.5	119.2	- 91.7
1963	14.1	51.4	- 37.3
1962	11.7	19.3	- 7.6
1961	18.3	10.1	+ 8.2
1960	43.1	8.9	+ 34.2

Note: Data exclude government plants and rural cooperatives. As of January 1, 1971, 42 applications for rate increases aggregating $659.1 million on an annualized basis were still pending.

TABLE 8–S
ELECTRIC POWER COMPANIES' RETURN ON EQUITY CAPITAL

	Common % of Capital		Earned on Equity	
	1962	1970	1962	1970
American Electric Power[F]	33%	33%	14%	14%
Central & Southwest[N]	40	43	14	15
Cleveland Electric Illumination[F]	48	42	12	15
Houston Lighting & Power[N]	44	42	15	15
Middle South Utilities[N]	36	34	11	14
Public Service Electric & Gas[F]	32	33	14	11
Southern California Edison[F]	37	35	11.5	11.5
Texas Utilities[X]	39	38	15	15

F Uses flow-through of tax savings from accelerated amortization in financial reports.
N Normalizes tax effects of accelerated depreciation.
X Financial and tax reports are similar.

Quality of Earnings

The eight companies, as well as other utility companies, have differences in the quality of the earnings. The primary accounting points are: (1) flow-through of tax savings; and (2) interest charged to construction. Under the first (flow-through), the companies take accelerated depreciation for tax purposes and straight-line depreciation for stockholder reports. The tax difference is treated as additional profit. The alternative methods are to apply half the savings to deferred tax reserves or to depreciate on a straight-line basis for tax and stockholder reporting.

The effect of these procedures on utility earnings can be seen in Table 8-T. Although depreciation continued at about the same percent of revenues, income taxes became a smaller share of revenues, while profits became slightly higher compared to revenues. The profit before depreciation and taxes actually declined.

TABLE 8–T
COMPOSITE ELECTRIC POWER INDUSTRY TAX DATA

	1960	1962	1964	1966	1968
Depreciation as percent of revenue . .	10.2	10.7	11.0	10.8	10.8
Income tax as percent of revenue	12.5	11.5	10.9	9.9	9.3
Earnings as percent of revenue	13.3	14.0	14.6	15.0	14.1
Total percent	36.0	36.2	36.5	35.7	34.2

In the 1960s, regulatory commissions in many states required that interest on money tied up in plants under construction should be capitalized with the hardware construction costs. The change in this category was substantial. In 1965, interest charged to construction was 9.5 percent of total interest cost, and in 1970 it was 22.25 percent of interest. Had the industry in 1970 used the same accounting as it had a decade before, profits would have been lower by about 3 percent of revenues.

TABLE 8–U
ELECTRIC POWER INDUSTRY REVENUES AND INTEREST CHARGED TO CONSTRUCTION
($ millions)

	1960	1965	1970
Industry Revenues	$10,116	$13,400	$19,804
Interest charged to construction	99	94	403
Interest charged to construction as percent of revenues	0.98%	0.71%	2.03%

TABLE 8–V
ELECTRIC POWER PER SHARE DATA

Company	Interest Charged to Construction		Reported EPS		EPS Ex. Interest Charged to Construction	
	1960	1970	1960	1970	1960	1970
American Electric Power . . .	$.13	$.86	$1.17	$2.30	$1.04	$1.44
Central & Southwest	.07	.21	1.45	2.85	1.38	2.64
Cleveland Electric Illumination	.02	.60	1.65	3.02	1.63	2.42
Houston Lighting & Power . .	.05	.25	1.09	2.56	1.04	2.31
Middle South Utilities	.08	.27	.76	1.61	.68	1.34
Public Service Electric & Gas .	.25	.61	1.35	2.46	1.10	1.85
Southern California Edison . .	.08	.42	1.29	2.70	1.21	2.28
Texas Utilities	.06	.34	1.56	3.33	1.50	2.99

Most industrial companies do not capitalize interest on money tied up in plants being built. Many professional investors and analysts consider that the utility company earnings have been of lower quality in recent years because this capitalized interest has come to equal a fifth on earnings for the industry.

Utility stockholders are not considered as owners but rather as investors whose money is hired. To the company, the real cost of equity capital is the cash dividends paid. There must be stockholder capital and earnings to supply the coverage of bond interest and amortization, or else the bond ratings would fall. The argument is that however the earnings may be reported they will accommodate growing dividends.

On the list of eight stocks, Cleveland Electric increased its dividend about 8 percent a year. Ohio Commissions specified flow-through accounting in 1962, and the image of the stock deteriorated thereafter. The attitude of regulators is that the stockholders should be concerned only that rates are sufficient to accommodate dividend growth, which they do. In practice, it is easier for regulators to approve rates that accommodate desired dividends than it is for industrial corporations to earn profits required for dividends.

Growth, Pollution, and Bond Rollover

The cost of eliminating pollution from power plants is thought to be a threat to electric utility earnings. Another worry is the maturing of low interest rate bonds that were issued decades ago and must be refunded at interest rates prevailing in 1971.

These two factors that tend to raise costs fall unequally on electric power utilities. The need for power companies to control pollution has been recognized for about 15 years. Companies that were growing faster had more opportunities to build major new plants, which overcame their pollution problems in the aggregate. Companies with slower growth had relatively more expense in correcting pollution problems.

In Texas, the use of natural gas fuel has always made pollution a negligible problem. Unrealistic federal regulation of natural gas prices in interstate sales also helped Texas utility companies. Gas producers were unwilling to sell gas at prices authorized by the Federal Power Commission; so they concentrated their sales contracts in Texas, where buyers and sellers agreed to prices that were not subject to arbitrary reductions by the FPC years after the fact. The power companies in Texas had opportunities to contract for gas supplies for decades in advance at prices that were lower than they would have been if the other consuming states had been buying gas at prices producers were willing to accept.

Utilities with Growth and Adequate Profits

Growth in revenues should be 7 percent. The common stock equity should be near 40 percent so that equity dilution is not a current problem. The return on total capital should be in line with current interest rates, or earnings on plant should be fairly close to 8 percent. The nine stocks listed in Table 8-W meet these specifications in most respects. This group is expected

TABLE 8–W
UTILITIES WITH GROWTH AND PROFITS

	Earned on Total Capital 1970	Equity Ratio
Central & Southwest	8.6%	43%
Cleveland Electric Illumination	9.1	42
Florida Power & Light	7.8	41
Houston Lighting & Power	9.0	42
Kansas Gas & Electric	8.1	41
Northern Indiana Public Service	8.9	39
Oklahoma Gas & Electric	8.5	33
Texas Utilities	8.4	38
Tucson Gas & Electric	8.0	37

to have an earnings progress superior to that of the economy; the stocks had been in a bear market since 1961. For instance, Florida Power and Light had a high in 1961 of $85, and since then has sold that high only once, in 1964. Between 1961 and 1970, net income increased 87 percent, which is over 7 percent growth. Cleveland Electric in 1971 was selling about in line with its 1961 high. Since 1961, earnings increased on a 7.75 percent trend. These stocks are worth getting to know better.

Comparison of Utility and Industrial Stocks

Relative yield studies show that dividends of electric utilities have grown a little faster than industrial dividends (DJI or S&PI). Since the early 1960s, relative yields of utilities moved from near parity, or ratios of 1.0 compared to industrials, to a relative yield of 1.5.

The foregoing discussion indicated that utilities were able to recover their higher interest costs. Most of them have authority to pass on higher fuel costs to customers. I thought that the market had been accentuating the negatives and not paying enough regard to dividends, and that the yield of utility stocks eventually would come back in line with industrial yields.

Natural Gas Pipeline Companies

The main pipeline movement is natural gas. With the growth in quantities delivered, this should have been a good business for investors. Unfortunately, federal regulators basically have been hostile and biased in favor of consumers to a degree that probably costs them more in the long run. Although there is a certain amount of lip service to the notion that the return on investments is to permit the pipeliners to finance their growth, the companies have been hard put to get rate increases needed to cover the higher costs of purchased gas.

For a number of years, the pipeline companies were not permitted to charge prices for gas produced from owned properties on parity with gas purchased from petroleum producers. They were held to a utility rate of return on a risk commodity.

In 1970, the regulatory environment seemed to become more favorable, but when the pipeliners were given the right to produce gas and charge it into the pipelines at field prices they got carried away on their capital investment standards. At the December 1970 federal lease sales in the Gulf of Mexico, pipeline

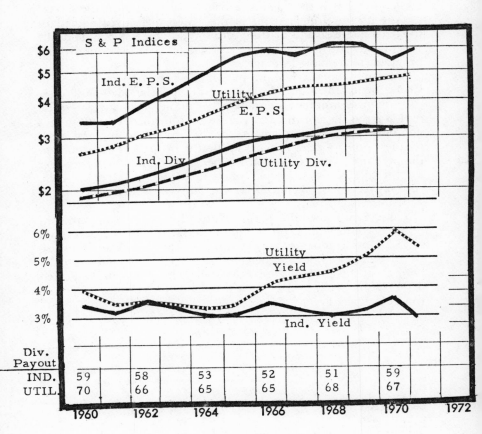

Figure 8-1

companies bid prices for exploratory concessions that staggered the petroleum industry.

Entrepreneurial risk takers in the oil business differ from the regulated industry management in that the first invest stockholder money in what is regarded as a risk venture, whereas the second usually borrow three-fourths of the capital employed and plans to factor the lease and drilling into the rate base. A couple of the pipeliners went further and set up investor-participation drilling programs to get more leverage.

Although superficially the pipelines seem to be making giant strides with their multihundred-million-dollar debt-and-stock-issue-financed annual programs, the whole procedure is quite dull as far as the stockholder is concerned. Tenneco management's February 1971 announcement that it aspired to increase each business group's sales to $500 million is of little consequence to the investor who could hardly be excited about the 10-year 31-cent total increase in per share dividends to $1.32 in 1970. (By my analysis, Tenneco profits are overstated because of generous accounting.)

Table 8-X shows the performance of pipeline companies in terms of return on capital, plowback rates, and senior capital ratios. Most companies report lower profits for taxes than are stated to stockholders. When tax rates are between 20 and 35 percent, profits probably are overstated. If the companies reported depreciation as allowed for by federal income taxes, profits would be lower by 20 to 35 percent.

TABLE 8—X

Company	Common Equity as % Capital	Earned on Net Plant	Earned on Common Equity	Income Tax Rate	Dividend Growth Rate	Depreciation Rate
Columbia Gas	45%	7%	12%	36%	4%	3%
El Paso Natural Gas	25	7	10	25	0	3.75
Northern Natural Gas . . .	32	6.5	13	40	5	3.5
Panhandle & Eastern Pipelines	27	7.5	20	25	6.5	3.5
Southern Natural Gas . . .	44	9	18	30	3	3.5
Tenneco	25	7.5	18	20	3	4
Texas Gas Transmission . .	35	8	14	40	4.5	3.75
Westcoast Transmission . .	26	6	3	0	2	2

Earned on common equity at 50% tax rate: CG, 9%; El Paso, 7%; N.N.G., 11%; P.E.P., 13%; S.N.G., 13%; Tenneco, 11%; T.G.T., 12%.

9

Growth Industries

A growth industry is one that grows 7 percent or more per year from internally generated products and techniques. Sales of a growth industry never decline in any year. Usually, research and patents are important. Profits on capital tend to be much higher than those in most industries.

Growth industries include: ethical and proprietary drugs, hospital supplies, and cosmetics; computers (equipment, services); photography; clothing patterns; petroleum modifiers; electric photography; travel service; credit information; nuclear fuel; and a multiple growth company.

In most instances, the growth industries are the creation of one or two companies within their industrial group. Small competitors do exist in some groups, but their growth is overshadowed by that of the leading companies. For example, Eastman Kodak and Polaroid handle over 90 percent of the photography business, and Xerox dominates the electric photography field. Leader in credit information is Dun & Bradstreet, and 3M Company has a virtually unique position as a multiple growth company. Other growth industries and their company leaders are: travel service, American Express; clothing patterns, Simplicity; petroleum modifiers, Lubrizol; nuclear fuel, Kerr-McGee.

Drugs, Hospital Supplies, and Cosmetics

This industrial sector is the most reliable large growth industry group. It has many able managers, hardly any union labor, and a $750 million research pool that really invents new products. At least a dozen companies have long growth records with a high payout of dividends.

Drugs

The drug industry stands as one of the better run, higher profit business structures on the U. S. corporate scene today. Their stage of business could be described as generally lacking the cyclical shortcomings and overall outperforming the majority of industries on a score of measures. As an industry, it does not require heavy capital investments for manufacturing facilities. It is not in the category of capital-intensive or labor-intensive industries. The drug group's success depends on the ability to create needed therapeutic agents and to merchandise these compounds aggressively in world markets.

TABLE 9—A
GROWING DRUG COMPANY SALES
($ billions)

	Total Sales of Products	Pre-tax Earnings	Foreign Sales	U.S. Human Ethicals	Percent Generic	Hospital Purchases
1968	$10	$1.5	$1.8	$3.6	8.2%	$.676
1969	11.2	1.7	1.9	3.9	9.0	.758
1970	12.6	1.9	2.2	4.4	10.0	.875

In recent years, ethical drug producers have tended to diversify into related consumer areas, such as proprietary drugs, cosmetics, and toiletries. Some of this movement is fostered by the dearth of new ethical drug discoveries. This slowdown of new compounds reduces the high profit flow that such drugs typically generate. The drug companies continue to pour vast amounts of dollars into research and development programs, which may hold promise of greatest rewards. In some instances, they are duplicating one another's efforts (both Pfizer and Smith, Kline & French developed doxepin for relief of psychoneurotic depression).

Diversifying into consumer-related areas is relatively uncomplicated for ethical drug companies. The requisites are a broad product line, a steady stream of new products, good management, and sufficient financing — ingredients that are within the reach of many ethical drug companies.

Problems have been encountered, however, when the move has been to unrelated technical areas (chemicals, electronics). Some managements of the acquired nondrug companies scooped up the high-priced stock they received in the acquisition and left for new pursuits. In several instances (Upjohn, Searle), losses were absorbed to upgrade the quality of operations and strengthen the ranks of personnel. As they move into consumer goods diversification, drug producers can encounter initial profit dips because of marketing strategy changes that involve costly mass media promotion programs as compared to the traditional ethical drug type of promotion using detail men and journal advertising. Smith, Kline & French absorbed losses of Love cosmetics for three years until Love began to pay its way in late 1971, but the basic profitability of the company made the losses an easy burden to carry.

Research Experience. U. S. drug producers spent about $600 million for research programs during 1970, but the rate of new ethicals introduction has slowed down. Only 11 new chemical entries were marketed in the United States in 1969. In addition to the extended approval time encountered by new ethical compounds awaiting FDA approval, the time factor and high dollar cost of developing these products is a concern of drug managers over the progress of these programs. There is some thinking that the industry is working from a base of research knowledge established several decades back. Medical treatment is more complicated today, and the focus is on disease prevention and chronic physical and mental diseases. Newer frontiers include therapeutic possibilities such as enzymes and agents that affect nucleic acid metabolism.

Even though the number of recent new ethicals has been low, the dollar sales potential of several products is impressive. After 2 years, Sterling Drug was able to ring up $20 million volume on Talwin, a nonnarcotic analgesic that may have a $40 million sales potential. Pfizer's 1969 introduction of Sinequan, a psychotherapeutic compound, eventually could realize about $30 million from domestic sales.

After 5 years, Lilly's group of cephalosporin antibiotics registered annual sales of over $60 million. With recent introduction of oral versions of this compound, and more such varieties in development, this line may become a $100 million group for Lilly in the world market. Upjohn had sales of $50 million on its Lincocin, with exceptionally strong marketing abroad. Schering, a newcomer to the antibiotic market, pulled a surprise with Garamycin. Antibiotic manufacturers allude to the promise that antiviral agents will offer better treatment for viral diseases than do the specific and unprofitable established vaccines.

Overseas Sales. Total overseas sales of drugs by U.S.-based companies continue upward — at $2.2 billion in 1970. In the 1964-69 span, foreign sales had increased by 93 percent, while total sales rose 66 percent. The Japanese market offers promise of greater sales potential for U. S.-based pharmaceutical manufacturers. The international market for prescription drugs is now 3 times larger than the U. S. market, and it could become as much as 11 times greater if health-care levels in developing nations approach those achieved in the well-developed countries. U. S. ethical drug manufacturers in many instances have managed to market their new research creations first in foreign markets while they await FDA approval for domestic marketing. The process has been a relatively common sequence. The finished product is fabricated in foreign areas, where only a small manufacturing facility and few personnel are required. The need for the therapeutic agent is as common as it is in the United States, and only a local marketing group is required to spread the good word of the new discovery.

Puerto Rico. In addition to conducting an established and profitable drug business in foreign regions, some domestic manufacturers establish production facilities in Puerto Rico, where with up to 17 years of tax-free status stateside manufacturers are able to shave at least 5 points or even more off their federal income tax rate, depending on the breadth of their operation. U. S. producers are vying for Puerto Rican bases of manufacturing for major line ethicals, which are approaching patent expiration. The drugs, produced at a lower unit cost, are shipped back to the

United States and marketed under the familiar brand name at a selling price lower than, but one not so low as, new generic name versions of the drug.

The impact of the consolidation of the tax-free Puerto Rican profits immediately elevates the company's earning base. Further elevations are gained as more integrated operations are established and more compounds are shipped back in finished form. As more major U. S. drug manufacturers respond to the lure, the relative advantage among the drug companies is lost.

From an investment viewpoint, an item worth inspecting is the quality of earnings reported for stockholder purposes as more of a drug company's profits originate at such offshore facilities. Even though such profits are consolidated, they generally are not available for stateside use. Thus, if a company conducts a good segment of its manufacturing in Puerto Rico and derives 75 percent of its sale from within the United States, its reported cash position is not readily available for corporate needs in the United States; the company may have to resort to financial markets to meet domestic capital requirements. But the lure is nearly universal — Abbott, Baxter, Lilly, Smith, Kline & French, Searle, Parke Davis, Becton-Dickinson, plus others. The immediate thrust is higher reported earnings, with a lower production cost base from which to match probably lower selling priced generics. In many instances, the payback period is from four to five years. Thus, with such a fast recovery domestic drug manufacturers show little concern about a possible elimination of the tax lure — they will take it while it lasts.

Generic Drug Manufacturers. The effects of generic label selling do not occur until the patents on an ethical drug expire. Then, as the manufacturer of the new generic drug offers the drug at reduced prices, the original brand-name producer continues to sell its drug under its familiar label but at slightly lower prices. The generic label manufacturers sell the drug under their own brand names, not under the chemical ingredient name. (In one instance, a generic label drug manufacturer gained a court injunction forbidding pharmacists to substitute other brand drugs for the company's product, which was physician prescribed.)

The main expense of new generic drug manufacturers is in amassing costly clinical data to prove that their products have the same therapeutic effectiveness as the parent agent. Ironically, the selling prices of recent generic label compounds have been rising, while prices of ethical brands generally have been declining.

Drug Sales to Hospitals.   An estimated 20 percent of the annual domestic ethical drug sales are made to hospitals. Today, hospital pharmacies that fill prescriptions for outpatients are gaining, and the institutional volume buying power could influence generic purchases, depending on therapeutic equivalence with lower costs. This trend would seem to augur strongly for greater sales volume of generic-labeled ethicals through these institutions, but generic label sales account for about 8 to 9 percent of the drug volume today. If England with its 20 years' of socialized medicine is any indication, trade experts expect that generic prescribing in the United States could level off at the 10-percent range of prescription sales.

Thus, the increasing assistance to senior citizen patients is likely to crystallize more drug dispensing from the hospital pharmacy. This trend is likely to afford the hospital combine a greater leverage in trade discounts, currently unobtainable on independent purchases. These social developments, and health industry evolutions, will put pressure on the drug industry's selling prices.

With the thrust to diversify, drug executives should emerge as more balanced corporate managers. They will extend their responsibilities to budget profit schedules on a more flexible approach in guiding complex, varied businesses. The diversification need not dilute the importance of ethical pharmaceuticals, but the shift could ease the responsibility of this one line of merchandise to support the corporate structure.

Drug Stocks. According to the quality measurement system, most drugs rate as Grade I or II stocks. Standard & Poor's index includes the following major drug stocks: Abbott Laboratories, American Home Products, Bristol-Myers, Merck & Company, Pfizer, Richardson Merrell, Schering-Plough, G. D. Searle, Sterling Drugs, and Warner-Lambert. Other major companies include Eli Lilly, Smith, Kline & French, Johnson & Johnson, Baxter Laboratories, and Upjohn.

The companies, of course, have grown at different rates. Charts in Chapter 6 showed that Pfizer grew slightly faster than the group and that Smith, Kline & French leveled off to slow growth in profits. American Home Products has a long growth record, averaging about 10 percent; Sterling's long growth record is in line with the group.

In recent years, Johnson & Johnson, Schering, and Eli Lilly speeded up growth and gained at 15 percent or more yearly. In the early 1960s, Bristol-Myers and Merck were the fastest growing companies. Drug companies have speedup periods when new product efforts are particularly fruitful, and in any period usually three or four companies make exceptional progress.

In the long run, it has been hard to find better investment performance than major drug stocks as long as the companies have been as profitable as the average of the industry. Dollar cost averaging of purchases has worked to investor advantage in this group. Some examples of price ratios for drug stocks are given in Chapter 11.

TABLE 9–B
PERFORMANCE OF DRUG STOCKS

	High	Low	Last
Post-tax Profit 1955–70	10.3	8.2	9.4%
Profit as percent of book value	24.6	17.9	23.0%
Growth in Earnings 8%			
Growth in Dividends 8%			

Cosmetic Stocks

Cosmetic companies are the highest profit large stock group. Since 1960, they have had profits of about 24 percent on equity. Avon Products (described in Chapter 6) has an outstanding record among all U. S. companies and is the only company that has been more consistent and more profitable than IBM. For most of the 20th century, it has earned about 35 percent on stockholder capital and has sustained growth at about 17 percent. Avon *is* about half the cosmetics industry. Its sales totaled $850 million in 1971.

Other companies in cosmetics and toiletries have had their ups and downs. Fifteen years ago Gillette was as profitable as Avon Products, but it lost the touch. Bristol-Myers, classed as a drug company, really had its best growth when Clairol hair colorings were at their height of popularity. Chesebrough-Pond's had a particularly good record in the decade up to 1971, but its success was not altogether attributable to cosmetics, since it had a number of toiletries that usually are not regarded as cosmetics. Vaseline is its biggest product, and Q-Tips is another important product.

The standard cosmetics firms such as Max Factor and Revlon have slower growth periods in recessions. Revlon is diversifying more in drugs. Some cosmetics firms come apart in hard times; examples are Helene Curtis and Alberto-Culver.

International Flavors and Fragrances is a popular stock because it is supplier of chemicals that provide tastes and smells. The stock has been expensive for some years, but it is worth knowing about because eventually there will be a bargain day and its growth program is aggressive.

Computers

Computer industries supply machinery and programs for use with equipment, provide computing service, and rent time. There is over 10 percent growth in the use of computing equipment; the development of time sharing is an important part of computing; and rapid adoption of new applications is fostered by decline in the cost of supplying the functions of computers to users. A central fact is IBM's ability to sustain its leadership position through improvements in equipment and types of service offered to customers.

The computer business is a very large worldwide business, by all odds the largest rapidly growing industry. By the end of 1971, U. S.-based companies had an estimated $40 billion worth of computing equipment installed for the use of customers, and 6 well-known American companies have placed at least $1 billion worth of equipment in customer locations.

The industry is distinctive in that it continues to own most of the equipment and receives rent from customers for use thereof. The effect is that the revenue of the industry grows almost exactly in proportion to the growth in customers' use of computing machines. This rent revenue sets it apart from most machinery manufacturing, in which income varies with cycles in shipments of machines.

Users of computing equipment also buy what is called software from the industry. Software is the automatic instructions and routines that the computers require for the specific chores of each user. Most users are regularly buying additional software each year, and they have growing needs for machine maintenance by the manufacturer's personnel.

What Computers Do for Business

The basic purpose of machines for accounting-type work was to automate clerical operations. At the time when electronic computers entered the business arena, scientists concerned with nuclear and rocketry design used them to work engineering problems when manual solutions were not practical. The scientists wanted to retain much of their data and calculation in the computer, and that led to the use of electronic memories on magnetic tape.

The scientists found the need for methods whereby a number of different people could use the giant systems, because one person could use only a small fraction of available time. Since it was not convenient to have a parade of scientists jumping in and out of one chair, and most people wanted to leave some setting on the console keyboard for the next step in computations, they invented time sharing, whereby different workers could be switched in and out of the computer. The next step was to permit different terminals to access common data memories. A little later they added memory in the terminal locations away from the main computer, thereby enabling the computer to scan what is on the memory at a remote station.

Leave the network concept aside for a minute and consider the superhuman chores the computer can perform. It can make millions of calculations all day long. It can balance a set of books as soon as the last item of data is given to it. It keeps track, with instant status reports, of every airline seat operated. It tells everyone who cares to know the prices at which thousands of stocks are quoted and trading, together with ratios and sales volume. This kind of information simply was not available in the precomputer era.

As we get further into the application of the communicating computer, it will be possible to operate a business with hard information where now much business is done with estimates. In a few years, all bank branches will have data about deposits, withdrawals, loans, and so on, on computers in such fashion that headquarters will know every fact about its operations from minute to minute. To the degree that business decisions can be improved with instant knowledge, the computer gives us something new. In addition, it can do the calculations that people can't keep up with, as well as speeding the routine chores.

Computer Problems

Computing is subject to the normal complaint that the supplier oversold the customer on what it would do and how much equipment would be needed. The worst problems revolve around the software programming for large systems that are supposed to serve a whole bunch of remote users in real time. My observation is that customers really want the performance of the supercomputers in networks with common memory.

The problem is for the software programmers to conjure up electronic proxies for the workers who make the old system function. Individual workers know how to help machines function through their understanding of mechanical idiosyncracies, but the automatic system must have manmade operating systems that can respond to requests for data, to calculate the balance, or to do whatever. A man would be hard pressed in trying to describe what he does each day so that electronic programs could take over many of his functions. A person who works at a job long enough learns shortcuts, but a computer cannot work like a human brain; it does not know how to take shortcuts. This is partly why it takes longer than predicted to bring a big system up to performance requirements.

A similar situation arises when smaller computing systems are to displace other methods. Usually, the organization has its routines set with people trained to put data into the system in set formats. Whenever the computer is installed, it must receive its work in a different manner. It does not produce end-products exactly like the old or in the same time sequence. You cannot perform certain jobs at intervals but must adapt to the way the machinery works.

However, when a computer finally is performing it improves efficiency and enables a business to do things not previously feasible. One example, cited earlier, is inventory control, in which computers are really essential to keeping track of all items in process and correlating them with current sales and orders to make inventory adjustments.

Computer Equipment

The main manufacturers provide the machinery that performs the work described. They are also the primary source of the software programs that help the machines do the required jobs. These manufacturers are very capital-intensive in that they continue to own the products they supply for customer use. Four or five years are required to get the full sales price from what they sell; so they have great demands for money. Hence, the business has come mainly into the hands of companies that had financial strength before they got into computing.

As a group, companies that started from scratch as computer makers were unprofitable in 1971. Control Data began as a computer maker but now earns all its profits as a finance firm. Scientific Data Systems is an unsatisfactory division of Xerox. Digital Equipment Company, the profitable substantial company, was not in the business computer field where rental of systems is the rule. DEC sells minicomputers and small time-sharing systems for engineering work but will enter the large-scale computer market in 1972.

The bulk of the world's business computers is supplied by six companies. Among them, one, IBM, supplies 67 percent of the U. S. market and does around 55 percent of the overseas business.

TABLE 9–C
ESTIMATES OF MARKET SHARES OF INSTALLED EQUIPMENT

IBM	67%
Honeywell Information Systems	9%
Sperry Rand–Univac	7%
Burroughs	5%
RCA (withdrew in 1971)	4%
NCR	4%

A major share of the government-supported British market is served by a domestic supplier, which is really not a factor in world markets. Japanese computers are just starting up. Control Data competes for business applications computing, but it really is not a factor in accounting markets.

Burroughs and NCR make most of the accounting machines used in the world. The modern machines have electronic computing and memory features and are semiautomatic computer systems; defining the market to include accounting machinery that incorporates electronic components, Burroughs and NCR probably each have about 10 percent of the market.

IBM earns almost nine-tenths of the profits earned from supply of computing equipment and services, as you can see from Table 9-D. I estimate that the share of profits from computing and accounting in the total company profits for each of these companies are as follows: IBM, 85 percent; Sperry Rand, half; RCA, none; Honeywell, half; Burroughs, all; NCR, 33 percent.

This data is not supplied by the companies and is presented here only to give you a general idea.

TABLE 9–D
COMPUTER COMPANY PROFITS
($ millions)

	1970	1971 (Est.)
IBM	$1,017	$1,079
Honeywell	58	66
Sperry Rand	72	57
Burroughs	67	74
RCA (withdrew in 1971)	92	def.
NCR	30	1

IBM. Only a handful of companies earn $1 billion annually, and among those the one whose growth rate has been over 15 percent compounded for 57 years is IBM. Other big companies, such as General Motors, Standard Oil of New Jersey, American Telephone, and Royal Dutch Petroleum, have long since slowed down to the pace of the world economy.

IBM is mainly in the business of helping to automate clerical work. It has many skills, such as salesmanship, low cost manufacturing, depth in research, and aggressiveness. However, the factor that keeps IBM in the lead is its ability to get results for customers.

The long-term policy of leasing equipment to customers with only a one-month rental requirement has worked well for the development of IBM. With a limited commitment in terms of capital, a customer is able to secure the use of high cost machinery that calls for alteration in methods of operation. This leasing policy has helped IBM to overcome sales resistance that might otherwise mean a slower rate of adoption of its products and services by customers. The rental policy has made it difficult to compete with IBM because of the capital needs.

The rental business has been attractive for the stockholder who tends to be sheltered from the profit effects from fluctuations in the volume of shipments that coincide with new model introductions. With minor exceptions, business and profits follow the same growth trend as the increase in value of equipment installed at customer locations. It is possible for IBM to have down years in the quantity of product shipped without much change in the rate of its earnings growth.

In spite of its good performance, IBM continues year after year as an underrated stock, assuming that the values of all listed stocks are correctly reflected in the marketplace. Although it has growth three times as fast as the Dow Jones Industrials and has avoided profit declines altogether, its price reflects a price over earnings ratio of two to two and one-half times that of the Dow Jones Industrials. It took only five years for the triple growth rate to give overwhelming advantage to the IBM stockholder.

In the first quarter of 1971, the market value of IBM was almost equal to the total market value of all stocks listed on the American Stock Exchange. (There are 114 million IBM shares, and their price changes are usually equal to the Amex list changes.) The importance of this stock is hard to overemphasize. Since it earns about nine-tenths of the profits of the largest dynamic industry, it is easy to understand why IBM-watching is a primary concern for professional investors. More than one trust institution has 10 percent or more of its managed funds invested in IBM. While they worry over IBM, their main problem is to manage the other 90 percent well enough to have it keep up to IBM. The following reply to an editorial on antitrust factors appeared in the New York *Times* on February 20, 1972.

To the Financial Editor:
Your article "How Big Is Too Big?" (Feb. 13) raises three large questions which ultimately can only be answered through due process of law.

We at I.B.M. are completely convinced that no American court will ever see reasons for, or merit in, partitioning I.B.M.

T. VINCENT LEARSON
Chairman, International
Business Machines
Corporation
Armonk, N. Y.

There are two sets of antagonists to the good position of IBM in the U. S. economy. One is a group of lawyers who take U.S. government jobs as stepping-stones to high-salary jobs in corporate law practices, helping businesses to protect themselves from what the lawyers prove in Washington to be the menaces of antitrust law. In order to damage IBM, they must invent some new law that Congress has not enacted, and they must get the better of Mr. Learson, one of the greatest business strategists in history.

The other antitrust antagonists of IBM comprise a group of incompetent businesses that sought to cut themselves in on more than a reasonable share of the markets created by IBM. These businesses express indignation that IBM would make competitive responses to their attempts to displace IBM products from IBM systems in customer locations. In my opinion, if the competitor-initiated antitrust suits against IBM prevail, American investors may as well join the welfare state.

IBM's Competitors.   One might think that the half-dozen companies that vie for the third of the computer business not held by IBM would grow fat on the crumbs from such a feast. For every advantage gained from participating in this fast-moving large business, there is some offset.

In theory, IBM prices are firm and high enough for competitors. Competitors must offer more value to get business away from the dominant company, and they also compete among themselves to some extent. Since IBM rents machines, competitors must accept the same slow payback on the products they ship; so they have had to raise hundreds of millions of dollars every year to stay in the race. Competitors are under pressure to show some product innovation ahead of the leader, and at the same time they must be prepared to provide equipment equal to whatever IBM brings out of its enormous engineering facilities. Each competitor must service somewhat delicate machinery as promptly and as regularly as IBM but with one-tenth as much service personnel as IBM. In addition, IBM has about 10 times as many salespeople as each competitor (or at least it seems that way). They spend their time assuring users of competitive equipment that once they recognize the error of their ways and come back into the fold their computing problems will disappear.

IBM's competitors are good companies. They have a lot of qualities that have sustained them over many decades. They get business in competition with IBM; however, if they fall down and IBM gets a customer back, he won't be a prospect again for a generation. Two types of computer operation are remaining effective in competition with IBM. Three companies, NCR, Burroughs, and Sperry Rand, have been in the accounting machinery business about as long as IBM and have established clientele. Two other companies, Honeywell and RCA, needed new product areas in which to apply their electronic engineering competence, and they have tried to copy IBM methods as closely as possible. Their marketing ploys have been to find gaps in the IBM line or to take advantage of the timing requirements implicit in IBM's business base.

In some cases, the competitors have taken design approaches that could give interim advantage over IBM. Although IBM is enormous, it is able to attain practical advantage by applying its resources through in-depth attack on a fairly narrow technical line. Its catalog contains many model numbers, but at any given time all the models are related to one another, and consistent architecture is employed throughout.

In the 1960s, when multiprogram use of computers was increasing, computer designers found that with ingenious methods they could manage to have several on-line users working simultaneously with the high-speed memory inside the main computer — a feat that required closely controlled switching capability. IBM scientists simply did not like this approach with its demands for more precision in the midst of high-speed operation. IBM designs continued to incorporate what to some customers seemed like redundant quantities of magnetic core memory. The scientists reasoned that within a few years the costs of components and their speed of functioning would be so favorable that the straightforward machine architecture with reserve capacity would be more satisfactory.

In 1972, IBM announced the development of machines with "virtual memory." This advance is based on the use of high-speed fixed disc memories of the type pioneered by Burroughs. With the fixed disc memory it is possible to transfer program instructions quickly to and from the main central processor memory and, thereby, expand the effective capacity of the main memory so that it can handle a greater volume of work in a given time span. By this move, IBM confirmed that the more elegant computer architecture had proven out and was ready to be combined with modern integrated central processor memories to enhance the capabilities of large computer systems.

In the meantime, Burroughs Corporation, the most prominent exponent of the complex systems for maximizing the use of high-speed computer memories, was engaged in a challenging effort to test its computer architectural concepts. Burroughs had secured good results with an earlier model computer, its B5500, which performed the multiprogram work in fine style, and it had designed a much larger system that scaled up the operating concept and method. Although the machines would perform their basic functions adequately, Burroughs had its hands full in trying to get the systems to perform in the scaled-up configuration.

By 1972, Burroughs had achieved commercial success with its design approach, and, as noted above, IBM had adopted certain of its concepts.

Characteristics of IBM's Competitors. After the foregoing outline of IBM's superiority, you may wonder why we are interested in its competitors. As I said, these are good companies that have been able to stand up with the most forceful industry leader.

Burroughs Corporation achieved one of the most remarkable redevelopments ever accomplished by a troubled old company — and did it entirely with internal abilities. Burroughs gained its computer know-how by building equipment for military and space agencies. It was the first company to make comuter logic and memory components available to the small users of book-keeping equipment. Most of its profits in the 1960s came from its electronic accounting machines, which continued to be distinctive products in the market into 1971.

During the 1960s, Burroughs' product designs and their market acceptance permitted the company to lower its costs of goods sold from over 60 percent to 50 percent, and in any manu-facturing industry the company that gets products out of the factory for 50 percent of the sales dollar will prosper. Additionally, this cost reduction was accomplished in a period when Burroughs was engaged in a costly buildup of its medium- and large-scale computer division.

Burroughs was the first one on the market with working terminals that could perform some of the preliminary work before being accessed by the central computer. The advantage of its design was that the time-shared network could do its work with a lot less time on the telephone lines than is possible with terminals that must be on line with the central computer in order to function.

Burroughs management claims that it succeeded because its organization has a thorough knowledge of the ways in which customers work with its machines. Product planning has been well integrated with its marketing. In 1971, Burroughs was in a challenging position and had its hands full in getting per-formance with its big computers, which were intended to enable customers to operate multibranch integrated computing systems.

In summer 1971, Barclays Bank announced that its Burroughs 6700 system was functioning as projected and that two more systems would be installed. Acceptance of these systems was of great importance to Burroughs and assured that it would have a major new source of profits. By the end of 1971, the more sophisticated investors recognized that Burroughs had become the most proficient challenger for a growing share of the business computer market, with 1971 shipments up to about a 7 percent share. The year 1971 was important for Burroughs in that the company proved its technical competence and reached financial self-sufficiency after years of heavy demand for outside capital.

Honeywell, Inc. is the most pretentious of the challengers in the computer business. Its computer business began as a joint venture with Raytheon, which sold out to its partner when Honeywell wanted to direct the effort toward the business computer market in an era when all the challengers were concentrating on the tropical garden of federally funded scientific computing. Honeywell believed that the future lay in the areas where IBM was concentrating its efforts.

The real start of Honeywell growth came in 1963, when it marketed its H200 series, which satisfied a market need just prior to the introduction of the IBM System 360 series, first announced in early 1964. Honeywell got a lot of customers who wanted some extra performance promptly. It went on from that initial impetus to build the strongest marketing organization next to IBM. It stressed the popular-sized systems that were the major products in IBM's business. It worked to build a following of satisfied customers in general industry and obviously had to offer customers more performance for their money.

Providing a somewhat lower cost performance than IBM does not require drastically lower prices. IBM likes to persuade customers to acquire systems that have some excess capacity that they will grow into. A competitor such as Honeywell proposes that the new customer take only what he needs this year and promises to provide the extra capacity as soon as it is needed. By 1970, Honeywell was claiming that it was Number 2 in the business.

In the meantime, General Electric Company had become discouraged with its attempts to become a factor in the computer industry. It had not done well in the medium-scale computer market, where Honeywell was at its best, but GE-Bull was selling a well-accepted small computing system that was competitive with IBM's System 3 small computer.

In the fall of 1970, the GE computer operation was merged with Honeywell; GE received Honeywell securities and a minority interest in Honeywell Information Systems. Then Honeywell really did become the Number 2 computer business, with a market balance about in proportion to total world markets. The value of Honeywell's computer products shipments in 1970 was about $860 million and represented for the combined computer divisions an increase of 13 percent over 1969.

In 1971, I estimated that the enlarged Honeywell would have cash flow reinvestment of around $270 million — $40 million from retained earnings and the balance as depreciation. Measuring this cash plowback against assets, the cash plowback return was about 12 percent. Honeywell needed an additional $75 million of new outside capital. Its balance sheet was leveraged with about 46 percent debt. It was earning profits on the computer operation at an estimated 3 percent of sales, which was not much in light of Honeywell accounting policies that included capitalization of some cost items that are more commonly expensed. However, the company was able to generate the cash for about three-fourths of its ambitious growth program in computing.

Honeywell stock has great volatility. In both 1962 and 1970, the stock price fell to less than half its bull market peaks. Earnings from its climate control products and its aerospace business are cyclical. Honeywell has a long growth record; by one means or another, it has achieved growth on a per share basis of about 10 percent a year. It is an interesting stock to watch; about three times in each decade there has been a big capital gains opportunity.

The Univac Division of Sperry Rand has gradually declined in relative position. It makes a good line of large computers, known as its 1100 series, which were used largely in engineering applications and were effective for time sharing. It has not been effective with these machines in business data processing, which is the main computer growth market. Univac also competes effectively with its 9000 series of smaller business computers. The company has a position in the industry and is making about half its profits in the Univac Division. It would like to hold its position and profits and shows little interest in challenging for leadership. Univac's takeover of the RCA computer business was essentially the purchase of a customer base that Univac had been unable to secure with a straightforward product and sales effort.

NCR was the last of the old-line office machine firms to succeed in computers. It has a good line of smaller-scale computers, which pulled the company up to about a 4 percent market share. It is a company whose weaknesses offset the strong areas. It waited eight years before it modernized its accounting machines to incorporate the electronic computing features that Burroughs began to sell in 1963. In the midst of exploiting the success of its Century series of computers, it made some disastrous acquisitions that diverted management attention and company resources from its main purposes. In 1972, NCR made a defensive agreement with Control Data for manufacture of computer peripheral equipment in order to overcome excess capacity.

I should explain why Control Data does not figure in the business computer market. For practical purposes, its management really does not know the automatic accounting business. On top of that, its main technology is created in a laboratory in a remote forest by scientists who neither know anything about business data processing nor care to learn about it. In the market for large scientific computers, it was challenged in 1972 by Texas Instruments, whose very large new computer contained more advanced components and vector-optimized architecture than had previous supercomputers for scientists.

Minicomputers. Minicomputers are a product different from the IBM type of business data processing. Minicomputers are sold as major components of a great variety of electronic systems. As many as 70 companies have been in the market, which was originally developed by Digital Equipment Company, the only moderately large company with a major protion of profits from these products. D.E.C. now seeks to have a rising share of its growth from sales of larger computing systems.

With impetus from Texas Instruments, the minicomputer was entering a transition to semiconductor memories that would foster significantly lower prices. The entry of T. I. with its $2,850 computer would have some affect on market shares among suppliers, but low price could be met by other manu-facturers as they adopt the lower cost memory and logic components. The net effect might be more rapid growth in unit sales of minicomputers, with the declining prices offsetting some of the unit growth. The possible uses of minicomputers are almost endless, from routing of a high volume of telephone communication to manufacturing plant control to hospital patient monitoring and, in time, sharing computer terminals.

Of the small companies specializing in minicomputers, Data General Corporation was a 3-year-old firm that had achieved good profit rates on sales of about 2,000 minicomputers through 1971. The operations of numerous larger companies will benefit from minicomputers as they either make them or use them as components of other products. As often as not, the buyer makes more money than supplier. For instance, Varian Associates supplied minicomputers for Burroughs to incorporate in electronic accounting and data processing equipment. Varian had an operating loss in 1971, and its computers apparently were not very profitable, while Burroughs made money on the equipment in which they were installed. As noted above, the entry of Texas Instruments complicates business forecasting in this product area.

Computer Service

In addition to the business of providing the use of equipment and programs to customers, there is an associated industry that sells computer-based services. Some 400 computer service companies perform data processing for fees, operate computer systems on customer premises, operate time-sharing computer networks, prepare program software for customers, and perform research-type projects. A couple of dozen are fairly substantial; the top 10 had almost $1 billion of gross sales in 1971.

These activities have been growing at about two times the rate of computer equipment rentals. The reason for superior growth is that they have been able to employ more specialized and capable personnel than is readily available to the average computer user. Either they do the work at a lower price or they give the customer more performance for his dollar.

Compartments of Computer Service Business. The several elements of the computer service industry are: (1) the service bureau type of operation, (2) software and systems programming, (3) time sharing, and (4) facilities management. Facilities managers combine all four skills to perform computing tasks at prices less than their clients' original costs. Electronic Data Systems, Bradford Computer, and National Data Corporation, among others, have been identified as facility managers, but over a period of time a number of other companies, such as Computer Sciences, Planning Research, and Automatic Data Processing, will in one way or another become managers of systems.

Contract Service and Facilities Operation. Historically, the IBM Service Bureau Corporation has been the major supplier of data processing for a fee. IBM used SBC as a convenience for customers until they could be sold on in-house data processing systems. SBC never intended to supply service on a perpetual basis to customers. The independent vendor services offer to perform data processing indefinitely and assert ability to do it better and cheaper than the customer can do it himself. Where traditionally bookkeeping was done internally, the modern trend is to use contract service.

Contract service may be integrated with facilities management, an arrangement whereby the vendor manages and operates the customer's in-house computing facility. There is a trend toward use of equipment in the facility manager's location. Supercomputers can have lower processing costs, and the customer's work is introduced to the system via working terminals. Electronic Data Systems is the most aggressive practitioner of facilities management combined with remote processing on EDS computer systems.

TABLE 9—F
COMPUTER SERVICE COMPANIES

Company	Approximate Shares Outstanding
Automatic Data Processing	5,600,000
Bradford Computer & Systems	3,000,000
Computer Sciences	13,000,000
Computing & Software	5,500,000
Electronic Data Systems	12,400,000
International Time Sharing	2,104,000
Informatics	1,500,000
National CSS	1,054,000
National Data Corporation	1,950,000
ONLINE Systems	519,000
Planning Research	5,200,000
Rapidata	917,000
Tymshare	3,000,000
URS Systems	2,200,000
University Computing	8,000,000

User-Based Time Sharing. The time-sharing segment of the computer service industry has sought to exploit the potential of computers by offering full computer power on a pay-as-you-go basis to the computer-user community. Time is bought over the wire, and the vendor is a passive party in the work done. In the pure interactive time-sharing field, a few — Rapidata, Tymshare, ONLINE Systems, and National CSS — have turned profitable, but most of the contenders for this market either have fallen by the wayside in financial disrepair or have joined forces with other computing organizations. Remote batch processing, which is generally considered a part of the time-sharing industry, is led by University Computing Corporation's computer utility network. Difficulties beset Computer Sciences Corporation in its Infonet development, which is a combination remote batch and interactive time-sharing operations. The survivors of the 1970 debacle would appear to be major contenders for what promises to be a rapidly growing market.

While the growth of the major companies is, in effect, a transfer of activity from in-house processing to vendor processing, the network information and computing services appear to be developing, almost literally, something new under the sun. Table 9-F lists a few companies or divisions of companies that are providing some type of on-line computer-based service, which is developing revenues in a manner and from sources that did not exist prior to the start-up of these activities. These companies are providing remote batch computing, interactive time sharing, reservations, and credit card verification, and they are providing remote access to an infinite variety of software programs for performing special tasks. It could be argued that many of these activities could be performed in other ways or in more limited ways on in-house computing systems (certainly remote batch processing); however, in almost every case the activities are developing revenues and activity that did not exist before.

Ratio of Revenue to Capital. The handiest measure of proficiency in the computer service field is the ratio of dollars of revenue to dollars of paid-in equity and debt capital. This is a people-intensive business in which most of the machinery can be rented from computer manufacturers. In general, the companies have proven successful when they have secured about $2 of gross revenue for each $1 of capital. When revenue exceeds $3 per $1 of capital, return on capital seems to become satisfactory.

In the 1960s, several computer software firms were most

profitable when they had the high ratio of revenue to sales. Several of these reversed their profitability when they raised large blocks of capital to implement elaborate computer networks. It proved correct to downgrade the investment rating of such stocks while the ratio of revenue to capital was depressed, as in the cases of Computer Sciences and University Computing.

Automatic Data Processing. This company is described in Chapter 6 as a most exciting growth company, the best among computer services. Its founder-management group has over 20 years of experience in data processing and is expanding its computer services across the United States by acquisition and development of computing centers in major cities across the country. It is a well-financed company with virtually no long-term debt; it has a plan for major expansion and appears to have the momentum to carry it from its current sales volume of about $60 million to levels well in excess of $100 million within a relatively few years.

Electronic Data Systems — Glamor and Problems. EDS has been the primary practitioner of the facilities management type of computer service. It assumes responsibility for all aspects of operating the customers' equipment systems and also supplies processing capacity from its own computers. In 1971, EDS was a $100 million sales company with 3,000 employees. It is noted for the esprit of its organization and quality of training. Growth in revenues had been around 50 percent a year.

EDS was subject to a degree of stock market controversy because of its "Texas" style accounting, the unrealistic price at which the stock traded, extracurricular activities of its head in world affairs, and assumption of control of a Wall Street firm, F. I. Du Pont. Earnings of EDS have been increased about 20 percent by human resources accounting, whereby it capitalizes training costs of personnel to be prepared for specific customer contracts. Such expenses are amortized in 24 months. In the long run, the training investment is fully recovered, and in the meantime cash flow is adequate to cover the training expense. However, it is a permissive form of accounting that makes reported earnings moderately questionable. EDS came under attack in Congress in 1971 over the rates it charged for data processing in the medical benefits agencies.

EDS began trading as a public company at prices equal to about 300 times earnings, a ratio that no company can live up to. For several years, the stock labored under a gross overvaluation handicap. By the late fall of 1971, the price had finally reached a basis that could be supported. It would not be in the clear, though, until the question of its charges to medical health agencies could be cleared up and it showed ability to attract more clients in fields other than health service.

Independent Equipment, Supplies, and Financing Companies

In addition to the main computer systems companies and service firms, there are companies that make equipment to be used in place of some machines supplied by computer makers in their systems. Some companies lease computing equipment for rentals lower than those quoted by the manufacturer. Supply of magnetic tapes and paper forms is largely from companies other than computer makers. The magnetic discs used in computers are supplied by independent as well as by main manufacturers.

This is a quick gloss over several different industries. The substitute machine makers are engaged mainly in leasing of disc memory machines to be used in place of the units supplied by IBM but at lower rentals. IBM finances its machines with stockholder capital, while the independents borrow most of the money they invest in the disc drives. The independents assert that they have lower prices or some new features with advantages.

This business is a battlefield, and IBM has responded with strong competitive products and prices. Memorex and California Computer Products are prominent in the warfare. It is a hazardous area for investors.

In the 1960s, there was a big splurge of new companies that would buy IBM System 360 machinery from IBM and then rent to customers at lower rentals than IBM charged. They figured they could depreciate the machines over 11 or 12 years and finance with borrowed money, saving taxes on the capital invested. This idea blew out in the high interest rate market of 1970.

When IBM introduced its System 370 in 1970, its first new models were aimed squarely at machines owned by the leasing companies. The fallacy was in thinking that IBM System 360 machines could be kept on full rental for five to six years after IBM had fully depreciated its company-owned 360 equipment.

Suppliers of magnetic tapes and paper forms operate in a fairly settled business, where they have more of the market than

do equipment suppliers. Moore Corporation in paper forms
and 3M Company in magnetic tapes are stronger in these
products than are any of the equipment firms.

The situation for magnetic discs is fairly messy, since these
constitute a supply with value high enough for users to rent.
IBM invented the removable disc memories with its medium-
scale System 360 computers, and at the outset it was the sole
supplier. The disc is not terribly difficult to copy, and a
number of companies did so, causing a subsequent oversupply.
3M Company entered the fray in an unusual role as a price
leader; its position was that it had lower costs with its high-
volume new factories. Soon afterward most of the independent
suppliers of disc packs had lower profits.

Photography

Photography products include: box cameras, precision cameras,
microfilmers, X ray, color and monochrome films, printing,
processing materials, and sensitized papers. Sales of film and other
supplies are several times the equipment sales.

Production of quality-consistent film is a critical phase of
photography. More manufacturers make satisfactory cameras and
equipment than they do films. In the past, Kodak has supplied
most of the film consumed, and it supplied the film marketed by
its largest competitor, Polaroid. Part of the overwhelming
dominance of Kodak was a product of marketing vigor, but its
persistent advantage has been based on the uniform quality
of its films and supplies. This uniformity has been Kodak's main
strength in building a unique $3 billion sales business and at the
same time providing the film on which Polaroid built a $500
million business.

Other film makers exist, but their profits are insignificant
compared to those of Kodak and Polaroid. The relationship
between Kodak and Polaroid began to change when Polaroid
started to manufacture its own newly designed films. The new
Polaroid films are intended for new-model cameras, one a
portrait camera introduced in 1971. In 1972, Polaroid planned
to unveil a pocket camera with some remarkable features. The
shutter system is nonmechanical, being opened and closed by
electro-optical methods.

Growth Patterns

The combined photographic markets — pictures, graphic

arts, microfilm, and X ray — have had average growth of around 10 percent a year. Growth comes in surges, depending on new product introductions. In the last two decades, the surges were associated with pictures in a minute, amateur color, the Instamatic cameras, instant color, systems for microfilm retrieval, and other innovations. The most visible possible newer growth products are computer output microfilming and Polaroid's instant picture pocket camera. Kodak will offer a new 15 mm film camera with qualities similar to 35 mm.

Financial strength of the leaders is superior. They have high margins and no debts. The profits on capital of the leaders have been as shown in Table 9-G.

TABLE 9–G
PERCENT EARNED ON STOCKHOLDER EQUITY

	1965	1966	1967	1968	1969	1970
Eastman Kodak	23	25	23	22	21	20
Polaroid	30	38	33	26	22	14

Polaroid growth has been in surges, as shown in Figure 9-1. It raised $100 million via a stock offering in 1969, which increased book value 35 percent on an offer of 3 percent more shares. The added capital had not been employed effectively in 1970, which is why the earned on equity fell off. Capital expenditures and research totaling $400 million had not yet matured.

Figure 9-1 displays the volatility of Polaroid stock and shows that investors were willing to discount the revival of growth in the mid-1970s. The stock is worth studying against the day when earnings resume growth. In 1971, Polaroid was seriously bogged down with start-up problems on its new film plants as well as by the need for new products to stimulate demand.

Clothing Patterns

Simplicity Patterns makes and sells low-priced paper patterns, which would not appear to be a one-company industry. True, it has competitors, but they are not available to direct investment. Fortunately, Simplicity, the best company, is listed on the N.S.E. It has almost $100 million sales in patterns and instruction textbooks and grows around 15 percent a year. The company has no debts or other complications. It just undersells competition and earns 12 to 13 percent after taxes.

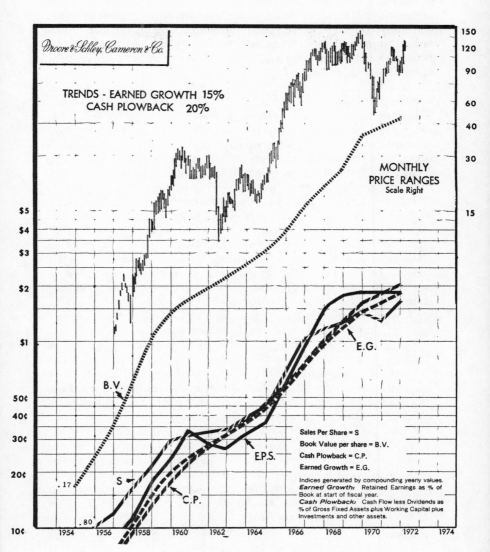

Figure 9-1. Polaroid

Petroleum Modifers

Of course, no one has a monopoly of petroleum chemical additives. (Additives are compounds to improve fuel combustion and emission residues or to provide lubrication.) However, one company has done more creative research and has grown much faster than the petroleum chemicals industry. Lubrizol has become a substantial growth company based entirely on creative chemistry in this field.

Electric Photography

In the 1970s, the 40 percent annual growth of Xerox in its heyday does not mean much. However, Xerography, a dry method of duplicating any number of copies on plain paper, is still a superior duplicating method that serves a growth market. Quality of reproduction is good, and although cost is higher than offset duplicating, the convenience and speed make it attractive. The company has always stressed the volume applications of its method and has pioneered an expansion in the use of medium-volume duplicating.

In 1970, there was some concern about whether the entry of IBM into the copying field would make a difference to the growth of Xerox. IBM introduced its copying machines at prices that were too high, and it had to reduce prices to become competitive. IBM started with equipment at the size and price scale where Xerox had success in the past. Xerox more recently has been emphasizing higher-performance equipment.

Xerography, or volume copying by dry printing as Xerox markets it, requires a depth of service support that Xerox has beyond the capabilities of all competitors combined. The company has about $1.5 billion of sales and rentals, or 25 times its sales a decade ago. So far, its position has not been threatened, and it continues to extend the business base.

Xerox profits in 1970 were 11 percent of sales and 24 percent of stockholder equity. Financially, it can support 15 percent growth as long as it can develop markets. The record of the stock is interesting. In the years of exploding growth, the stock traded at prices where the P/E ratio was about four times that of the Dow Jones Industrials. In 1966, investors started to allow for slower growth, and the stock traded at a yearly average price of about 95 for 4 years until the P/E ratio declined to about $2\frac{1}{2}$ times that of the averages, or about the same as IBM (see Figure 11-7). This is probably the ratio of price that will persist in the future.

Rank Xerox is an English company whose earnings growth is mainly based on its participation in Xerox international operations, which grow faster than the North American business.

Nuclear Fuel

Kerr-McGee is a growth minerals exploration company. Gas and oil production from offshore Louisiana is a dynamic source, accounting for half of the company's profits. The company is a major factor in the U. S. uranium business and also the major supplier of boron chemicals. It is operated with aggressive capital investment policies.

As an oil and gas company, it has some distinctions, such as pioneering offshore oil drilling; however, in nuclear fuel it is more distinctive. It is estimated to own about one-fourth of the U. S. uranium ore reserves, and the grade of its main mines at Grants, New Mexico, is fairly high. New exploration has revealed sufficient additional uranium to keep the company position in the greatly expanded market forecast by 1980, when uranium sales are expected to be four or five times those of 1971. In that year, about 25 million pounds were shipped by all suppliers.

Kerr-McGee is integrated forward into the uranium hexafluoride that is fed to gas diffusion plants for uranium enrichment. The company plans to continue aggressive expansion in its nuclear business; its goal is profits five to ten times the 1970 nuclear earnings, which were about one-fifth of company's total profits. In the meantime, Kerr-McGee has become increasingly prosperous through its offshore oil and gas operations. It also owns most of the mineral rights to Searles Lake in California, a rich deposit of boron and other caustic chemicals.

Growth has been 10 to 12 percent a year and could be better. The stock usually trades at a P/E ratio of about one and one-half times that of the market averages.

Travel Service

American Express Company has a variety of travel services that support its travelers' checks. Profits are derived largely from income on invested reserves held against travelers' check accounts. Growth in the company's income is proportionate to the trend in public expenditures for travel and interest rates on invested reserves.

The prospects for American Express are more complicated to forecast because of its entry into the insurance business through the 1968 acquisition of the Fund American companies. The merger worked well, since profits continued to grow 15 percent a year after the merger; not including profits on securities sales, operating profits went up 20 percent a year. Interest rates on municipal bonds and other securities helped the profit showing.

American Express Reservations is a computer-centered system for hotel room rentals. It is another marketing base for the company to expand its travel business and financial assets. Since the profits of American Express have grown faster than the travel business, the company needs something new to keep up the pace. This is an important growth company that belongs in most portfolios.

Credit Information

Dun & Bradstreet is synonymous with information about credit worthiness. Its computerized files hold data on 3 million businesses. These data are used by customers, largely in marketing, both as a credit check and as an information source on size and potential of a company. D&B earns a high return on capital, pays a generous dividend, and grows about 9 to 10 percent a year. It is a fairly large company with $300 million revenues.

With the merger of Corinthian Broadcasting and Dun & Bradstreet, J. H. Whitney & Company became the largest stockholder group of D&B. Corinthian stockholders received about 19 percent of D&B shares. The immediate effect of the merger on earnings was not so important as the possibility that extra energy from the Whitney group would help speed up growth.

In 1971, D&B was implementing a program to get its hundred-odd offices in line with the main company data banks. The idea is that if the information about companies is immediately available, D&B will sell more reports. When it took days to get a report, the D&B customer was apt to make a decision without bothering to make inquiry; now, with speedier responses, it could become more routine to use D&B information. Business information is about one-half of D&B operations. It also publishes airline guides and Moody's Financial Manuals and has classified telephone directory services.

Several smaller companies provide retail credit information to merchants and service companies and represent a business different from that of D&B. Retail Credit Company is the most prominent.

Multiple Growth Company

3M Company (Minnesota Mining & Manufacturing) is a

unique multitechnology creator of its own growth companies. It is one of the half-dozen highest quality companies, and one that has increased pre-tax profits in 28 of the last 30 years; the last setback was 3 percent, followed a 70 percent gain in 1950. It has extraordinary coordination of innovation and marketing.

3M stresses production techniques that make for quality and efficiency. Some of its competitive advantage is based on its skills in production. It has held on to a dominant position in pressure-sensitive tapes largely because of superior quality.

3M seeks market exclusiveness rather than penetration of markets created by others. Its new products tend to require longer market testing periods than is typical in industry. During shakedown periods, it normally spends a couple of years with pilot production models in its facilities or in the hands of friendly customers. Many of its new products call for a lot of experimenting until they come out right. For instance, the color copier was an unknown quantity as far as potential users were concerned, and customers have had to learn what to use it for.

3M is a fascinating organization in terms of its diversity of novel products from reserach. Possibly no other company conceives, perfects, and markets technically sophisticated products in a number of different industries all at the same time. Further, it moves the ingenious new products square into the territory of first-class business leaders.

A sample of the interesting gadgets coming on as significant products includes: a concrete block polishing and coating system to equal terrazzo finish; porous, transparent surgical tape; color photocopying; 90-second X ray film; electron beam microfilm recording; dry silver microfilm and copy paper; hairset tape; fluorochemical "light water," a fire extinguisher for volatile liquid fires; sound on a slide; a high-speed photocopying system; reflective woodgrain auto siding; synthetic athletic playing surfaces; traffic light switching by light beam from vehicle.

3M Industries and Technologies

A feeling for the virtuosity of 3M can be derived by listing the industries in which these different items are supplied and then considering the types of technologies involved. Industries include:

Construction	Beauty care
Medical	Fire extinguishing
Photocopying	Automotive

Computer output recording	Recreation
Information retrieval	Optics and traffic control

The various technologies involved in 3M industries include:

Synthetic fibers and films	Photography
Adhesives	Radiology
Medical pathology	Fluorochemistry
Optical imaging	Fire fighting
Electronic control	Audio reproduction
Photochemistry	Photocopying and printing
Chemical impregnating	Furniture manufacture
Electronic radiation	High voltage electricity
Computing	Traffic dynamics
Mechanical film and paper transfer	Resilient plastics
Information accessing and filing	

3M Specialty Areas

Most of the know-how of 3M relates to applications of synthetic materials, in which 3M seeks to combine raw materials that are available on a commodity basis into exclusive products for the convenience of the user. In recent years, it has become more skilled with dynamic systems to consume volume quantities of chemically treated paper, films and fibers, and liquid compounds.

The systems approach has led 3M increasingly into electronics and optics. Mechanical materials handling and liquid applications had to be mastered. 3M is working its way into photographic products through design of gadgets to use its microfilm and copy materials that employ an exclusive dry silver technology and electro-mechanical development. These gadgets include micro-fiche reader printers and the high capacity microfilm electron beam recorders that image film directly. These products bid fair to become the most successful in their fields.

3M and Pollution

We analyze the responses of industrial corporations to the social demand for improved management of processes that may cause air and water pollution as well as spoliation of natural resources. 3M Company anticipated most of U. S. industry in this area by about a decade. During the 1960s, 3M built up an engineering staff devoted entirely to design factors in its plants that affect the environment. This group now numbers 32

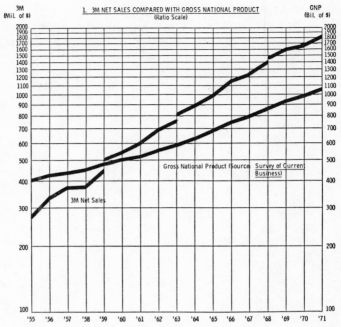

Figure 9-2.

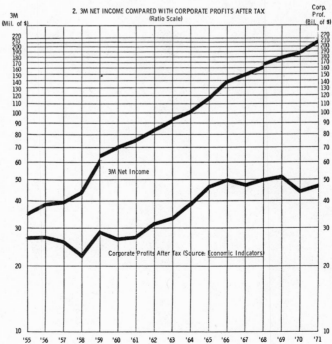

Figure 9-3.

professional engineers. The company advises that for practical purposes all its facilities conform to current pollution standards and that in some cases recycled materials, including water, now offset as much as 25 percent of the extra costs.

10

Emerging
Growth Companies

I~N~ the stock market, the borderline is not too
well defined between speculation and sensible investment in
fast-growing younger companies that at least have a track
record. The question of whether the speculation is in the stock
price or in the company bears on this point. A way to get
perspective in this question is to study thoroughly the American
Stock Exchange list of 1,200 companies. How do we sort among
1,200 stocks? I went through the list stock by stock in mid-1971
and could identify at most one out of four of the companies in
regard to the nature of its business and the status of its prosperity
or otherwise. If I can tell you about only 300 of the stocks listed,
then as far as I'm concerned the other 900 must be regarded as
speculations. Of the names I could give some information about,
perhaps 1 out of 10 could be classed as a growth stock, allowing
for some cyclical variability. The other stocks are about equally
divided into two groups: one, settled companies that tend to
perform about in line with the economy; the other, companies

in which the earnings situation is hard to predict or in which the stock price reflects speculation on new developments, making them hard to forecast with confidence.

Amex Index

In 1963, the American Stock Exchange began to issue an index of all its listed stocks. Analysis of this index has shown that it increased in value by a rate about twice as high as the indexes of the stocks on the New York Stock Exchange through 1968, but it declined more in 1969-70 and recovered more slowly. The Amex monthly pamphlet, *The American Investor*, which gives data on the Amex index, shows that the earnings of the constituent companies have grown about in proportion to the value of the index.

The index has been somewhat more volatile than the other stock market indexes. In the 1969-70 bear market, the Amex index declined almost 43 percent from high to low. It declined from a P/E ratio of 26 times composite earnings to about 12 times. The wide fluctuation in the value of the index shows us how much speculation is contained in the prices. At times, the speculative factor is negative in the sense that the stocks may be undervalued compared to the long-term pattern.

That the Amex index might grow faster compared to the N. Y. S. E. list is explained by the nature of the Amex list. It is constantly adding companies that have grown large enough and sufficiently profitable to qualify under the fairly stiff listing standards of the exchange. In some years, as many as 100 new stocks have become listed on the Amex, an indication that 100 stocks are in fairly dynamic stages of their growth trips. In the meantime, numerous stocks are transferred from the Amex to the New York Stock Exchange list. By definition, the stocks that move to the New York Stock Exchange are somewhat more mature than the companies being added to the Amex list. This should provide a bias in favor of higher growth for the Amex list.

I suggest that in working with the list you try to identify those stocks on the Amex list that can score enough quality points, using my method, to come up to Grade III. A few quite high grade stocks are on the list, but the interesting companies, from a speculative point of view, are those with profits of around $1-2 million but without the long records that are required for the highest quality ratings. The main concern you will have after you have made a list of interesting stocks is that a good deal of the time the stock prices contain a speculative factor.

Aggressive Investing

My observation is that investors do not base the majority of their decisions to buy or sell stocks on statistical analysis of the historical data. Very often they base decisions on judgments about factors that are expected to result in future profit improvement or decline. Statistical methods are not so universally accepted that their significance is fully reflected in market prices. From the following discussion, it may seem that good statistical results are well recognized, but I shall argue that while they are recognized, the future has not been altogether discounted.

Moneymakers

The investor's quest is to find corporate general managers who have proven methods for earning high profit rates on stockholder capital. The scarcest people in the business world are managers who have working formulas for making a lot of money in proportion to their capital. Plenty of business people have good concepts and ability to attract capital and personnel for ambitious undertakings; unfortunately, too many do not have the aptitude for turning out profits. I remarked on entrepreneurial aptitudes early in this book, and I find it most helpful in suggesting methods for analysis of smaller companies.

Standards for Smaller Companies

We select stocks of smaller companies instead of stocks of strong, large companies because the small companies are expected to have faster profits growth. Experience has been that profits have come from a few very fortunate speculations and that too many have done poorly. Subjects in this book are in order of their reliability as investment tools. Quality has worked well since I designed it; growth forecasting works well; stock prices are always tougher to predict, almost by their nature; and venturesome investing is the most difficult. The following standards are my attempt to avoid the seemingly inevitable failure of some portion of our aggressive investments.

Size of companies. If a company had earned $1 million for a couple of years, it had demonstrated its capability and was big enough to gain support from bankers and strong backers as well as suppliers. It should look better to its customers. It would still be small for institutional investors, but the aggressive investment funds might consider it.

Profit rates. I started to limit my selections to companies that earn 20 percent or more on stockholder capital, or almost double the average profit rates of the big U. S. companies as a group. Because 20 percent proves too exclusive, I decided that over 15 percent profit on equity would be all right if other factors were very positive. Retained earnings should be more than 10 percent of book value.

Profit persistence. Examination of smaller company records showed that venturesome stocks that gave analysts trouble in the 1960-70 period had previously suffered profits setbacks. The inference was that the nature of their operations predisposed them to future setbacks. The statistical services publish five- to eight-year records for small companies. Whatever data is available should show no profit declines in this analysis.

Debt. Companies that grow and prosper with little or no debt usually have more skill and commitment to earning high profits on capital. Most heavy-borrowing companies eventually have growing pains of some severity. Therefore, companies selected should have less than 25 percent debt in the capital structure.

Conservative accounting. Some companies report more profits to stockholders than to the tax collectors. They may tell the tax collector that an item has no tangible value but may assure stockholders that it has. Probably a majority of companies now use accelerated depreciation for taxes and straight-line depreciation for stockholder reports.

The easiest way to discover the amount by which profits reported exceed taxable profits is by looking at deferred tax reserves. Use of straight-line depreciation usually does not supplement reported profits by more than 10 percent compared to taxable profits. If the deferred tax reserve or deferred taxes for a year exceed 10 percent of earned surplus or reported earnings for a year, the investor usually can find capitalized intangible assets on the balance sheet. It is best to use a standard when deferred tax reserves are less than 10 percent of earned surplus and the increase in the deferred tax reserve is less than 10 percent of earnings for a given year.

Number of shares. In order to generate adequate trading interest in a stock, the number of shares should be over 1 million and over 500,000 should be owned by the public.

American Stock Exchange Growth Companies

To cull the Amex list statistically, begin with all the stocks that have 1 million shares and $1 million of after-tax profits.

These stocks number not quite 400, and after elimination of those with a lot of debt and profits of less than 16 percent on equity, fewer than 100 remain. Finally, of the stocks that suffered no setbacks once they were established, 28 had no setback in net income (not necessarily per share) since 1963, and 4 had good short records.

Table 10-A shows the stocks that met these standards: $1 million profits, 1 million shares, no profit decline since 1963, cash plowback above 10 percent, less than 25 percent debt, 16 percent profit on equity, and deferred tax reserve less than 10 percent of earnings.

TABLE 10—A

Company	Earnings as % of Book	Earned Growth	Sales 1970 ($ millions)	Profit 1970 ($ millions)
Alliance Tire & Rubber	30%	25%	$ 102.7	$ 9.7
Ames Department Stores . . .	29	28	48.19	1.44
Angelica Corporation.	27	23	58.35	3.44
Arctic Enterprises	40	40	80.24	4.70
Associated Baby Services . . .	19	11	31.53	1.54
Augat Inc.	33	28	8.40	1.26
AVEMCO Corp.	17	15	4.65	1.19
Carnation Co.	17	13	1053.4	41.88
Circle K	20	15	93.61	2.90
Globe Security Systems	28	28	40.84	2.13
Heck's, Inc.	30	26	52.89	2.23
House of Fabrics	23	23	44.34	2.07
Harvey Hubbell	26	13	118.46	9.39
Levitz Furniture	23.7	23	99.65	4.44
Mammouth Mart	24.5	14	106.25	3.40
New Process Co.	64	30	93.89	8.50
Pamida, Inc.	34	34	79.21	3.72
Petrie Stores	34.4	16	115.63	8.55
Prentice-Hall	28	15	128.30	15.44
Prudential Building				
Maintenance	45	30	51.80	2.18
Research-Cottrell	16	14	79.43	2.62
Rex-Noreco	30+	30	8.46	1.60
Rupp Industries	43.5	43	29.28	1.52
STP Corporation	41.5	30	85.94	11.60
Sternco Industries	27.7	27	46.45	3.59
Superscope, Inc.	18.0	18	57.20	3.13
Valle's Steak House	17	17	22.69	1.50
Venice Industries	33	33	22.14	2.14
Vetco Offshore	22	22	16.75	1.81
Bradford Computer	43	43	8.50	1.21
Delta Corporation of America.	35	35	14.91	1.26
Suave Shoe	36.0	36	42.59	2.03

Analysis of Companies

We started with the theory that moneymaking aptitude should be what we first searched for. Of the companies listed in Table 10-A, all but 5 earned 20 percent or more on equity and had high plowback of earnings. Here are brief comments about the companies.

Alliance Tire is an Israeli manufacturer that accounts for most of Israel's tire exports. It has grown around 15 percent a year. Truck tires are emphasized.

Ames Department Stores is an east coast discount chain that operates in small cities. This kind of stock must be closely monitored.

Angelica specializes in work apparel and uniforms, which it sells largely to employers. Expansion to retail stores implies some changes.

Arctic Enterprises is a snowmobile firm, which suggests that it is in an increasingly competitive field.

Associated Baby Services rents diapers and acquires related companies. The trend toward disposable diapers brings it into competition with Procter & Gamble and other big firms.

Augat Inc. has a modest specialty in components for mounting integrated circuits. It is a good specialty firm but with more potential competition.

AVEMCO is a small aviation insurance and finance firm with investment activities. It is exclusive underwriter of group accident insurance for the Aircraft Owners' and Pilots' Association. One would want to know more about this operation.

Carnation Company is a billion dollar growth company that just happens to be listed on the Amex.

Circle K is a fast-expanding convenience grocery chain in the southwestern United States. It is a narrow profit margin operation that depends on momentum, making it risky.

Globe Security Systems is mainly a uniformed guard agency controlled by Walter Kidde & Co. Growth showed signs of slowing down.

Heck's is an Ohio-West Virginia-Pennsylvania-Kentucky discounter that makes a fair number of acquisitions that tend to modify the sales mix.

House of Fabrics has exploited the home sewing trend with rapid store expansion. With 241 stores, it had room to grow.

Harvey Hubbell is a moderately large electrical control products firm that grows via acquisitions. Growth was coming harder, although it resisted the down cycle in capital goods.

Levitz Furniture was in a rapid store and warehouse expansion phase in 1971. It retails popular-priced furniture on a discount basis. Growing pains should be watched for. It is now listed on the New York Stock Exchange.

Mammoth Mart is a New England regional discount chain whose territory will receive some invasion by national discounters. It is pushing out of its territory, which it has pretty well saturated.

New Process has a nationwide low-priced apparel mail-order operation, which has gotten quite large. Profit margins are exceptionally high.

Pamida operates a midwest discount retail chain and rack-jobbing service. Profit margins have been fairly high.

Petrie Stores is a women's specialty chain with unusual distinction. Listing on the New York Stock Exchange was pending.

Prentice-Hall is a major publisher and leads its industry in quality and persistence of growth.

Prudential Building Maintenance services large buildings, including cleaning and operation. End of the office building boom in 1971 could affect growth, although the business is stable and profitable.

Research-Cottrell is an engineering construction firm that specialized in air-pollution control. Profit margins are not high, but growth is promising.

Rex-Noreco is a financial service firm in the mobile homes field. It was diversifying, which could make analysis difficult.

Rupp Industries is a recreation vehicle maker whose largest line is snowmobiles. Minibikes are a newer specialty. Very rapid growth means the company is unseasoned.

STP Corporation sells consumer-applied motor oil additives, whose merits are disputed by car makers and oil companies. The analytical problem is over the question of whether success is based on product performance or advertising vigor. The controversy led to an earnings setback in 1971.

Sternco Industries remained public after stockholders' protests against a takeover by American Home Products. It markets pet supplies and breeds pet fish, and distribution emphasis is on variety chains. F. W. Woolworth buys one-fifth of Sternco output. The Sterns also own competing Hartz Mountain Products. (The

AHP deal would have included Hartz Mountain.) The company is obviously an acquisition candidate. On its record, Sternco looks good.

Superscope is U. S. marketer of Sony tape recorders and has the Marantz hi-fi line. It is on the borderline in deferral of expenses. Expiration of the Sony contract in 1974 and changes in Japanese access to U. S. markets are important questions.

Valle's Steak House operates supersized steak restaurants in New England. One would have to know how far the personal management of the Valle family and the New England style can be extended south and west.

Venice Industries is one of the fast-moving participants in double-knit apparel. Its high profit rates are encouraging.

Vetco Offshore supplies underwater oil-drilling systems. One would have to understand the company's success in a seemingly competitive business. Vetco is a takeover prospect, partly because of its patent positions.

Bradford Computer, founded in 1967, is the youngest company on this list. It is a profitable company in a new industry, computer facilities management.

Delta Corporation of America supplies mobile home financing and insurance. Large mortgage lenders and insurers demand its services because of their lack of familiarity with the mobile home field.

Suave Shoe makes and imports casual shoes, priced from $2 to $4 a pair. As it grows, it comes more in competition with large companies.

Stock Price Histories

If we want to invest in the stocks of these smaller companies, we would still have to figure out what prices to pay. A beginning can be made by studying the price histories, as shown in Table 10-B.

Volatility

The Amex Median Monthly Price/Earnings Index shows that the 1969-71 high and low P/E ratios were 25-12. From its December 1968 level, the index declined 43 percent while the P/E ratio declined over 50 percent, an indication that profits continued to rise in 1969-70. Many of these stocks fluctuated more than the Amex index. They made their lows

TABLE 10−B
STOCK PRICE HISTORIES

Company	High, Low, and Median P/E Ratios, 1969−71	Percent Profit Increase, 1965−70
Alliance Tire & Rubber.	11−3−7	270%
Ames Department Stores	21−5−13	270
Angelica	26−12−19	120
Arctic Enterprises	30−6−18	4700
Associated Baby Services	18−9−14	100
Augat	39−15−27	500
AVEMCO	32−12−22	2000
Carnation	20−14−17	95
Circle K	35−12−24	160
Globe Security Systems	28−13−21	100
Heck's	27−7−17	230
House of Fabrics	39−16−28	430
Harvey Hubbell	18−10−14	43
Levitz Furniture	65−17−41	570
Mammouth Mart	24−9−17	215
New Process	37−10−23	355
Pamida	28−12−20	1600
Petrie Stores	30−13−21	185
Prentice-Hall	35−18−27	81
Prudential Building Maintenance	38−17−27	215
Research-Cottrell	95−22−58	480
Rex-Noreco	40−14−27	1500
Rupp Industries	20−12−16	1300
STP Corporation	27−16−21	170
Sternco	40−13−27	210
Superscope	37−6−21	265
Valle's Steak House	35−14−24	210
Venice Industries	24−9−16	740
Vetco Offshore Industries	33−7−20	550
Bradford Computer	80−28−54	−
Delta Corporation of America .	33−5−19	−
Suave Shoe	19−7−13	−

with the index and recovered with it. As a group, in 1971 they rose more than the index. All but three made all-time highs by mid-1971.

The Right Ratios

Quality and growth control the market price ratios accepted by investors. On this list, Prentice-Hall is the highest grade stock with a long growth record, and its P/E ratio has been about 1.75 times the P/E ratio of the Dow Jones Industrials index, which conforms to the ratio premium suggested in Chapter 11 for a high grade stock with 12 percent growth.

Carnation Company with growth at 13 percent was accorded very little premium in terms of P/E ratio. Unlike debt-free and more glamorous Prentice-Hall, Carnation is in the dairy products industry and had 24 percent debt raised for acquisitions. Investors usually do not pay such large P/E ratios for growth stocks in nonglamor industries. Carnation has paid only 30 percent of earnings in dividends, while Prentice-Hall has paid 50 percent. During the five years, both stocks gained about the same percent in prices.

Investors discriminate among smaller company stocks in the same way they do among the big companies. That they are wary of apparel manufacturers is shown in the lower P/E ratios. Soft goods retailers are modestly evaluated, and snowmobiles seem to be suspect, but services such as Prudential Building Maintenance seem to rate well. The newer types of marketers may sell at higher P/E ratios while investors are still discovering them. Examples are Circle K, Levitz, New Process, Sternco, and House of Fabrics.

As a group, the companies in Table 10-B were increasing capital over 20 percent a year from retained earnings, and growth rates had exceeded 20 percent a year in many cases. Major growth stocks that have settled back to around 15 percent growth trade at P/E multiples of nearly twice that of the DJI. The few that persist at 15 percent growth are rated between 2 and 3 times the P/E ratio of the averages.

While 20 percent long-term growth is too much to expect, some of these stocks seem likely to sustain growth at 15 percent. The ones that do can be expected to merit P/E ratios two to three times the P/E ratio of the DJI. It would be surprising if many of them remain long at P/E ratios above three times the averages.

The higher or lower ratings between glamorous and mundane industries can be expected to persist. Machinery, for example, may never rate with pollution and new technology.

In timing of purchases, you should find that at some time in most years the stocks will sell at the middle of the P/E ratio ranges of recent years. The investor is faced with the need to make an earnings extrapolation for the year ahead, because people who would buy these stocks make decisions based on such projections.

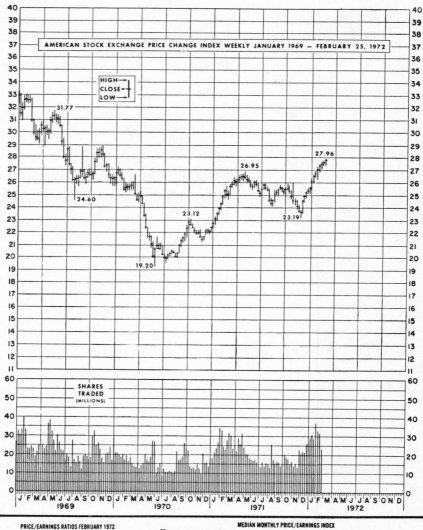

AMERICAN STOCK EXCHANGE PRICE CHANGE INDEX WEEKLY JANUARY 1969 — FEBRUARY 25, 1972

HIGH →
CLOSE →
LOW →

31.77
24.60
19.20
23.12
26.95
23.19
27.96

SHARES
TRADED
(MILLIONS)

J F M A M J J A S O N D J F M A M J J A S O N D J F M A M J J A S O N D J F M A M J J A S O N D
1969   1970   1971   1972

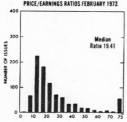

PRICE/EARNINGS RATIOS FEBRUARY 1972

NUMBER OF ISSUES

Median
Ratio 19.41

0 10 20 30 40 50 60 70 75

MEDIAN MONTHLY PRICE/EARNINGS INDEX

J A S O N D J F M A M J J A S O N D J F M A M J J A S O N D J F M A M J J A S O N D
1969 ——— 1970 ——————— 1971 ——————— 1972-

Figure 10-1.

To identify future growth stocks, of course, one must revise stock lists every year. The main benefit is that the investor always has his attention focused on the moneymakers.

11

Stock Prices and
Returns to Investor

You may find this chapter difficult, but here are a few things I hope you can get from it: (1) a general idea about the whole problem of stock prices; (2) some measures you can apply in the real world of ambitious investing; and (3) an interest in a thorough study of valuation problems.

Stock Returns

What returns should stocks provide their owners? A stock return consists of cash dividends and something for retained earnings. The only way to calculate whether or not a return is adequate is to assume that a stock was bought for an average price in a year, that dividends have been received, and that the stock was sold some years later.

Table 11-A shows a historic sample of the average yearly return on a group of stocks over different five-year periods. The information in the table is based on these factors: (1) stocks were bought at the year's mid price; (2) they were sold at mid price five years later; (3) dividends received were added to price gain; and (4) the compound annual return was calculated.

TABLE 11–A

PERCENTAGE INVESTMENT RETURNS BY QUALITY GRADE

Grade	1960-65	1961-66	1962-67	1963-68	1964-69	1965-70	1966-71
I. . . .	17.0	14.4	16.1	16.9	14.3	10.0	16.3
II . . .	14.0	8.2	15.9	16.3	14.6	8.1	8.7
III. . .	9.9	9.1	13.2	12.3	10.5	-0.3	6.6
IV. . .	15.0	9.7	11.0	10.2	4.4	-1.5	2.7
V . . .	6.7	3.1	9.1	14.2	8.1	-1.5	-1.2
S & P 425 Industrial Average	12.4	7.7	11.1	8.5	6.8	2.2	6.7
Dow Jones Industrials	11.0	8.7	9.1	8.7	4.6	0	2.5

If you had bought the 30 large, well-established stocks on the Dow Jones Industrials index at an average price in any of the five-year periods, your return would have been about 7 percent. With a group of Grade III stocks, the return would have been slightly over 9 percent. (Standard & Poor's 425 Industrials averages also returned about 9 percent.) With the 15 Grade I stocks, the return would have been almost 15 percent. In other words, if you had bought Avon Products, IBM, Merck, Coca-Cola, or 3M Company, for example you might have had a 15 percent annual return on your birthday.

In 1970, the high for IBM was $390 and the low $220, giving a median of $305. In 1965, the median price was $155. If you had bought IBM then, you would have received annual dividends of about $13 between 1965 and 1970, and you would have doubled your money, which equals 15 percent compounded for 5 years.

Start $1.00
End 1 year 1.15
End 2 years 1.33
End 3 years 1.56
End 4 years 1.77
End 5 years 2.00

If you don't like five-year doubles, burn this book!

Is the historic 7 to 9 percent earned on the averages good enough at the present time? The answer is no. Only 1.5 percent of the stocks listed on the N. Y. S. E. are Grade I by the quality measurement system. The valuation basis has to be the general market, and all stocks relate to the averages.

If the Dow Jones Industrials Averages always sold at prices to make dividend yield 4 percent, then its 4.5 percent dividend growth would give a total return of about 8.5 percent. If a major growth stock yields 2 percent, and its dividends increase 10 percent a year with no change in yield, the total return would be 12 percent. What the investor should seek is a basis on which he can buy and hold a stock with growth faster than the averages so that he is fairly certain to secure a gain in market value at the same percent as the growth in dividends and earnings, with the cash dividends on top of the growth.

Bond Yields and Stocks

From the late 1860s to the late 1960s bond yields were almost always about 3 to 4 percent lower than the apparent total yield on stocks, even in periods when bond prices were declining with a rise in yields. Long-term (30-year) bonds bought in 1960 declined about 25 percent to mid-1970, and the effective return was about 2.5 percent. In the same 1960-70 period, stock investors had a total return of about 6.5 percent from the Dow Jones Industrials and about 8.5 percent from the larger list on Standard & Poor's 425 Industrials Averages.

In 1970, the average yield on better grade bonds was 8 percent. In 1970, the DJI yield at the mid price was 4.375 percent. With a dividend growth at 4.5 percent, the total return would be 9 percent. By March 1971, prices of bonds had gained until the yields were 7.25 percent; the cash yield on the DJI stocks had decreased to 3.625 percent. Measuring total return, cash yield was down at least as much as the bond yields. The question is whether there is a persisting change in the ratio of bond yield and total return on stocks.

U. S. Interest Rates

Prior to World War I, America was an underdeveloped land that attracted European capital for exploitation of oil, mines, and manufacture. After that war, the U. S. dollar emerged as the safest currency and attracted more than its normal share of world reserves. In the depressed 1930s, the U. S. dollar was rated above all other currencies, and this condition persisted through World War II. At the end of the war, the United States had the only reserves of any consequence left in the world.

During most of this century, the U. S. dollar has been favored, and since World War II, interest rates have been about 2 percent below equivalent rates in Europe. In the 1960s and 1970, yields in Europe and in the United States came much closer together. Dollar holdings by foreigners became so large that they placed some pressure on U. S. yields to hold closer to foreign rates. Currencies of West Germany and the Netherlands were strong, the French franc was firmer, and even the British pound recovered some of its former strength.

My theory is that U. S. interest rates have been 2 percent below those of European countries for reasons that may not persist. In 1970, rates in Europe moved in concert with those in the United States. After devaluation or revaluation had occurred, the risk of holding dollars was reduced, and it was possible that the U. S. dollar might again be favored for holding of reserves. The biggest jump in interest rates on U. S. dollar investments occurred when our trade deficits rose to about $4 billion in 1968.

In the fall of 1971, I thought there was a good possibility that European interest rates would decline more than U. S. interest rates. I reasoned that a number of the governments would try to lower rates in order to discourage the inflow of money they did not want. In addition, the new U. S. economic policies would tend to depress business in other countries. With the dollar devalued, higher interest rates in the United States would attract money.

In September 1971, several central banks began to lower their interest rates. They said the action was to resist the inflow of speculative money; however, it was also evident that they were trying to prevent their currencies from rising relative to the dollar. I began to believe that for the first time in this century we would see interest rates in America higher than those in Europe.

Bond-Stock Ratio

The bond-stock ratio is published in *Barron's*, a magazine issued by Dow Jones & Company. *Barron's* compares the yield on its bond index with the earnings yield on its 50-stock average. An earnings yield is the 12-month reported earnings as a percent of market price. *Barron's* calculates it this way:

Yield of bonds ÷ Earnings yield

Over the years, the ratio has ranged between .50 and 1.25. Traditional analysis has held that: (1) the normal ratio is about 0.8; (2) the stocks were overvalued when over 1.00; and (3) the stocks were undervalued when near 0.50.

During 1970, the bond-stock ratio was above 1.00; when bonds went to 8.5 percent, the earnings yield was nearly 8 percent. In January 1971, when bonds moved to 7 percent yield, the earnings yield was 6.75 percent.

To some degree, stock investors indicated belief that earnings were below normal and that bond yields would decline until their yields were closer to the 4.5 percent Treasury Bill rates of early 1971. Earnings on a long-term trend would have been 15 percent higher in 1970.

Earnings yield on trend earnings, January 1971:   7.25 percent
Bond yields with normal curve of bond yields: 6.25 percent
Bond — Stock ratio, adjusted to trend: 0.86 percent

In other words, stock investors considered that they were just anticipating probable cyclical adjustments.

Since World War II, earnings yields on the DJI have ranged between 4.5 percent and 10 percent. During most years, the yield has been at 7.25 percent some of the times; 7.25 percent is equivalent to 14 times earnings.

Bond Interest Rates

My assumption has been that interest rates would fall back to 6 percent. Between 1900 and 1967, interest on bonds had been above 6 percent in only 2 years. The factors that made for high interest rates in the late 1960s were extraordinary. Nevertheless, we should try to judge whether stocks might have higher yields and lower P/E ratios if bond yields remain above 7 percent.

The suggested P/E ratio of 14 is actually lower than the real P/E ratio during most of the 1960s; however, it was a normal ratio in earlier decades when investors obtained some 3 to 4 percent higher returns on stocks than on bonds. There are two reasons to doubt that the total returns on stocks will be higher in the future than in the past. First, when bond yields are 5 percent, the bonds are too expensive and their yields too low to attract individual investors, and they also are too expensive by foreign standards. Bonds have not proven safer than stocks by enough margin to warrant a 3 to 4 percent differential in yield versus total return on stocks. Second, if American stock investors have secured 8 to 8.5 percent return for 100 years, it seems optimistic to think the market might return 10 percent in the future. In other words, investors will not expect a higher return on stocks and are apt to continue rating stocks in the same old way.

If bond yields are approximately the same as the estimated total return from stocks, bonds will compete with stocks for investor money. Then, switching emphasis between bonds and stocks will be more normal than it has been during the decades when bonds have been too expensive to appeal to individual investors. A balanced investment portfolio, in which the percentages of bonds and stocks are varied according to the market level, may then become the normal practice.

Little attention has been given to bonds in this book, partly because during too few market years have bonds been really competitive with stocks. The primary stress here is that high grade stocks, with relatively high growth rates, provide to investors long-term returns that are substantially higher than the returns obtained from the general market.

Relative Stock Prices

Seasoned stocks usually sell on some basis that relates to the averages. In general, when quality is high investors pay more dollars per share per dollar of earnings. They also pay premiums for cash dividends. Growth is accorded varying amounts of premium, depending on rates and projections.

The following standards were used in relating stock prices to the averages.

Quality is determined by the quality measurement method described in Chapter 3. For lower quality, you demand a higher return.

Dividends are rated according to the percent of earnings paid out in cash.

Growth rates are determined by the methods explained in Chapter 6.

Rate of return standard is based on the record of the Dow Jones Industrials. According to my method, the DJI Averages fit Grade III. The average has returned about 8.5 percent over the decades, although the range has been from negative to about 18 percent for various 10-year periods, depending on the purchase and sale dates selected. Its dividend has been 55 to 60 percent of reported earnings, which grew about 4.25 percent a year. The median dividend yield was 4 to 4.5 percent.

The arithmetic of relative prices is a little complicated. In developing the technique, we took many samples of stock price ratios, compared the companies for growth and quality, and compared the yields (or P/E ratios) to the averages. Difference in quality requires a higher return, or lower price, for lesser quality.

Quality and Rate Return

Taking the five quality grades, when the averages are at about 14 times earnings, the range of normal rate of return is about 3 percent from high to low, which gives the following scale, *where no difference in growth is projected:*

Grade	Average Percentage Rate of Return
I	7
II	7.75
III	8.50
IV	9.25
V	10
Ungraded	11

Taking Grade III as standard at 8.5 percent return, a difference of 1 percent in return makes a difference of 12 percent in price. The premiums paid for best quality are modest, because investors overrate medium grade stocks of large companies. However, prevalence of a wider scale for rate of return based on quality cannot be demonstrated. That is why owners of quality stocks almost always come out ahead.

Quality Premiums and Discounts

Clearly, the differences in market rating for quality are not very great. I treat Grade III (medium) as the standard. The P/E ratio of Grade III is treated as 1.0. Premiums or discounts are expressed in tenths (or hundredths if we want more refinement); so the P/E ratio of a Grade IV stock should be 9/10 of the P/E ratio for a Grade III stock. Grade III is equal to the market averages.

Premiums for Growth

The stock market hardly ever agrees with theoretical arith-

TABLE 11–B
PREMIUMS AND DISCOUNTS FOR QUALITY

Grade

I	+0.2
II	+0.1
III	0.0
IV	-0.1
V	-0.2

metic about premiums for growth. The P/E ratios in Table 11-C are based on the theory that a growth rate will persist for 15 years. In 15 years, 5 percent growth will increase 1.0 to 2.1, and 15 percent growth will raise 1.0 to 8.15, which is nearly 4 times 2.1. Therefore, if you pay 3.7 times the P/E for 15 percent growth, you should get the same return on your money if both end up at about the same P/E after 15 years. It makes one pause to realize that a P/E ratio of 60 is discounting 17 percent annual growth for 15 years.

TABLE 11–C
THEORETICAL P/E RATIOS FOR GROWTH RATES
(dividend payout at 30 percent * of earnings)

Growth Rates	P/E Ratios	Ratio of P/E to 5 percent Growth P/E
3%	9.5	0.77
5	12.5	1.00
7	16	1.28
10	24	1.93
12	31	2.5
15	46	3.7
17	60	4.9
20	90	7.3

* The 30 percent payout is used in this example because higher growth rate stocks seldom pay 50+ percent.

Table 11-D shows what investors usually pay for various growth rates in terms of P/E ratio. Except in bull markets, investors usually are willing to discount a superior growth rate for only about eight years ahead before the growth is presumed to slow to the average growth rate.

The main differences for growth apply to superior growth. The stock market usually does not pay growth premiums that are as great as the ratio of a company's growth to the growth in

TABLE 11–D
USUAL RANGE OF P/E RATIOS FOR GROWTH
(dividend payout at 30 percent of earnings)

Growth Rates	P/E Ratios	Ratio of P/E to 5 percent Growth P/E
3%	10.5	0.84
5	12.5	1.00
7	14.1	1.15
10	17.5	1.42
12	20.2	1.62
15	25.0	2.00
17	28.7	2.30
20	35.3	2.87

U. S. corporate profits, but some later examples indicate that in some cases the market does pay a theoretical premium (see Table 11-C). Table 11-E gives the differences from the usual range of P/E ratios for growth. Growth at 5 percent is the ratio of 1.0. Differences are expressed as tenths and hundredths, plus or minus from 1.0.

TABLE 11–E
RATIO PREMIUMS OF DISCOUNTS FOR GROWTH

Growth Rates	Most Usual Ratio Differences	Theoretical Ratio Difference
3%	–0.16	–0.23
5	0.0	0.0
7	+0.15	+0.28
10	+0.42	+0.93
12	+0.62	+1.5
15	+1.00	+3.7
17	+1.30	+3.4
20	+1.87	+6.3

Dividend Payout Discounts and Premiums

For dividends there is an added complication in that when growth is high the dividend is a smaller part of the return expected by the investor. For that reason, P/E ratios are a little less sensitive to the payout as a percent of earnings. Therefore, differences at 5 percent growth and at 10 percent growth are shown in Table 11-F. A 50 percent payout is used as normal.

TABLE 11—F
RATIO DIFFERENCES ACCORDING TO DIVIDEND PAYOUT

Percent of Earnings Paid in Cash	Differences in Ratio of P/E to P/E at 50 percent Payout	
	5 percent Growth	10 percent Growth
0%	−0.43	−0.38
10	−0.38	−0.30
20	−0.33	−0.23
30	−0.18	−0.16
40	−0.09	−0.08
50	0.0	0.0
60	+0.09	+0.08
70	+0.17	+0.14
80	+0.24	+0.20
90	+0.34	+0.23

These differences may seem to be quibbling. It is true that this is theoretical arithmetic, but if it helps our objectivity it is better than guesswork unaided.

Dividend Payout Rates

Table 11-G shows that in terms of P/E ratio investors pay about 60 to 80 percent more for stocks that pay out 50 percent of profits in cash dividends than for stocks that pay no dividends. It is simple arithmetic that when dividends can be paid while sustaining a growth rate investors value a stock more highly than they do when all earnings are reinvested to support the same growth rate.

However, the cash dividends are not rated the same as retained earnings. If they were, then a 50 percent dividend payout stock would be even more prized. Cash dividends are taxable to individuals, and they do not assume that they will be reinvested with compounding growth. Furthermore, there are values attached to the company beyond its current earnings.

The various assumptions made in this kind of calculation can give one an accordion-type shift on the ranges of P/E. For instance, a change in the assumed total rate of return can reduce a premium from, say, 60 percent to 40 percent. Nevertheless, this kind of table can be a helpful guide in figuring dividend payout rates.

TABLE 11–G
DIVIDEND PAYOUT RATES

Percent of Earnings Paid in Cash	P/E Ratio Grade III	Ratio of P/E to P/E at 50 percent Payout	Quality Adjusted P/E Ratios Grade I	Grade V
assumed growth rate of 5 percent, perpetual				
0%	8.0	0.57	9.2	6.8
10	8.8	0.62	10.0	7.5
20	9.6	0.67	10.9	8.1
30	11.4	0.82	13.0	9.7
40	12.8	0.91	14.4	10.8
50	14.2	1.00	16.2	12.2
60	15.5	1.09	17.8	13.2
70	16.8	1.18	19.2	14.3
80	17.8	1.24	20.4	15.2
90	19.0	1.34	21.6	16.1
100	20.0	1.40	23.0	17.0
assumed growth rate of 10 percent, perpetual				
0%	16.5	0.62		
10	18.5	0.70		
20	20.5	0.77		
30	22.5	0.84		
40	24.6	0.92		
50	26.7	1.00		
60	28.5	1.08		
70	30.2	1.14		
80	32.0	1.20		
90	33.7	1.23		

Relative P/E Ratio

The relative P/E is simply the P/E ratio for the stock divided by the P/E ratio on the averages. (The Dow Jones Industrials Average was used here, but other indexes are used for these ratios.)

	Market	EPS	P/E
Dow Jones Industrials Average	850	60	14
Any Stock	50	2.50	20

$$20 \div 14 = 1.42 \text{ (relative P/E)}$$

The ratio of P/E in the section above is the same calculation as in this example. I treated 5 percent growth as 1.0, or the parity standard, since the 5 percent rate of growth is close to the trend of the averages.

TABLE 11–H
SAMPLE OF RELATIVE P/E RATIOS

Company	Historic Rel. P/E	(q) Quality Grade	(p) Plowback Growth	(d) Dividend Payout
Eastman Kodak	1.9	I	11	50%
Monsanto	1.0	III	5	55
Polaroid	3.5	II	14	15
Abbott Laboratories	1.5	II	9	45
Merck	2.0	I	11	65
Pfizer	1.5	I	9	50
Avon Products	2.8	I	16	65
Gillette	1.5	III	9	60
Amerada Hess	1.0	IV	11	8
Gulf Oil	0.85	III	6	50
Kerr-McGee	1.4	III	10	33
Louisiana Land & Exploration	1.6	II	12	67
Mobil Oil	0.8	III	7	50
Pacific Petroleums	2.2	IV	8	40
Fedders Corp.	1.2	IV	10	25
Georgia-Pacific	1.5	III	8	45
Johns Manville	0.9	IV	5	50
Carborundum	0.7	IV	7	40
TRW	0.95	III	8	40
Crown Cork & Seal	0.9	II	12	0
Holiday Inns	2.0	III	14	20
Howard Johnson	1.5	III	11	20
Marriott Corp.	2.3	III	11	0
McDonald's	1.9	III	18	0
Associated Dry Goods	1.15	III	7	50
S. S. Kresge	1.45	II	13	25
R. H. Macy.	0.95	III	7	40
J. C. Penney	1.3	I	10	45
Sears, Roebuck	1.55	I	8	50
Woolworth	0.85	IV	6	50
Burlington Northern	1.00	III	1	70
Santa Fe Industries	0.90	V	3	70
Southern Pacific	0.75	V	3	50
Union Pacific	0.8	V	3	50
Columbia Broadcasting . . .	1.25	III	9	55
Capital Cities Broadcasting .	1.30	IV	15	0

(Continued on next page)

TABLE 11–H *(continued)*

Time	1.2	V	4	70
Times Mirror	1.3	III	10	25
Anheuser Busch	1.4	II	11	40
Coca-Cola	1.90	I	13	60
General Foods	1.20	II	7	60
Kraftco	0.95	II	7	60
Pepsico	1.35	II	11	40
Standard Brands	1.05	III	7	60
Emerson Electric	1.6	I	11	45
General Electric	1.6	III	6	70
Whirlpool	1.0	III	11	50
Burroughs	1.8	II	12	20
Digital Equipment	3.2	III	15	0
Honeywell	1.6	III	9	25
IBM	2.5	I	10	40
Minnesota Mining & Manufacturing	2.0	I	10	50
Sperry Rand	1.25	IV	7	20
Xerox	3.0	I	17	30
Cenco Instruments	1.5	III	10	15
Hewlett-Packard	2.5	III	12	10
Schlumberger	1.3	II	10	30
AMP, Inc.	1.5	I	15	30
Texas Instruments	2.0	III	10	25
Motorola	1.8	IV	9	·20
Magnavox	1.3	III	8	50
RCA	1.3	IV	8	45
Zenith	1.6	IV	5	60
Raytheon	1.0	III	11	20

(q) See Chapter 3.
(p) See Chapter 6.
(d) As percent of reported earnings.

A historic relative P/E ratio should be challenged before we accept its future persistence as probable. Although the record suggests that most stocks will trade in patterns that repeat, in numerous examples the ratio of price to earnings or to yield did change. We can measure three factors for their influence on stock prices. Volatile though the stock market may be, we should still be able to apply objective standards.

I know of no method now being used widely to validate price ratios of stocks, although judgments are made constantly about the correctness of prices for particular stocks. The widespread use of the price-earnings ratio is in itself risky because reported earnings are the more variable statistics among company accounting data. I have mentioned that most stocks report earnings that deviate widely around long-term trends; therefore, in discussing growth forecasting I have urged study of earnings plowback, sales, and book values. Nevertheless, almost every stock analysis describes the stock price compared to earnings and states whether the P/E ratio is high, low, or normal.

The problem is further aggravated by the definition of earnings against which price is compared. The P/E ratio can be retrospective; it compares price to earnings for the latest reported 12 months. The P/E ratio can be extrapolated from a forecast of earnings. The forecasts of earnings for companies with variable growth or just plain cyclicality may vary by 30 percent. Ten security analysts may forecast that the 1972 earnings for a stock whose 1971 earnings were $2.75 a share will be from $2.60 to $3.30. If the current price is 60, they extrapolate P/E ratios of 23 times at one extreme and 18 times at the other. Some will be bullish while others are bearish. Nevertheless, this is the popular tool and we must cope with it.

Discussion of Samples

	Quality Premium	Growth Premium	Dividend Premium	Statistical Relative P/E
Abbott	+0.10	+0.33	-0.05	1.38
Merck	+0.20	+0.52	+0.12	1.84

In this calculation, Merck is two grades above the averages, and Abbott is one grade higher. The growth of Merck is 6 percent better than the averages, and Abbott is 4 percent more. Merck has a higher payout, and Abbott's is lower. When you consider how tentative these growth calculations are, I think the closeness of the calculated ratios to the historic ratios (these are statistically rough also) indicates that such procedures are useful. The historic relative P/E for Abbott was 1.5; for Merck, 2.0. Both have long records, and their growth premiums could be explained by market evaluations implied by my theoretical differences for growth.

	Quality Premium	Growth Premium	Dividend Premium	Statistical Relative P/E
Gulf Oil	0.0	+0.07	0.0	1.07
Louisiana Land & Exploration	+0.10	+0.52	+0.13	1.75
Kerr-McGee	0.0	+0.42	−0.13	1.29

For Louisiana Land & Exploration and Kerr-McGee, the historical relative P/E ratios (see table) are close enough to the calculated so that we can reason that their market standing is settled. The relative P/E ratios for international oil stocks have been about 20 percent lower than for the averages for many years. Investors long anticipated the problems with oil exporting countries that came to a head in 1970 and 1971.

	Quality Premium	Growth Premium	Dividend Premium	Statistical Relative P/E
IBM	+0.20	+0.42	0.00	1.62
Honeywell	0.00	+0.32	−0.20	1.12
Sperry Rand	−0.10	+0.15	−0.23	0.82

IBM's quality is so much higher than other stocks that my Grade I standard does not fully rate this factor. With respect to the growth premium, IBM did grow over 15 percent for half a century, and the theoretical ratio difference can be applied. As I mentioned before, the relative P/E ratios were determined for a large sample that includes companies in slower-growing industries. If the company grows faster than the industry, investors reason that the company's growth must eventually slow down. When a company is growing at the same rate as its industry, investors usually will buy the idea that it can sustain its established growth rate.

IBM is a special situation in that, for practical purposes, it *is* the computer industry. Investors' projections for IBM indicate confidence that it can grow at least 12 percent for many years. This pace is about 70 percent of its rate of gain in the 1960s. My theory is that if IBM grows only 10 percent a year in the 1970s, investors will be rewarded on purchases of the stock when its P/E ratio is twice the P/E of the DJI Averages.

For years, Honeywell traded at an average P/E ratio of over one and one-half times that of the averages. Investors have credited Honeywell with ability to generate new growth activities to support its long-term trend; its progress in computers is the modern basis for confidence.

In 1969 and 1970, Sperry Rand lost its premium and sold below parity with the averages. Investors concluded it might not hold its position in the computer field. It has maintained its position and bids fair to grow at its historic rate, probably about 7 percent a year, but quality and low dividend payout suggest a P/E ratio lower than the averages.

	Quality Premium	Growth Premium	Dividend Premium	Statistical Relative P/E
Coca-Cola	+0.20	+0.72	+0.08	2.00
Standard Brands	0.0	+0.15	+0.08	1.23

The market rating of Coca-Cola confirms the usefulness of the adjusted relative P/E ratio. Standard Brands has not been rated quite so high as my method suggests could be supported. The stock has been something of a wallflower, and I am not inclined to emphasize the idea that the rating should be higher.

	Quality Premium	Growth Premium	Dividend Premium	Statistical Relative P/E
R. H. Macy	0.0	+0.15	−0.09	1.06
J. C. Penney	+0.2	+0.42	−0.05	1.59

Analysis of retailer P/E ratios shows that the stocks may have been somewhat undervalued in the past. In 1970 and 1971, most of the major retail chain stocks were strong in price, and their relative P/E ratios rose above my adjusted ratios, shown here. The premiums over what I find to be normal were about the same size as the discounts I saw in the historic trading record; stocks regularly range above and below normal. As a result of the rise in relative P/E ratios, these stocks no longer offered price appreciation any greater than their earnings growth. The difference in market rating between Macy and Penney remained about the same in all periods, which confirms the usefulness of the measures of quality and growth applied. The greater popularity of retail stocks in 1970-71 is explained by the popular belief that the consumer would be key to recovery from the recession.

	Quality Premium	Growth Premium	Dividend Premium	Statistical Relative P/E
Johns Manville	−0.1	0.0	0.0	0.9
Georgia-Pacific	0.0	+0.24	−0.09	1.15

Johns Manville stock usually has sold at a P/E ratio a little lower than the Dow Jones Industrials, and the record indicates that it should have. Georgia-Pacific grew somewhat faster than its plowback rate in the 1960s because of aggressive use of borrowed capital, and it also issued quarterly stock dividends whose market value was enough to have dividends equal or exceed 100 percent of profits. If one treats the small stock dividends as equivalent of cash, the adjusted relative P/E ratio would be about 1.5, consistent with the record.

	Quality Premium	Growth Premium	Dividend Premium	Statistical Relative P/E
Capital Cities Broadcasting.	−0.1	+1.0	−0.38	1.52
Times Mirror	0.0	+0.42	−0.20	1.22

The market histories of Capital Cities Broadcasting and Times Mirror agree with the calculated ratios shown here. The quality of Capital Cities was suspect in the early 1960s, when its capitalization was largely debt. However, debt went from 60 percent of capital in 1965 to 23 percent in 1970. In 1971, its market price was in line with the adjusted relative P/E shown here.

	Quality Premium	Growth Premium	Dividend Premium	Statistical Relative P/E
Howard Johnson	0.0	+0.52	−0.23	1.29
McDonald's	0.0	+1.45	−0.38	2.07

The adjusted P/E ratio of Howard Johnson is a little lower than the record. "HoJo" has been in an aggressive expansion effort, and its quality image could be a shade higher than I measure. The historic relative P/E ratio of 1.5 discounts a growth speedup.

McDonald's relative P/E ratio of 1.9 was lower than its record would warrant in another industry, where its exclusive management skills might seem more credible. *Datamation* magazine has given coverage to the exceptional skills of McDonald's in inventory control computer programs. They even account for the hamburgers given to the police.

	Quality Premium	Growth Premium	Dividend Premium	Statistical Relative P/E
AMP, Inc.	+0.10	+1.00	−0.16	1.94
Texas Instruments	0.0	+0.45	−0.20	1.25
Motorola	−0.10	+0.33	−0.25	1.00

These theoretical relative P/E ratio obviously deviate from the historic. AMP stock had been rising on a 15 to 20 percent annual trend. It started at a low P/E in the early 1960s and moved up to a 70 percent premium in 1970. The upgrading may persist above the historic 1.5 relative P/E.

The Texas Instruments situation is more sticky. Its average EPS gain in the 1960s was 10 percent. If you apply the theoretical P/E ratios I gave for growth differences, you can validate a 2.0 relative P/E for 10 percent growth. Sales per share grew 15 percent in the 1960s, and that would support a higher relative P/E; investors may reason that in a boom period profit margins will recover to bring EPS also to the 15 percent trend. Texas Instruments is a unique stock, and a high relative P/E is apt to persist.

Motorola's historic premium could be supported if it reasserted past 11 percent growth in the future. Motorola has a very long record; so investors are confident in its continued cycling around trend. In mid-1971, I thought the confidence was overdone; investors were paying too much for the possibilities.

The three electronic stocks, a group with earnings and price volatility, show that the judgment of appropriate relative P/E ratios requires a good deal of thought and care. The Motorola graph (Figure 11-4) shows just how difficult forecasting can be.

You may want to argue with our historic relative P/E reading, but in the long run arithmetic catches up with overpriced stocks.

P/E Ratio Sources

Statistical services supply the records of P/E ratios for listed stocks. The S&P stock reports list the high and low P/E ratios for past years. The current P/E ratio of the DJI (see Table 11-I) appears in *The Wall Street Journal* once a week. Standard & Poor's *Outlook* includes P/E ratios on S&P averages; *Barron's* magazine also publishes P/E ratio data. The P/E ratios of stocks traded on exchanges are available on all the stock quote monitors for the latest 12 months.

TABLE 11–I
P/E RATIOS* OF DJI AVERAGES

	1971	1970	1969	1968	1967	1966	1965
End of 1st Quarter . . .	17.5	14.1	15.4	15.5	15.2	17.2	17.5
End of 2nd Quarter . .	16.8	13.2	15.1	16.2	16.7	14.9	17.3
End of 3rd Quarter . . .	15.9	15.2	14.0	16.8	17.7	12.9	17.7
End of 4th Quarter . . .	15.8	16.2	13.7	16.4	17.1	13.6	18.6

TABLE 11–J
CALCULATION OF RELATIVE P/E FROM A STOCK

	1970	1969	1968	1967	1966
E.P.S. for 12 Months Ended:*					
March	1.05	.90	.82	.71	.67
June	1.05	.92	.85	.75	.70
September	.95	.96	.86	.77	.70
December	.90	.97	.88	.80	.70
Market Value at End of Quarter:					
March	15	17	16	13	11
June	13	15	17	13	10
September	12	16	19	14	11
December	13	15	18	15	12
P/E Ratio+ at End of Month:					
March	15	19	19	17	16
June	13	16	20	16	14
September	13	17	22	18	16
December	14	15	21	19	17

(Continued on next page)

TABLE 11–J *(Continued)*

	1970	1969	1968	1967	1966
Relative P/E (P/E ÷ DJI P/E) for Same 12 Months:					
March............	1.07	1.23	1.25	1.15	.96
June	.98	1.05	1.23	1.00	.95
September.........	.85	1.20	1.31	1.07	1.22
December	.86	1.10	1.28	1.10	1.25

*This is not the quarterly earnings.
+These P/E ratios are all retrospective.

Relative Graphics

On the following pages are graphs that show the relative P/E ratios, relative earnings, and relative prices.

Relative earnings is plotted on the graphs so that we can see whether earnings are gaining on the averages, losing ground, or staying even. This ratio compares the earnings of a stock to the earnings of the Dow Jones Industrials Average. We use the same series of 12 months' earnings that we used to calculate the relative P/E ratios. A relative earnings ratio trend that is rising strongly from left to right is evidence of superior growth.

In the 1962-70 period, earnings of the averages were most strong in the first half and were flat or declining in later years. Therefore, a stock with regular yearly growth tended to look much stronger after 1966 than before. If a relative earnings trend lost ground in the later years, it was even more cyclical than the averages.

Relative price ratio shows how the stock price is moving in relation to the level of the averages. The ratio is simply the price of the stock on a date divided by the price of the index. You can see numerous patterns; some stocks range much more widely than the averages, and some gain consistently. In comments with some of the graphs, I try to show what you might look for in studying relative price.

The symbols used in the graphs are: RE, relative earnings; RP, relative price; RP/E, relative price/earnings ratio.

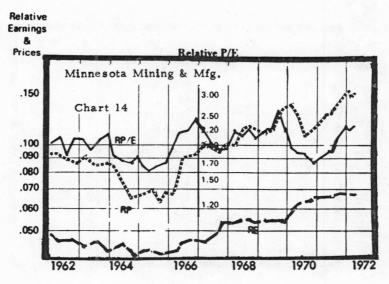

Figure 11-1

3M Company (Grade I)

3M (Figure 11-1) is the classic established big-growth stock. Regularity of growth means that it can be slightly outpaced by the DJI in a boom but moves out in a slow period. The relative P/E has cycled around 2.0 for years. The quality, 50 percent payout, and even growth fully support the 2.0 relative P/E. The relative price line shows that the stock fell behind in the 1964-65 bull market but gained on the market after the December 1965 all-time high of the Dow Jones Industrials.

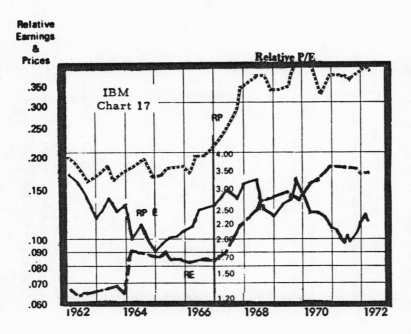

Figure 11-2

IBM (Grade I)

IBM (Figure 11-2) has cycled from a relative P/E of 2.0 to 3.0 for a long time. In the years shown, relative earnings almost gained 200 percent on the DJI. Investors have been increasingly nervous about IBM growth prospects in 1970-71. Even if growth slowed to 10 percent, it would be hard to justify a relative P/E below 2.0. Note that the relative price line was rising fastest after the earnings of most corporations stopped rising in the mid-1960s. IBM earning gains have come in surges.

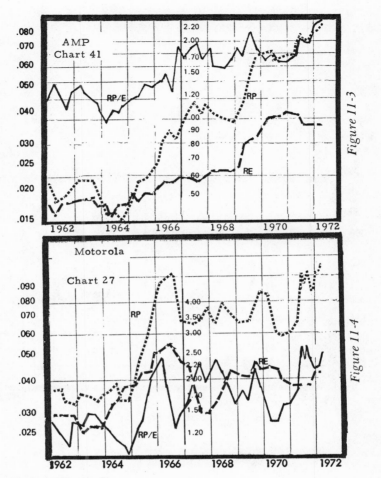

Figure 11-3

Figure 11-4

AMP, Inc. (Grade I)

The relative P/E of AMP (Figure 11-3) has had a steady upward trend, which was confirmed by the relative earnings trend that moved well ahead of the market. The premium of 60 to 100 percent over the averages in terms of P/E seems to be justified by the record. RP (relative price) gained more than earnings from 1964 to 1970. AMP does have growth interruptions, and it had as high a relative P/E as could be expected.

Motorola (Grade IV)

Motorola (Figure 11-4) has some wide profit swings and has not been much more dynamic than the averages. The relative P/E range between 1.5 and 2.5 makes this an expensive stock. The stock was overpriced much of the time between 1965 and 1971.

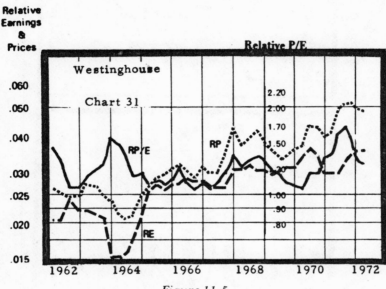

Figure 11-5

Westinghouse Electric (Grade III)

Relative earnings of Westinghouse (Figure 11-5) made a little progress, which was matched by price. The stock seems to be a buy when the relative P/E is 1.0 and a sale at above 1.3. In this example, the relative P/E seems to have a settled range from high to low.

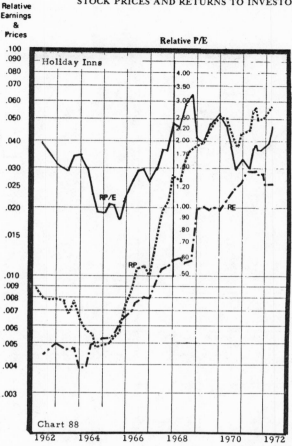

Relative
Earnings
&
Prices

Relative P/E

Holiday Inns

Chart 88

1962   1964   1966   1968   1970   1972

Figure 11-6

Holiday Inns (Grade III)

Volatility in relative P/E is evident. The largest motel chain, Holiday Inns (Figure 11-6), with 180,000 rooms, had had growth much faster than the lodging industry but slowed in 1971. Analysis of hotel-motel capacity showed that it was getting ahead of demand. Most of the revenue growth was coming from higher room rates. This graph shows a declining trend in relative P/E, which should lead us to inquire whether professionals might foresee a change in the growth trend. When such rapid growth merits a relative P/E of under 2.0 after the strong market through mid-1971, it pays to be wary.

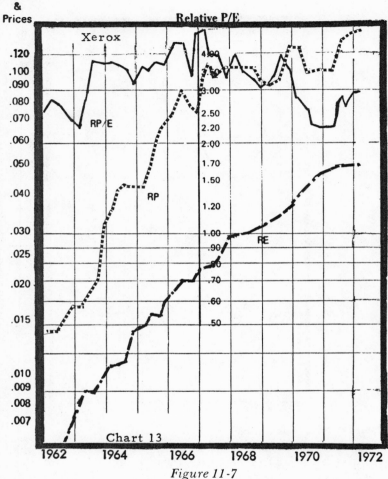

Figure 11-7

Xerox (Grade I)

Xerox (Figure 11-7) is a classic example of the inability of even the strongest growth stock to remain at a relative P/E above 3.0. Nothing bad happened to earnings. The relative P/E went down to about the usual relative P/E of IBM and then showed signs of leveling off. We believe it will persist at around 2.5.

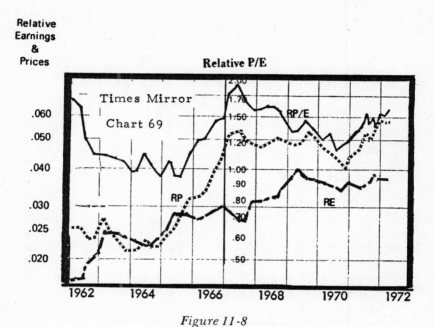

Figure 11-8

Times Mirror (Grade III)

Cyclicality, in spite of above-average long-term growth, held Times Mirror (Figure 11-8) down to a relative P/E of 1.25 and made it vulnerable above 1.5. Attempts to diversify hurt its earnings in the late 1960s. In 1971, growth in earnings resumed. In the 8 years, relative earnings rose from 2.4 to 3.6 percent of the earnings of the Dow Jones Industrials Average; therefore, it grew 1½ times as fast, or about 7 percent a year.

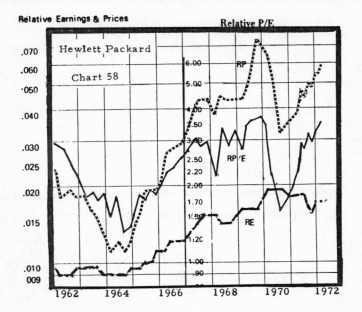

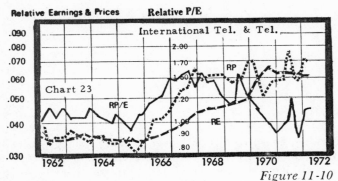

Figure 11-10

Hewlett-Packard (Grade III)

Growth has come harder for Hewlett-Packard (Figure 11-9). As the market recognized this problem, the stock dropped from a relative P/E of 3.0. No matter how good a company becomes, a relative P/E at 3.0 + puts the stock in danger. With growth much over 10 percent improbable in the future, Hewlett-Packard will be hard put to perform when the relative P/E is above 2.0.

International Tel. & Tel. (Grade III)

Although relative earnings were far better than the averages, investors show suspicion about conglomerates. ITT (Figure 11-10) was at a record relative price in June 1971, just before Justice Department pressure resulted in the agreement to divest several subsidiaries. It fell back to a relative P/E of 1.0. If the stock remains at a relative P/E of 1.0 and grows faster than the averages, it will be a good holding.

Relative P/E by Group

Standard & Poor's publishes full data on its group indexes, and in several groups all the stocks change at about the same rates in earnings and prices. The next two examples are groups that display group behavior.

Oil Group (Graph 11-11).   Oil stocks are cycle-resisting, which explains the occasional declines in relative earnings. The 1957 relative earnings was accentuated by high profits during the Suez crisis. The group had earnings growth 2 percent faster than the averages.

Over 24 years, international oils grew 7.75 percent a year, while S&P trend earnings gained at 5.75 percent a year. During 24 years of 2 percent better growth, the big oils never sold at a P/E as high as the slower-growing averages, although return on capital was higher in 14 out of 24 years.

The relative P/E has been highest when relative earnings were behind boom earnings of the market averages (see Figure 11-11). This point suggests that investors have repeatedly stressed cyclical stocks when a boom is expected and have paid up for oil stocks when the boom seemed mature.

The relative P/E of the international oil group was 0.57 in the fall of 1971, the lowest since 1961. Although the earnings of the S&P 425 gained on the international oils from 1961 to 1965, the big oils gained from a relative P/E around 0.6 to above 0.9. The record shows that investors have been wrong often.

Chemical Group (Chart 11-12).   During two decades, the chemical group had a declining trend in relative P/E ratio, and in the 1960s relative earnings lagged the averages. In the decade through 1970-71, sales of the chemicals increased 140 percent, while sales of the S&P industrials gained 89 percent. However, the chemicals profits gain was only 32 percent, or less than half of the 68 percent profits increase of the S&P industrials. The chemical stock group was interesting in early 1972, when profit margins had begun to rise while sales growth continued to exceed the sales growth of all industrial products. The relative P/E ratios had always been higher than the averages, but they were still relatively low.

Relative Yield and Relative Dividend

In discussing relative P/E ratios, I said that earnings cycles

GRAPH OF INTERNATIONAL OIL STOCKS VS. S&P 425 INDUS. INDEX

INDEX OF RELATIVE EARNINGS & RELATIVE P/E RATIOS

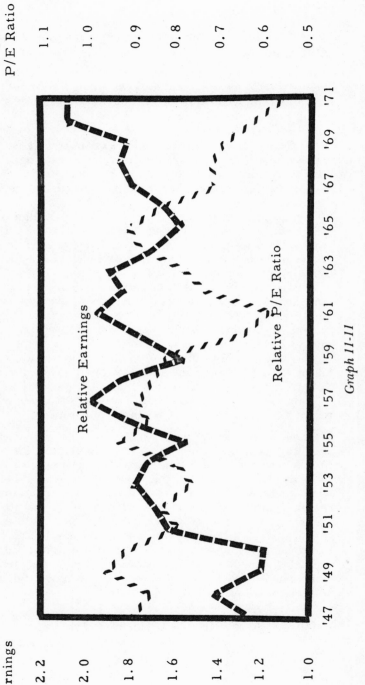

Graph 11-11

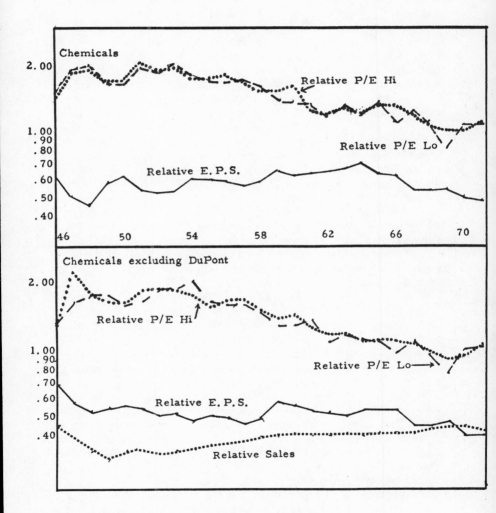

Chemicals

Relative P/E Hi

Relative P/E Lo

Relative E. P. S.

46   50   54   58   62   66   70

Chemicals excluding DuPont

Relative P/E Hi

Relative P/E Lo→

Relative E. P. S.

Relative Sales

Chart 11-12

make it difficult to estimate what the correct ratios might be for certain stocks. In 1971, I began to study whether dividends might be more useful in some cases — a study that led to the relative yield. I believe this is the first time the relative yield has been proposed as a guide to stock price valuations.

There is plenty of evidence in favor of using the dividend instead of earnings. For instance, the dividend payout of the market averages is equal to more than half of the earnings. Earnings fluctuate much more than do dividends, and at any given time there is considerable uncertainty about what the P/E ratio is compared to the current earnings. There is hardly ever a serious question about the current dividend yield. In some of our price evaluation work, we note a considerable difference in the portion of market price that can be attributed to dividend yields and to discounting of future earnings growth. For higher growth stocks, those with growth in the 10 percent and upward range, the earnings being realized or expected in the future are a main consideration in the price evaluation. On the other hand, for the vast bulk of stocks, which grow at a 5-6 percent or even a 7 percent rate, the dividend is a big factor in the valuation.

In thinking about investor attitudes toward stocks, it becomes evident that individuals trade their stocks less than do institutions and that the main contact individual investors have with the companies is through the quarterly dividend checks. It is quite likely that the public does not think of P/E ratios in the way professional investment people do. The dividend is of importance to the individual in evaluating a stock. Most individual investors do not have a particularly good idea of what earnings to expect from a company before they receive a report to notify them of what profits have been realized.

Stockholders know that dividends are taxable income, and no one likes to pay taxes. If not most, at least many investors know that it might be more advantageous for a corporation to reinvest the earnings paid out. The dividend, however, evidences a corporation so well managed that it can earn real cash profits that can be disbursed to stockholders and still have enough money to pay for sustained growth.

Fifty years ago corporations issued simple reports that said business was good enough so that dividends could be paid at a rate indicated by the enclosed check. In other years, they might say that business was not so good and that dividends were less. Since the 1930s, corporations have offered stockholders more and more financial statistics. For a while, such reports seemed to make the corporations better in the eyes of stockholders. The 1960s probably spoiled the image of more detailed earnings reports, and they were taken less seriously as it became apparent that a good-sized minority of corporations adjusted their reports to make the business look better than it was. We do not know whether public attacks on business over environmental and social matters, as well as challenges to the whole work ethic, had as much influence as skepticism about reports. In sum, a lot of things helped cast doubt on corporate financial reports.

To use dividends for valuing stocks, we need guides to tell whether the cash dividend yield of a stock makes it cheap, expensive, or in-between. Earlier I explained how to judge whether a price-earnings ratio is fair in proportion to quality, growth, and dividend payout. We examined techniques for comparing the ratios of stock prices to general stock market standards. In this section, dividends and yield of the Dow Jones Industrials are used.

Definitions

Relative dividends. The dividend of a stock is divided by the dividend of the Dow Jones Industrials Average to get a ratio. For example, a dividend of $1 divided by the DJI dividend of $33 gives a relative dividend ratio of .03. We calculate this ratio periodically over a number of years to see if it is growing faster, slower, or the same as the averages.

Relative Yields. The dividend yield of a stock is divided by the concurrent yields of the Dow Jones Industrials to provide a ratio above or below 1.0. If the Dow Jones Industrials yields 4 percent, a stock with a yield of 2 percent would have a relative yield of 0.5. If the stock had a yield of 5 percent, the relative yield would be 1.25. We examine the record of relative yield for guidance on how the stock usually has traded in terms of relative yield. If the record is consistent, we can make judgments based on this ratio history. It is also possible to calculate what the relative yield should be, as explained in Table 11-K.

The numbers in Table 11-K are ratios of yields on stocks to the yield of the DJI expressed as 1.0. This table is constructed with the DJI yield at 4.5 percent. When the yield of the DJI is other than 4.5 percent, the ratios are somewhat distorted but are close enough to be useful.

Assuming the current level of the Dow Jones Industrials to be

TABLE 11 – K
RELATIVE YIELD RATIOS
(based on dividend growth discounting)*

Forecast Dividend Growth	Grade I	II	III	IV	V
1	0.96	1.06	1.22	1.35	1.46
2	0.88	1.0	1.14	1.24	1.38
3	0.83	0.93	1.05	1.15	1.29
4¼	0.78	0.86	1.00	1.08	1.18
5	0.72	0.80	0.93	1.05	1.13
7	0.64	0.72	0.82	0.89	1.0
9	0.56	0.62	0.72	0.79	0.87
11	0.45	0.55	0.63	0.70	0.78
13	0.42	0.49	0.56	0.61	0.69
15	0.38	0.42	0.49	0.53	0.60
17	0.34	0.37	0.42	0.48	0.56
19	0.29	0.33	0.38	0.42	0.47
21	0.26	0.29	0.33	0.38	0.41
23	0.23	0.26	0.30	0.33	0.37
25	0.20	0.22	0.27	0.29	0.33
28	0.17	0.19	0.22	0.24	0.28
30	0.15	0.17	0.19	0.22	0.25

*DJI dividend growth of 4.25 percent. Normal DJI yield, 4.5 percent.

normal, a relative yield at the ratios shown in Table 11-K means that we are paying for the growth rate in the left column. The quality measurement is used to determine which quality column to use. The relative yield of 1.0 in Grade III growth at 4.25 percent is calculated for 4.5 percent yield. Therefore, if a relative yield is 0.5 and the cash dividend yield is 2.25 percent (half the standard DJI yield), a Grade II stock, for example, would be priced for growth at about 13 percent, which would be correct for a market level where the DJI was at 4.5 percent yield.

Graph 11-13 is a plot of data from Table 11-L. A 4.25 percent trend is placed through the dividends. The years from 1935 through the late 1940s are estimated to have been below trend. The vertical bars represent the yearly price ranges of the average. A duplicate of the dividend plots is placed on the chart to where the price would have been each year if the yield had been 4.25 percent. It is clear that when the prices were below the 4.25 percent yield line, prices rose or were steady in the following years (except for 1941 and 1942, when the United States got into World War II). When the prices were above the 4.25 percent

TABLE 11 – L
DOW JONES INDUSTRIALS

Year	High Price	Low Price	Dividend	Yield at High	Median*	Yield at Low
1940	153	112	7.06	4.6	5.4	6.3
1941	134	106	7.59	5.7	6.4	7.1
1942	120	93	6.40	5.3	6.1	6.9
1943	146	119	6.30	4.3	4.8	5.3
1944	153	134	6.57	4.3	4.6	4.9
1945	196	151	6.69	3.4	3.9	4.4
1946	213	163	7.50	3.5	4.0	4.6
1947	187	163	9.21	4.9	5.3	5.65
1948	193	165	11.50	6.0	6.5	6.95
1949	201	162	12.79	6.36	7.1	7.9
1950	235	199	16.13	6.86	7.5	8.1
1951	276	239	16.34	5.9	6.4	6.85
1952	292	256	15.48	5.3	5.6	6.0
1953	294	256	16.11	5.5	5.9	6.3
1954	404	280	17.47	4.3	5.2	6.25
1955	488	388	21.58	4.4	5.0	5.65
1956	521	412	22.99	4.4	5.0	5.58
1957	521	420	21.61	4.15	4.6	5.15
1958	584	437	20.00	3.4	4.0	4.6
1959	679	574	20.74	3.05	3.3	3.6
1960	685	566	21.36	3.1	3.5	3.8
1961	735	612	22.71	3.1	3.4	3.7
1962	726	536	23.30	3.21	3.8	4.35
1963	767	647	23.41	3.05	3.4	3.65
1964	892	766	31.24	3.5	3.8	4.1
1965	969	841	28.61	3.0	3.2	3.4
1966	995	744	31.89	3.2	3.6	4.3
1967	943	786	30.49	3.2	3.5	3.9
1968	985	825	31.34	3.2	3.5	3.8
1969	969	870	33.42	3.4	3.6	3.8
1970	848	627	31 53	3.7	4.3	5.0
1971–May	951	831	proj. 33.00	3.4	3.7	4.0

* Median DJI yield seems to be moving back to 4%. Normal Relative Yield of 1.0 should be about 4%.

yield price line, the market gained more slowly or declined. During most of the 1960s, stocks were overpriced by this measure, and not until 1970 did the DJI sell as cheaply as in 1958, when a seven-year uptrend began, albeit punctuated by a sharp decline in 1962. During the years when the federal government is trying to pump up the economy with easy money, the market tends

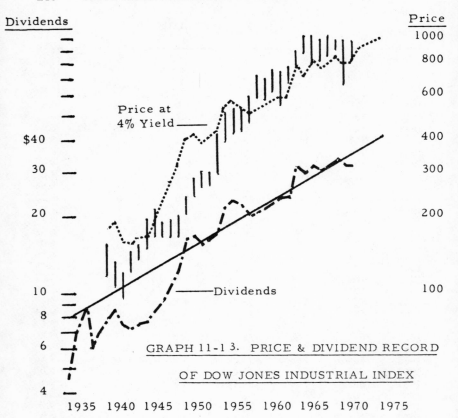

GRAPH 11-1 3. PRICE & DIVIDEND RECORD
OF DOW JONES INDUSTRIAL INDEX

to run ahead of dividends. By the time dividends rise above $40, there is apt to be some effort to stem inflation again.

There is a 100-year history of 8.5 percent total return from U. S. stocks. Growth at 4.5 percent and yield of 4.25 percent gives about 8.5 percent. Investors got 8.5 percent in the capitalist era, and I do not see much promise for improving the return.

The DJI yield record, Table 11-L, shows the history of dividends since 1940. Growth has come in spurts; dividend growth in the 1960s was complete by 1966. A similar spurt in the 1970s would raise the DJI dividends to around $43 by 1976. Quite possibly the market will have discounted this amount by reaching a new trading range centered on 1,000.

Arithmetic of Standard Yields

Dividend is assumed to grow for eight years at the rate
estimated. It reaches 50 percent payout and thereafter grows at
the rate of the averages. Tables were calculated to terminate all
stocks on a 4 percent yield basis on 50 percent cash dividend
payout. Table 11-M shows the results of this computation for
the five quality grades.

TABLE 11 – M
RELATIVE YIELD STANDARDS

Standard Investment Return:	I, 7.5%;	II, 8.0%;	III, 8.5%;	IV, 9.0%;	V, 9.5%;

Dividend Growth	Required Cash Dividend Yield for Standards				
	I	*II*	*III*	*IV*	*V*
3%	3.8%	4.2%	4.8%	5.3%	5.8%
5	3.3	3.7	4.2	4.6	5.1
7	2.9	3.2	3.7	4.1	4.5
10	2.4	2.6	3.0	3.4	3.7
15	1.7	1.9	2.2	2.4	2.7
20	1.2	1.4	1.6	1.8	2.0
25	0.9	1.0	1.2	1.3	1.5
30	0.7	0.8	0.9	1.0	1.1

Where dividends grow at the rates indicated, stocks bought at
the yields shown will provide standard investment returns on
the assumption that all sell on a 4 percent yield basis 8 years
later. The eight-year period was used because American investors
have been willing to project superior growth rates for eight years
except in periods of great stock market enthusiasm or in depres-
sions and wars.

Discounting arithmetic usually underrates stocks that actually
grow at rates higher than the discount rate. However, we want to
secure a return that equals or betters a stock's rate. If we pay
higher prices for stocks than are called for by the relative yield
ratios in Table 11-K, our investment gains will almost surely be
less than the growth rate.

We have found that in three- to five-year periods most stocks
gravitate toward relative yields (or relative P/E ratios) consistent

with an eight-year discount period. Even if stocks grow at 15 percent a year for half a century, they still come around to an 8-year discount basis.

Some stocks remain at relative yields of 1.2 to 1.5 compared to the averages, even while growing as fast or faster. Owners of international oil stocks have had returns superior to the averages by the difference in yield and often, in growth.

I compared the relative yield ratios in Table 11-K to relative yield graphs and found that they seem to fit behavior of numerous higher growth rate stocks. Because of market bias, more dynamic stocks tend to perform better from these ratios that do average growth rate stocks. When stocks deviate, sooner or later they come around to these ratios. The graphs are shown in following pages.

Dividend Growth

Investors accept a stock dividend yield that is lower than the yield of the market averages when they expect the dividend to grow faster than the 4 to 4.25 percent dividend growth of the averages. Earlier I mentioned that most stocks have dividend payments equal to about half of profits. In such cases, dividends seldom increase faster than the growth in earnings. Most companies that are in faster growth phases pay dividends equal to less than half of profits. In the long run, as growth companies become large their dividend growth tends to speed up, for perhaps a decade, until about 50 percent payout is reached. In the decades of the 1950s and 1960s, when IBM profits were rising 15 percent a year, the dividend increased over 25 percent a year until it reached 50 percent payout in 1970.

Forecasting Dividend Growth

The following method for predicting dividend growth can be used when the current payout is lower than that for the majority of stocks. This explanation began with Table 11-L. Table 11-N shows which dividend growth rates to apply when the dividend payout is less than 50 percent of earnings.

Figure 11-14 permits us to solve for yield and growth at discount rates of 7.5 to 9.5 percent. If desired, we can solve for higher or lower discount rates.

Usefulness of Relative Yield and Relative Dividend

The relative yield will work well on bank stocks, utilities,

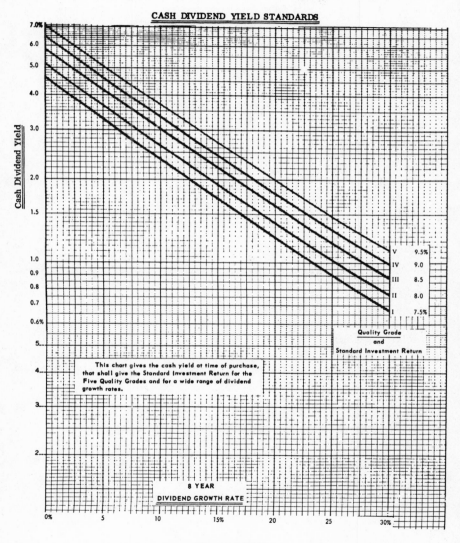

Figure 11-14.

TABLE 11 – N
DIVIDEND GROWTH FOR EIGHT-YEAR DISCOUNT METHOD

Earnings Growth Rates	Dividend Payout as (%) of Earnings				Earnings Compound to (%)
	20	30	40	50+	
3%					
4	17%	11%	7%	4	136
5	18	11.5	8	5	147
6	19	13	9	6	158
7	20	14	10	7	171
8	21	15	11	8	184
9	22	16	12	9	198
10	23	17	13	10	213
11	24	18	14	11	228
12	25	20	16	12	246
13	27	20	16	13	264
14	28	21	17	14	286
15	29	22	18	15	307
16	30	24	19	16	328
17	31	25	20	17	355
18	33	26	21	18	378
19	34	27	23	19	405
20	34	28	24	20	433

retail, and food stocks. It works well on oil stocks with settled dividend policies. The relative yield may be more useful than the relative P/E ratio on companies whose earnings are cyclical. In 1970, to rate General Electric stock yield would have been of more value than the earnings, which were affected by a long strike.

Examples of Relative Yield

In reading the relative yield charts for these examples, keep in mind the following.

Relative dividend is a solid line, scaled from the left.
Annual dividend rate in quarter for stock is divided by annual dividend rate for Dow Jones Industrials.
Relative yield is a broken line, middle scale *inverted*. (To show relative yield corresponding to price position, the relative yield is inverted.)
Yield at end of quarter for stock is divided by the yield of DJI at end of quarter.

Banks (Figure 11-15)

The First National City Bank had dividend growth of 7 percent, about 2.5 percent faster than the averages.

BankAmerica has had little tendency to improve its relative dividend compared to the dividend of the Dow Jones Industrials. In the boom period through 1965, both lost ground slightly and then recovered through 1970. Examination of the relative yield ratios suggests that only wide deviations in this measure are worth noting.

First National City has a settled pattern in which its relative yield varies between 0.8 and 1.1 times the yield on the Dow Jones Industrials Average. When its relative yield rises to above 1.0, it is fairly certain to gain on the averages. It can gain in a period of slower earnings for banking because the market will have discounted a slowdown by deflating FNC to a relative yield of 1.1.

BankAmerica's dividend growth has been slower than its earnings gains because it needed to retain more of its profits than was the case for FNC. The BankAmerica relative yield ranged between 0.95 and 1.25 until earnings coverage of dividends improved by 1970. The stock found support at a relative yield of 1.1 in 1971 due to higher earnings.

Over the years, investors should obtain a better return on these stocks compared to the averages by making purchases when they are at relative yields of 1.0 or above.

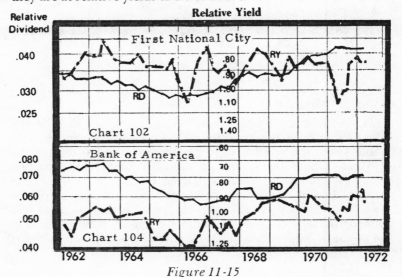

Figure 11-15

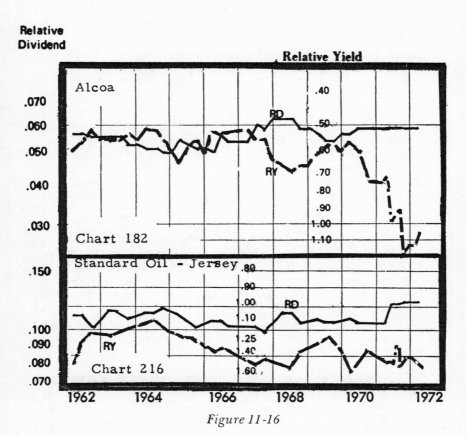

Figure 11-16

Alcoa and Standard Oil of New Jersey (Figure 11-16)

The relative dividends of these two large industrials moved at
about the rate of the Dow Jones Industrials Averages. In most
of the years, the relative yield of Jersey was about double that
of Aloca. This is an example in which investors have been dead
wrong on one of the stocks, if not on both. Even if the market
continued to overrate Alcoa, the sacrifice of dividend would make
it an unsatisfactory investment. It is apparent that investors have
consistently secured greater total return from Jersey than from
the averages. The record caught up with Alcoa in 1971.

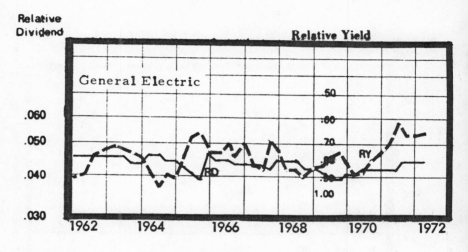

Figure 11-17

General Electric Company (Figure 11-17)

During the 1960s General Electric lost ground to the Dow
Jones Industrials on its relative dividend. Throughout the period,
General Electric's relative yield consistently reflected a yield
lower than that of the Dow Jones Industrials. The overall
performance of the stock price was below the progress of the
Dow Jones Industrials. Except in bull markets when it does seem
to lead the upturn, holders of this stock sacrificed both current
yield and performance.

Caterpillar Tractor (Grade III) (Figure 11-18)

Sensitivity to the business cycle shows up on Caterpillar's relative dividend record. Its biggest dividend gains were made when the Dow Jones dividends were strong. There appears to be a consistent trading pattern as indicated by the relative yield. You can buy the stock at a relative yield of 0.9 and sell it at a relative yield of 0.7.

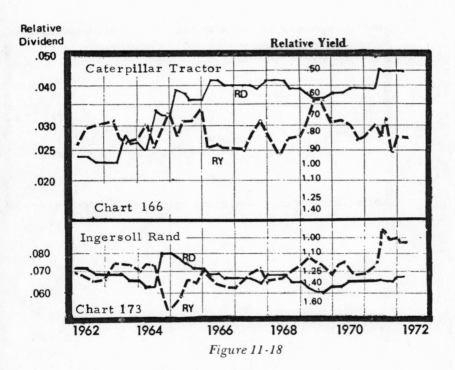

Figure 11-18

Ingersoll-Rand (Grade II) (Figure 11-18)

The IR dividend actually lost ground to the averages; however, between 1962 and 1971 the dividend payout improved from 100 to 50 percent. This explains the trend in relative yield from 1.4 to about 1.15. The June 1971 price with a relative yield less than 1.0 made the stock fully priced.

Merck (Grade I) (Figure 11-19)

Merck has one of the best relative dividend trends among large company stocks. The fluctuations in relative yield suggests that the stock is clearly contracyclical. The peaks in relative yield occur near market bottoms. In this example, the range is established so that we may forecast price action based on the record.

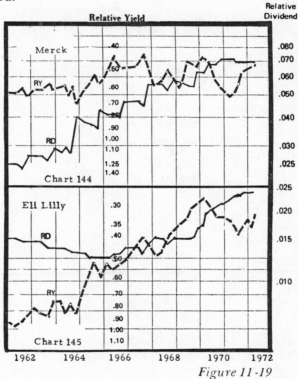

Figure 11-19

Eli Lilly (Grade II) (Figure 11-19)

Lilly entered a growth phase in 1966. The relative yield shows a drastic upward reevaluation in the image of the stock until early 1970. A downtrend became visible from early 1970, which means that the relative yield was rising. The market was revaluing Lilly in terms of growth expectations more in line with the industry. Products were maturing, and Lilly made a hasty cosmetics acquisition that investors questioned.

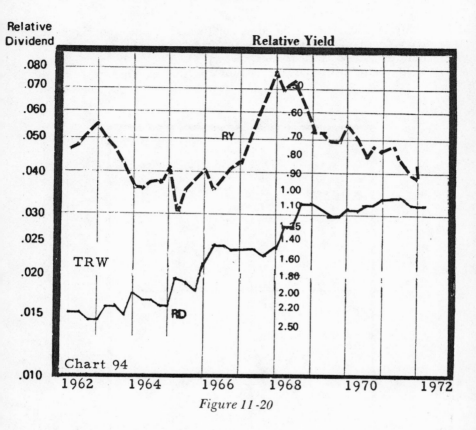

Figure 11-20

TRW (Grade III) (Figure 11-20)

The relative dividend of TRW has been unusual among industrial stocks. During the period shown, the relative dividend increased 100 percent compared to the DJI. The record of relative yield showed an unusual amount of change up and down for TRW. The main point that is clear is that when the relative yield on a large industrial stock, however well managed, gets under three-fourths of the yield of the DJI, the stock is unlikely to perform well in the long run, although in this case the stock continued to move to overpriced territory for a couple of years. Its May 1971 relative yield of 0.8 would be supported by a dividend growth of 7 percent.

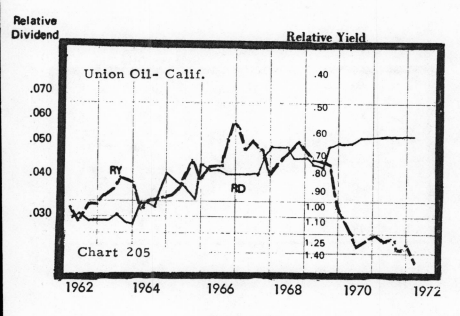

Figure 11-21

Union Oil of California (Grade IV) (Figure 11-21)

This is a 10 percent plus dividend record. The earnings decline did not start until 1969, and the relative yield held around 0.7 until the slump; but the subsequent reaction showed the risks in holding a slow industry stock with a yield lower than the averages. The relative yield of 1.3 in August 1971, on a 50 percent payout, took all the risk out of the stock.

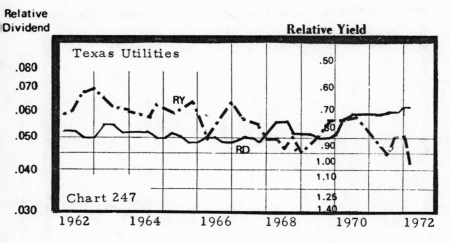

Figure 11-22

Texas Utilities Figure 11-22)

The relative yield of Texas Utilities had a downtrend on the chart, which means that the yield went up. This pattern was peculiar to utilities in the 1960s and in 1970, when their yields rose with bond yields. The earnings history and dividends of utilities is interpreted in Chapter 8.

The relative dividend grew on a par with industrials until 1970, when the dividend went up 7 percent in a year when profits gained 12 percent. The relative yield has an established range between 0.6 and 0.9. The trend in relative dividends could support a relative yield at the 0.8 level.

Pepsico (Grade II) (Figure 11-23)

Earnings of Pepsico grew about 10 percent, while dividend payout declined to 40 percent. The decline in relative yield discounted growth expectations as well as better dividend coverage. The relative yield of 0.5 called for 13 percent dividend growth, which is possible.

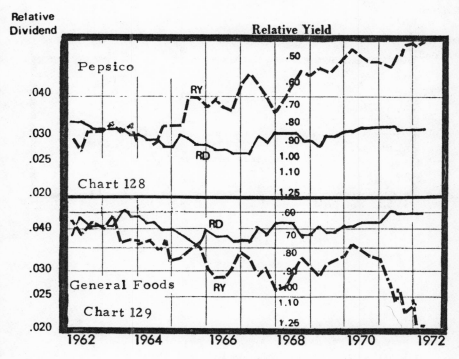

Figure 11-23

General Foods (Grade II) (Figure 11-23)

Dividends grow in pace with the averages. The relative yield at 0.7 in 1962 made the stock vulnerable. With good quality, the stock should at least sell at the same yield as the DJI.

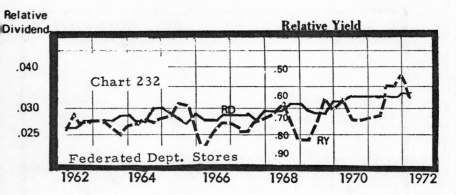

Figure 11-24

Federated Department Stores (Figure 11-24)

On a relative dividend basis, FDS has gained moderately compared to the averages and has proven cycle-resistant. This stock is recognized for quality superior to that of the averages, and the relative yield usually has been about three-fourths that of the DJI. There appeared to have been few opportunities to buy this stock on a bargain basis compared to the market and to have price gains better than the gains of the averages.

Updating and Using the Relative Yield Charts

On any date, ask for the latest 12 month's dividends of the Dow Jones Industrials Averages. Divide the dividend by the price of the averages on the date you are using. For your stock, also take the 12-month dividend rate and derive the yield based on the price on the date. Divide the yield of the stock by the yield of the averages. This gives you a ratio between the yield of the stock and the yield of the averages. Then this ratio can be plotted on the chart for the stock. See that the relative yield is inverted when you plot. The relative yield is inverted so that the plots will go in the same direction as the stock price.

12

Imaginary Information
and Values

About a century ago a whimsical author published
a textbook that he called *Pataphysics*, or the *Science of Imaginary
Solutions.* This in an era when science was taking itself most
seriously, even when its conclusions were founded on some
partially tested hypotheses. I happened to read the book 10 or
15 years ago and thought that there ought to be a discipline in
securities analysis called the "Science of Imaginary Values."

You may wonder if I am entering on a recapitulation of the
knavery of stock promotions. In practice, voluntarily adopted
illusions have vastly greater impact on stock market values than
do the few million dollars that the promotoers mulct the public
for each year. The market value of price changes in listed stocks
based on imagination runs into billions each year.

The impact of imagination on stocks and companies is a most
complex and little understood subject. The popularity of so-called
technical methods of stock price forecasting is based partly on
conviction that investors and analysts cannot forecast earnings

and growth with enough precision to have much bearing on the prices of stocks. The technical market analyst reasons that the effects of investor imagination can be read from stock price behavior as shown on charts. Some have great skill in trading stocks based on interpretation of popular enthusiasm or pessimism, which causes stock prices to rise or fall in amplitude that cannot be explained by progress or regress in the profits of a specific company.

In any given year, hundreds of stocks listed on exchanges have price changes that seem hard to explain on the basis of statistics. Stocks can have three kinds of price position.

1. Price can be explained in terms of current dividends, backed up by profits, where the evident rate of return is competitive with most bonds and stocks.

2. Price must be validated in the future by extraordinary increase in profits to an extent that dividends and profits would reach ratios to the current price that are comparable to the majority of stocks.

3. Price has declined to an extent that implies that the profit prospects for the company's future are much less than had been normal for the company in the past.

By the first example, I mean that stock has a price in relation to dividends and earnings that holds true for market averages. The second example pertains when the stock price is much higher than would be called for if the stock's future earnings growth will be similar to the expected performance of the majority of stocks. Such high-priced stocks are rated by the market as capable of exceptional future earnings growth. The third example applies when either the market projects serious trouble or there is a sharp slowdown in the growth pattern of previous years.

Most of the troubles that investors have result from buying stocks when their prices are too high. There is no way to assure that we will always be wrong in paying for ostensibly imaginary value or that we can always tell whether we really are faced with imaginary value. We might talk about a few examples, starting with the oil industry.

Nothing beats oil stocks for price changes based on imagination. This has been true for almost a century. Oil is a business devoted to quest for the big strike, and, of course, we do have them practically every year. When a company discovers oil that can become a big factor in its future profits, there is a tendency for some people to extrapolate from the first well announcement to a whole country full of gushers.

In valuing oil stocks, analysts may use certain rules of thumb to place values on the oil presumed to have been discovered. They assume that the oil will be produced in some number of years, and they calculate profits on the projected production. It is presumed that the company could sell the oil in place for a price based on projected earnings.

In the many cases, they are correct about the discoveries, but errors in timing and costs crop up in the forecasts of actual sale. Development of oil fields is a heavy investment business. Drilling all the wells and stringing the pipelines needed to get the oil to market usually takes longer than stock market speculators think. Usually, other people find more oil in the area of a big strike, and there is competition for the market. Mechanical problems crop up, and in most oil areas there is politics.

An example of how far ahead investors will discount oil profits is Pacific Petroleums, a large Canadian oil producer. Back in the 1956-58 period, the price of Pacific Petroleums stock was about $25 a share. The market then valued the company at $150 million. In 1956, total sales were $1 million, although sales went up to $10 million in 1958, but Pacific did not have a profit until 1962. In the 10 years from November 1958 to May 1968, Pacific stock never again sold as high as 20. In those years, its capital increased from $100 million to $350 million, and it acquired all the Canadian oil properties of Phillips Petroleums Company. It became a big gas and oil producer, realizing the values that were imagined in 1957 at the high. Unfortunately, no one got a return on his money for a decade.

The imaginary value was in the price paid. Pacific Petroleums would have had to grow to about three times the size it did in the decade in order to reward the 1958 buyer. On a per-share basis it did grow about 500 percent.

Occidental Petroleum (OXY) was a two-way imaginary value situation. It had been built up rapidly over two decades. Profits reported had equaled or exceeded the expectations of investors who believed in the wizardry of Dr. Armand Hammer, its president. It even discovered oil under its corporate headquarters in Los Angeles.

Then, in 1966 it took over an oil concession in Libya — acreage that had been discarded by other oil companies. At the time the *Oil & Gas Journal* reported on a major strike in Libya by OXY, the stock market response was not very lively. It was difficult to visualize Libyan oil sales by OXY that would be greater in quantity than those that Standard Oil of New Jersey was producing. After the *Arab Oil Review* (published in Tripoli) described Dr. Hammer as being almost like an adopted brother of King Idris, and the company described its plans to get the oil to market, investors became enthusiastic and bid the stock up 200 percent. That was not the end of the excitement, though, for thereafter King Idris was bumped off his throne, and his successor demanded much higher oil royalties and taxes. By the middle of 1970, when the successors to King Idris had been, in turn, bumped off their pedestals by army insurgents, OXY stock had retreated all the way back to where it had been when the Libyan oil was discovered.

Perhaps people should have recognized that after the rapacity of the Libyan leaders had been satisfied, the costs would be passed on to European consumers, and OXY would still have profits from Libyan oil. In many weeks during 1970 and 1971, it appeared that the third OXY profits from Libyan oil would evaporate. Imaginations went to extremes in the investor attitude that the Libyan operations represented a negative value for OXY stockholders. As it turned out, the company's earnings problems in 1971 came from excess costs of tanker charters rather than from Libyan oil.

Natomas Corporation (NOM) was an even more extreme example of the ups and downs of stock market imagination. NOM was a steamship company that earned about $5 million on its stockholder book equity of $60 million. The stock usually sold at seven times earnings until mid-1967, when the company discovered oil in Indonesia. The stock price was 14 in June 1967. By June 1969, its price was 114. In June 1970, it again sold at 14. In 1969-70, there were 3,750,000 common shares. The 100-point swing meant that in mid-1969 the market rated the Indonesia oil at $375 million, and in the 1970 market panic it valued the oil at zero. In March 1970, NOM sold at 60, suggesting that now the Indonesian oil was worth $175 million.

Major oil companies say that a tropical country oil venture should return its investment in three years. On this basis, NOM should have profits and depreciation at over $50 million a year from Indonesia to support $175 million valuation. The oil from Indonesia should be marketable at prices between $2.50 and $3.00 per U.S. barrel measure.

We do not know how the Indonesian oil deals will work out on profits, but the best experience anyone has had has been in Venezuela, where Standard Oil of New Jersey used to realize about 60 cents a barrel in cash flow through its subsidiary, Creole Petroleum. In the Persian Gulf, oil companies have realized about 25 cents a barrel. Taking the best experience, let us say that NOM could realize 50 cents per barrel on Indonesian oil if it produced 100 million barrels a year, or about 300,000 barrels a day, which is greater than the total production of Phillips Petroleum Company in the United States.

The interesting thing about oil prospects overseas is that American investors do not know how to value overseas oil production. Even competent statistical services are reduced to guesswork. In its January 1971 *Oil Industry Survey*, the Value Line projected 1974 cash flow for NOM of $30 million, with net income near $20 million, and it suggested that the stock might sell at 15 times earnings. In the same issue, it projected a P/E ratio of 9.5 for Royal Dutch Petroleum (Shell). Inevitably, NOM would have to sell some oil to Shell in order to reach the market. (This supposition became fact when Shell and Natomas announced that Shell would get half-interest for bankrolling development of the discoveries.) The service tried to strike a balance in forecasting the price action of NOM, recognizing that investors might take an optimistic view of the prospects for NOM.

I like the oil industry examples because there usually is as much oil as the enthusiasts expect. The imaginary factors are almost entirely in the timing of profit realization and what it is worth.

Imagination about Things that Are Not

We need to talk about normal profit rates in order to understand many imaginary value problems in stocks. Most of us who invest in stocks are to some degree concerned with management of property and people for profit. At work, we are fully aware of competition, and we know any time we get a profit on our business that is better than we expect, new competition will appear. Curiously enough, we are often willing to believe that some promotional-type fellows, operating a business that is strange to us, can earn profits on capital that will be higher than we would expect under very favorable conditions in our own business. Over the centuries, books have told how crowds go mad over some sort of speculative ventures, but I am thinking more about the mistakes in judging values that are made by people who should know better.

During the 1960s, a new version of the diversified corporation became popular. Whereas traditional diversified companies grew by careful acquisitions or by building divisions in new product areas, the conglomerators, as they were called, employed the great razzle-dazzle of stock market publicity to help popularize their securities, which were traded for stock of target acquisitions. One theory was that if the conglomerate's stock was accepted at 30 times earnings it could then pay 18 times earnings for a stock that usually traded at 12 times. It therefore did not matter if an excessive price was paid for an acquisition, because the conglomerate would pick up earnings per share to justify the fancy price at which its stock was trading. After a while, the conglomerators decided that it might be smart to offer bonds in exchange for acquisitions. Then the interest on the bonds would be deductible from the profits of the acquired company, and all the profits after interest would go to the acquiring company. Sometimes, the bonds offered were convertible, a feature that made it possible to use a lesser amount of bonds for the acquisition.

At the height of enthusiasm for this wheeling and dealing, about two dozen of these structures had been built up, with acceptance of market values about five times what the constituent subsidiaries had been worth in the early 1960s. The presumed justification for this markup in values was that the conglomerator management was so skillful that it could infuse new life into the acquired units, which then would become more profitable. This reasoning was accepted because most investors do not know how difficult it is to make profits with machines, workers, product designers, salesmen, and others. When it was all over, conglomerate stocks had declined back to the values of the companies they had acquired. A few actually did improve their acquired subsidiaries, and a couple had to be reorganized and liquidated.

Hotels-Motels in 1971

In February 1971, hotels in the United States had the lowest occupancy rates since 1933. In that month, all the stocks of motel-hotel chains went up and as a group sold at 30 times 1970 earnings, which had been relatively good. The chains had managed to have somewhat better occupancy than hotels, because they were still enjoying growth from new motels on the interstate highway network and had been able to make rate increases stick in 1970.

In the winter of 1970-71, the rate structures began to give way, and one could ask for and get discounts in modern motels and hotels. Analysis of the trends in public travel showed that it was not growing so fast as the chains, which grew at the expense of older hotels and motels. In the meantime, little noticed among investors was the rise of budget motel chains; they build on lower value real estate and rent clean, simple rooms for $8 to $10 a night.

Hotels started to go broke. In March 1971, the Geronimo Hilton in San Juan closed its doors. We could surmise that as more hotels went broke they might be reorganized by the mortgage holders, who could operate them at cut-rate prices just to pay off the mortgages, perhaps waiving interest. One could guess that travelers would find they could save $8 a night by staying at a less plush establishment. There was reason to suspect that the hotel-motel industry might be starting an era of price competition with profits eliminated. Hilton Hotels' stock was at $50 with $1 dividend. Profits in 1970 had been about $2, down 15 percent from 1969. It was widely assumed that profits would turn up, but we wondered if trouble was not just beginning.

Building Materials and Paper

During 1970, there was great enthusiasm for forest products stocks, with Georgia-Pacific and Weyerhaeuser at record highs at year-end. It was widely assumed that there would be a housing boom after the recession and that plywood and lumber would be in high demand. Wood product companies were admired for their participation in paper manufacturing, which accounted for 30 to 35 percent of sales.

About mid-March 1971, investors began to smell that the odor of wood products was not so sweet as they had previously sensed. The idea of paying 30 times earnings became suspect after reports of lower 1970 profits were exposed. A few other problems were given more attention: (1) wood products companies pollute streams, desecrate the environment, and use insecticides; (2) displacement of grocery bags by rolls of polyethylene bags became visible, and paper manufacturing had proven severely vulnerable to the recession; (3) the stimulus to the west coast lumber and plywood business from Vietnam was recognized; (4) smaller or modular houses were not such big consumers of plywood as were 60-foot ranchhouses; (5) bonds at 8.25 percent were continuing to preempt the investor money flow, and mortgage rates were just too low to be attractive for capital; (6) lumber and plywood is used in commercial and industrial construction, which was entering a decline; (7) the chart readers began to see tops on their building stock charts.

Since only about three housing booms have occurred in the century, professional investors may see only one in their working careers. Therefore, they are tempted to think it is something big when it comes. In the 1960s, there had been a prodigious commercial building boom that did nothing visible for stock investors. We actually felt its effects when its demand for funds sucked all the money out of the stock market.

Misleading Information to Sustain Values

My opinion is that willful creation of imaginary information is of less concern for investors than are the more innocent types of misleading information. In 1971, a newspaper article about the head of the airline pilots union explained how much money the pilots' association spent on research into the condition of airline company finances. In one case, a company used its financial operating problems as an argument in bargaining with the pilots over pay. On investigation, the pilots concluded that the situation was worse than the company management described.

Being an unusual group of employees, the pilots recognized that the company was most concerned about its image with financial backers, and that it had reason to be. The pilots subsequently moderated their compensation demands and, in addition, contributed to a fund to help attract patronage. In public, neither party said that the airline was not a good situation for investors. The company said the recession created some problems; the pilots said that they were statesmen and would consider the best interests of the airline. In truth, management and pilots wanted to keep financial backers comfortable lest they lose their jobs. They were saying that they would work for the welfare of the company so that the confidence of investors would be justified.

It is sometimes said that analysts look to company managements for optimistic stories. One company chief executive explained that company managements try to give those who interview them the more positive view of the situation because analysts always come in quest of favorable information. This is not altogether true.

Professional analysts contact company managements in search of objective information. We all prefer that news be good but do not want to be misled. The fact is that investors must be able to sift the stories and data. If you talk to executives with marketing duties or bias, you must expect them to talk toward their goals; the factory manager will tell why he is becoming more efficient. Companies are like people: some always paint a rosy picture; some are very cautious; a few are quite realistic in reporting about themselves.

The Viatron Imaginary Event

You may know about the spectacular bankruptcy of Viatron Corporation, which lost $30 million in 1970 on $12.5 million sales after having had large losses in the previous couple of years. All of the money lost had been raised from private and public investors in the late 1960s.

The facts are that Viatron designed a compact keyboard terminal for data input to and acquisition from central computer systems over telephone lines. It offered to rent the terminals for $39 a month at a time when major computer firms and a number of smaller companies were offering computer terminals to rent from $120 a month up. Viatron promised deliveries within a year, although it was not then set up to produce the terminals.

One of my associates brought in the descriptions given out by Viatron at the trade show where it announced its product. The proposal was of much interest, and we knew that in the mid-1970s what they offered should be feasible at the price. In fact, we had recently discussed the prospects for such products and their probable costs with management of the company that Viatron implied would be the source of the metal oxide silicon components to be built into the terminals.

In the effort to be sure we would not miss a good thing, we called the company that was expected to supply components to ask if they would be able to deliver those specified by Viatron on its time schedule. We were told with authority that the supplier would not have such components in volume production at those prices when Viatron planned to use them. We checked with other possible suppliers and could find no source ready to meet the prices and schedules. Consultants whom we relied on for help in evaluating such products came to the same conclusion. The specifications were great, and no one could deliver at the price for a few years.

Thereafter, Viatron continued to make claims about its coming success. It persuaded investment banking firms to raise many millions of dollars for it from public investors as well as private sources.

Because components were not available when Viatron assumed they would be, it was late on deliveries of any terminals and made many fewer than it took orders for. Costs were much higher than it had estimated, and since it rented the terminals it received only a fifth of its total sales price the first year.

Possibly the parties concerned with creating Viatron and raising its capital thought they could do what they planned. What the founders and backers must have overlooked was that no one was really experienced in management of such a complex business operation. They probably did not understand why IBM and its rivals require the 200 + percent markups over factory costs that they charge on novel products, and they must not have understood the amount of marketing, support, and service costs required. They must have assumed that the semiconductor industry would and could do almost anything to get in on the bonanza Viatron was offering.

13

Money Markets, Interest Rates, and Stock Prices

MONEY markets are the supplies of money from personal, business, and public savings related to the demands for money from borrowers and other seekers of capital funds. Interest rates are the prices that people demand or pay for use of one another's money. Some mechanical relationships, which I will explain, exist between interest rates and stock prices. These relationships are not altogether consistent, but they are good guides to direction. When interest rates are declining, stock prices tend to rise; rising interest rates usually are followed by falling stock prices. While profits of corporations have a lot to do with stock prices, the interest rates on money loaned and borrowed have more immediate correlation.

Money Supply

Money supply is the currency in circulation, in demand deposits, and in savings accounts. Some definitions of money include personal and corporate holdings of short-term Treasury securities and even life insurance values; the smaller figure is the one usually referred to as money supply. Economists theorize that the economy needs money supply in some ratio to Gross National Product. We need some quantity of money in our personal or business pockets to facilitate turnover of goods or to pay for service. Although many people manage with a week's pay, to function above the subsistence level most of us need a bit more cash, and a business usually needs about one month's cash supply. If we don't have enough cash, we get along on hand-to-mouth buying, but when we have a surplus we usually try to get some return on it.

The theory is that growth in the economy or national income requires an equal growth in money supply. Inflation is believed more likely when money supply grows faster than does the supply of goods and services. Hard times are associated with a money supply that is too small. This sounds simple enough, except that there is no popular measure of excess use of money supply or too much hoarding of cash. One must consult a professional economist for help in interpreting what they call the velocity of circulation.

Most investors really do not have the tools for measuring money supply turnover in a really helpful manner. As often as not, the symptoms have to be seen before the effects. Money is in short supply during a boom phase. Usually, by the time the economy has slowed down from overworking the money supply, money has become easy, and liquidity is restored when business is slow.

Investors should be aware of money supply and turnover in securities markets. In a sense, the value of securities that can be traded in public or private markets and the borrowed money used for securities ownership represent a kind of money supply and an indication of circulation velocity.

Traditionally, we look at the amount of money borrowed in margin accounts carried by brokerage firms. This data is published regularly by the N. Y. S. E. and also is published in Federal Reserve Board reports. By itself, it gives a fair idea of trends.

In the 1960s, an additional class of borrowed money for the stock market was invented in the conglomerate movement; this class is not easy to measure, but it is not hard to understand. The conglomerators created vast quantities of bond and preferred stock new issues, exchanging these issues for stocks of companies they acquired. While the trend was running strong, this paper was accepted as a new form of money because, in effect, the exchange provided former holders of more or less nondescript stocks with new paper worth more than their previous holdings.

For a time, the paper gained in value and seemed good to hold, but after a while some people felt a new market verve and started to trade the new paper for even more exciting stocks than they had had before. Whoever bought the paper theorized that it had some quality and potential; however, some people who thought the conglomerate had been great then decided to cash in, and some of the latecomers discovered it was not so good as they had thought. In a fairly short period of time, billions of dollars worth of new paper stimulated the securities markets and then evaporated as a force. It became dominant as a factor in stock markets.

The big expansions in stock market money and the equally dramatic contractions are hard to measure. Not since the 1920s had there been a bull market based on the use of market paper as a sort of money.

In the late 1950s through 1961, we had another kind of expansion in stock market money. There were the same number of stocks with imaginary values, but at that time the credit was available from more traditional sources. In that era, interest rates in the United States were much lower than world interest rates, and by 1958 demand for money for industrial construction had declined, remaining slack for a considerable period thereafter. Bank credit was readily available for carrying of securities.

The point about money supply as it concerns the stock market is that there are big changes in the effects on stock prices from money, but each time the effect is different. Investors must attempt to evaluate the situation at any given time in order not only to figure out what is going on but also to estimate where we are in a trend.

Federal Reserve Board Policies

Since the Federal Reserve Board (FRB) is an independent agency responsible for adjusting the money supply in an even manner, and since most of its directors are elected by private banks, it is surprising to learn how closely its actions coordinate with political considerations. The Federal Reserve has almost always followed policies that agreed with the ideas of the incumbent President; the only significant exception was over the Treasury bond price peg under Harry Truman. Otherwise, the federal government normally has applied its tight money policies in the first year and a half of a president's term, and usually has applied somewhat stronger tight money pressures during Republican administrations. It could be argued that Chairman Martin, appointed by President F. D. Roosevelt, was a Democrat; however, both President Eisenhower and President Nixon expressed preference for the FRB policies that were followed in their administrations. Possibly, Chairman Martin gave President Nixon a stronger dose than he bargained for though, since Martin had previously cooperated with the inflationary policies favored by President Johnson, who did not like tight money in any circumstances.

Chairman Burns, a Republican-appointed economist, has been described as possibly the most conservative economist in the United States. He took over his job when it was obvious, even to those who think all business should be transacted with gold coins, that the money stringency for our type of economy had gotten out of hand. When a man has the ultimate responsibility for a vital function of an economic society, he tends to adapt his opinions to the visible situation. As Burns has said in his talks, we now have some unprecedented factors in the American economy.

World Money Supply and Demand

In the 1960s there developed a pool of money that proved to be outside the control of major central banks. In the 1968-71 period, we saw the first really powerful manifestation of how this money can respond to worldwide demands for capital and how it can alter the effects of central bank policies concerned with easing or tightening money supply for domestic economic objectives as well as with fostering foreign trade.

Traditionally, the Federal Reserve Board was able to change the rate of money supply growth in the United States when it wanted to stimulate or slow down economic activity, and its policies usually had the intended effects. In the late 1960s, both the speedup in growth of money supply and the subsequent policy of restraint achieved much greater effect in the U. S. economy than the policymakers anticipated. The boom in the mid-1960s boiled hotter than expected, and the restraint had more violent effects than had been foreseen.

In the United States, President Lyndon Johnson was blamed

for trying to develop his Great Society programs while maintaining a Southeast Asia military beachhead on a grand scale. After 1968, President Richard Nixon attempted to deflate the inflationary conditions in the U. S. economy and encouraged the Federal Reserve Board to reduce money supply growth, a policy that the Board was eager to adopt. Subsequently, President Nixon appointed the conservative Arthur Burns to be chairman of the Reserve Board, and he forthwith instituted the most aggressive policy of money supply expansion seen in the United States in 35 years, reversing the previous policy.

The four key men in this economic drama responded in a manner suggested by early training. L. B. J. learned social economic policy from President Franklin Roosevelt, who was inaugurated in a deflated economy when massive financial stimuli could be applied without the least concern about inflation. Roosevelt's war was one for survival when there was no concern for economic consequences; L. B. J.'s Great Society programs were volatile fuel sprayed on an already hot economy.

President Nixon learned about economic restraint from President Eisenhower, who may have been lucky that his program for cooling a boom came in an era when the U. S. economy was still managed by the depression-hardened generation of managers who had done their building on a conservative, even though a little overoptimistic, basis. Nixon became President when an expansion boom had been financed on credit to a much greater degree than in the 1950s, and a boom based on credit is much more sensitive and delicate than is a stockholder-financed boom.

In the 1960s, the expansion of capital assets overseas was a vastly greater factor in economic activities than it was in the 1950s. Japan depended largely on borrowed capital, and credit was a big factor in financing Germany's expansion of exports. In world trade, the goods in transit and customer credit may be funded outside the exporting country or with funds borrowed in different currencies. The shipping may be financed from almost any source, including dollars exported from the United States.

Capital generated through profits on financing the trade transport and insurance, as well as the sale of petroleum by Arabs, has become a tremendous factor for international working capital. Because world trade was so prosperous, demand for funds became increasingly intense and exceeded the capital generated in the big manufacturing export countries. As I understand what happened, the Federal Reserve Board's 1968-69 cutback in money supply growth coincided with the peak of demand for capital to finance world trade. When U. S.-owned overseas bank branches sought Eurodollar deposits to relieve their shortage of deposits at home, they helped to raise foreign interest rates drastically.

The Eurodollar interest rates attracted some funds that were temporarily invested at interest in the United States by commercial parties whose money is outside the jurisdiction of any government. This drain, of course, deflated the U. S. money supply growth faster than American officials apparently had planned on. I have not seen an analysis of just how the ocean of extranational money aggravated the decline in stock and bond values in the United States during 1969 and 1970, but I am fairly sure that it did.

As the unfavorable trade balance of the United States became severe in 1968, the extranational capital pool sought to avoid the possibility of loss from dollar devaluation. Its loans in dollars were made on quite short terms, and it sought to hedge itself to obtain an advantage. The extranational capital pool, a lot of it indirectly owned by Americans, was invested carefully to minimize risks from the weakening condition of the U. S. dollar.

Really what Burns meant when he described unprecedented factors in the American economy was that the Federal Reserve Board had to conduct monetary policy with an overpriced U. S. dollar. Thus, whatever the FRB did could be offset or amplified by movements of international capital.

Prior to devaluation of the U. S. dollar and the forcing of other currencies upward, the extranational capital pool had sought to hedge and had moved aggressively into the stronger currencies, thereby causing some of the weakness in the U. S. bond and stock market. The mid-1971 level of the U. S. bond market made it fairly clear that extranational capital was not interested. Analysis of stocks showed that there was price strength, mainly in the most dynamic growth stocks and in some that were expected to benefit from business cycle upsurging. The defensive yield-type stocks in the United States continued at bear market levels.

With the new currency values, the scene was set for increased interest in U. S. bonds and stocks. To attract the extranational money, the dollar would have to be stabilized, and prospective rates of return on securities would have to be high enough. In

1971, the United States continued to offer the best bond values in history, and stocks in staples industries were reasonable. In addition, the markets were broad, and large quantities could be traded; so billions of dollars could readily enter and leave the U. S. securities markets.

In September 1971, we could not tell whether there would be a big movement of money into U. S. markets, but we could see the requirements being met. The dollar was getting closer to a sensible exchange rate, and declines had begun in foreign interest rates. There were two reasons for decline in European and Japanese interest rates. Central banks have ability to press interest rates down as part of their programs to prevent more than the desired amount of upward revaluation of their currencies. The Swiss had to go as far as to apply negative interest to keep out excesses of foreign money. The other factor favoring lower interest rates was the expected exports decline to the United States and some deflation in countries that had a large favorable trade balance with the United States.

As I explained in Chapter 11, U. S. interest rates have been lower than in most other countries during this century. It would be novel for interest rates in the United States to be higher, but there was a good possibility that this phenomenon would occur. If it did occur after sufficient U. S. dollar devaluation, the Federal Reserve would have a new, unprecedented factor to cope with.

Possibly enough extranational capital would flow to the United States to raise U. S. bond and stock prices relative to other markets. Quite possibly the money would be flowing in when the Federal Reserve would be striving to slow down money supply growth. At some later time, extranational money might be pulled out of the United States when easier money was desired. It seems to me that we have substantial new forces in our money and securities markets that are as novel to the experts as to investors.

Savings Bank Data

It is important for investors to be aware of the ratio of personal savings to disposable income in the United States. It seems not to be essential to know the reasons for change in the rate of savings; although that information refines our knowledge, it does not alter the effect. The stock market responds to increases or decreases in liquidity in the banking system. When savings are above normal, liquidity is rising; a low savings rate means people usually are spending too much money. If they are buying larger amounts of stock, that really is not saving money.

Normally, the U. S. public puts about 6 to 6.5 percent of disposable income into savings. When they save less than 6 percent, they probably are borrowing more than usual at the same time; when the savings rate goes above 7 percent, the public is rebuilding liquidity, and people usually borrow less. The circumstances are different in each turn of the cycle, but the stock market factors are about the same. In the 1970 market cycle phase, individual saver-investors had the good judgment to buy a lot of bonds, particularly A. T. & T. 8¾ debentures, because they saw the various bond issues as the best securities buys for making money. They did not buy the bonds for financial protection, even though they accomplished such a result. Really, they thought they had a better chance of making more profit from the bonds than from stocks.

It was not until after stock prices had justified people's worst fears and job security had become a serious problem that personal savings really began to rise in the second half of 1970. When savings did turn upward, the buying support behind the stock market became solid. In that instance, the stock market made a recovery of 10 to 15 percent before the savings rate turned positive.

14

Portfolio Suggestions

The management of a personal or fiduciary portfolio is a competence separate from the analysis of companies and stock prices, the subject of this book. I will try to pull together the ideas in the book and suggest ways in which the investor may use them to advantage. The assumption in this chapter is that the investor will use orthodox methods of buying and holding stocks and bonds: he will seek to identify established company stocks whose records are such that there is reason to believe that past patterns can be repeated. This assumption does not exclude the possibility of building a fortune through speculation; it merely recognizes that it is difficult to learn successful speculation.

Use of Techniques

Before making any other value estimate on a stock, subject the stock to the quality measurement described in Chapter 3. If the quality is high, the investor can have confidence that the management will take care of problems that the outsider cannot always foresee. When the quality is low, you can assume that everything about a stock will be harder to predict both for the investor and for the company management.

Take time to consider the arithmetic of growth. It takes money to finance growth, and the companies that generate high rates of cash flow compared to gross operating assets are better postured for sustained strong growth. It is easier to make useful forecasts for the growth of companies with higher rates of cash plowback.

The rate of return measures in Chapter 11 were taken from market history. We can get a reasonably accurate measure of the total return from stock investments at various levels of the market, and also we can identify the normal levels for stocks at given times. With the arithmetic provided, we can get an idea of what growth of dividends we are paying for.

It pays to seek a return as high as 25 percent a year, but it is difficult to achieve such performance. Readers who manage businesses, with full attention and great knowledge of operations, know how hard it is to accomplish such returns for their own companies. It is almost impossible to know as much about a company run by strangers.

When stock prices are quite high or quite low, the investment climate may get emotional. News stories seem to stress the prospects for worsening conditions when they are bad or brightening when they are good. If you use the price valuation methods explained in Chapter 11, you will have a better idea of where we are in the market cycle from a price point of view.

Cycles and Investment Timing

You can look at the stock tables on the New York Stock Exchange for the first 3 months of 1971 and see that the typical stock had a high price that was 25 percent higher than its low price. This fluctuation goes on year after year, and is fairly certain to continue. I discussed the relationship of bond yields and stock yields and gave some ideas about the problems in using this kind of measure. The ratio of bond yields and stock yields has very long cycles, and the investor has a big problem in deciding whether to look at the stock market itself for guidance on its cyclical behavior. A simple measure of the position of the stock market is the Dow Jones Industrials Averages. While this list is not truly representative of the market as a whole, it contains the large stocks that represent the major fraction of the market value of all listed stocks. The Dow Jones Industrials sold at a yield level nearly as low as 3 percent on a number of occasions, and almost always the averages declined within the following couple of years. You will also note that the yield on the Dow Jones Industrials has gone above 4 percent in the majority of years.

In 1970, the yield reached 5 percent for the first time since 1957. Over the last 100 years, the yield on the Dow Jones Industrials reached or exceeded 5 percent quite a number of times. We can estimate that in the future the yield on this average probably will exceed 5 percent a number of times, but this may be mainly in the panic years. It is not necessary for the investor to wait for the panic years to make all of his stock purchases, but it is debatable whether he should be adding new money to his stock account at times when the yield is under 4 percent. Based on past experience, the one time when an investor can safely commit himself in the stock market full bore, and even borrow money, is when the yield on stocks does get to around 5 percent. When the yield on the Dow Jones Industrials falls as low as 3 percent, you should be cutting back on the amount of investments in stocks and be putting your seed money back in the bank.

High Quality Stocks versus Cyclical Stocks

Although it is a little difficult to prove statistically, my general observation is that the highest grade stocks tend to be early in market cycles, which means that they will stop going down before the general market, or at least as soon. They tend to finish their upward cycles before the speculative stocks become popular in the market. When the market is down, you should start with stocks that rate in Grades I or II using the quality measurement system.

The foregoing comments suggest that in almost any period when the market is turning upward, the highest grade stocks will tend to be bought first and will usually have the strongest gain in the first 6 to 10 months of a bull market. It is not unusual for a stock such as IBM or Avon Products to accomplish three-fourths of such a gain as it makes in a bull market during the first 8 to 10 months of a 2-year upward trend. Having acquired excellent stocks at bargain prices, many investors will find that in the long run they are just as well off to lock them up in a box and keep them. Others want to operate on a policy of switching between different categories of stocks in the attempt to perform better at each phase of a market cycle.

Reliable forecasts of the price timing of cyclical stocks for future market cycles cannot be made. Cyclical stocks are those of companies engaged in production of consumer durable products, such as automobiles, appliances, and household goods, as well as various types of industrial equipment and materials.

The problem in dealing with cyclical stocks is that the market may favor certain cyclical stocks before the anticipated upturn in earnings is at hand, or it may wait out the turn in business before favoring some cyclical stocks. During 1970, investors favored stocks of building materials suppliers in anticipation of more prosperity for these companies when an anticipated housing boom should have come to pass. As things turned out, the bull market in these stocks was over by the end of 1970, before any significant improvement in the profits of these companies had occurred.

Among cyclical stocks, the chemical industry formerly was regarded as a growth industry and was one of the first groups that investors would buy when they were expecting better things of the stock market. It appears that the timing of price moves up or down for this group continues to be about the same as the market as a whole. Since the timing of drug stocks and other high grade stocks is about the same as chemical stocks, and there is also a growth advantage, the chemical stocks are really not much use to investors who want to switch among different groups to participate in different phases of the stock market.

You often will find that mining and other metals are on the late side in business cycles. This lateness often will prove true for industrial machinery stocks. Their business usually picks up after prosperity has set in for awhile, and capital spending picks up.

The banking industry has a degree of cyclicality, particularly its stock price fluctuations. This cyclicality occurs even though banks have very steady dividend policies and most of them raise their dividends four out of five years. They do not seem to follow a set pattern of earliness or lateness in bull markets, but one characteristic about them may be helpful in judging whether they will outperform the market. An index of bank stocks shows that when the average yield on a group of bank stocks is approximately the same as the current dividend yield of the Dow Jones Industrials, the bank stocks will tend to perform better than the DJI. When the yield on a bank stock sample falls to about 75 percent of the yield on the DJI, the banks are likely to perform less well than the averages.

At a time when growth stocks might have performed well in the market, I cannot recommend switching to cyclical stocks. It is better to use our energies in the search for stocks that may be coming up as future growth stocks or for proven stocks that have good prospects for improved progress. My method is to study the stocks we know as growth stocks or those whose renewal efforts seem ready to flower or the emerging companies.

Ideas in Late 1971

The following are ideas that offered promise in late 1971. They cover various industries and begin at the top of the quality scale.

In Chapter 6, I showed a graph of Pfizer Inc., which had begun to pull out of a dull period. My associate, George Sasic, believed that new drug products were rewarding and that Pfizer would surpass its long-term growth trend in the early 1970s.

Ira Hersch showed us how a major expansion effort by W. T. Grant should lead to a period of higher growth for this steady old retail chain. Growth in retailing is a function of store expansion. The net increase in square feet of store space was at a rate above 15 percent a year. It seemed highly probable that Grant's growth would exceed the historic 7 percent trend. Grant had made an all-time high in 1971, but it has reacted to a moderate price.

Among emerging companies, we were interested in Ryan Homes. The company had a 20-year record, but had been public for only three years. It had a remarkable profit margin improvement as access to financial markets allowed it to handle its own mortgages and also to take on longer range real estate site development. It had only 0.25 percent of the housing market, so it might be able to sustain earnings growth near 20 percent.

Honeywell has been a problem company that has seemed unable to coordinate earnings progress with its capital investment. In 1971, it obtained more orders for the large computer models acquired from GE than that company had booked in several years. Honeywell appeared to have arrived as a serious contender in the computer industry.

Redevelopment of formerly troubled companies is always an interesting subject. Ernest Levenstein showed how Brunswick Corporation was blossoming as a combined leisure and hospital supplies growth company. Although the stock had gained steadily for three years, it had only begun to live down its troubled period in the early 1960s.

I was interested in the American banks with foreign branches that could benefit from the different interest rates and money flows between the United States and foreign markets. First National City Corporation conducted 40 percent of its business through 633 overseas offices, and it had a 9-month earnings gain of 19 percent in profits in 1971, a year when U.S. banking was flat. It had a highly professional organization that sought to enhance its growth rate from the 8 percent in past years to as high as 15 percent. The stock had not attained a higher P/E multiple in spite of its evident prospects.

Pollution was an interesting subject in 1971. The most prominent supplier of chemicals for treatment of discharge water from industrial plants was Nalco Chemical Company. Its growth seemed to be speeding up as pollution chemicals and engineering services became relatively more important.

In Chapter 8, I gave some statistics about the above-average growth of packaged food and beverage companies and also about the exceptional records of reenergized companies directed by skilled merchandising executives. In late 1971, our work concerned two examples of this know-how. One was rather conservative and the other visibly aggressive.

Kraftco has begun to emerge from a plodding period during which it had suffered some attrition in profits of the milk and ice cream business and also needed substantial modernization of its manufacturing plant for cheese and convenience foods. By 1971, its capital expenditures were dedicated to growth, and its merchandising energies helped it to gain in the snack foods markets, particularly due to its innovations in convenience packaging. Profits progress was evident at a time when the stock price was relatively low.

Another food and beverage company that had great promise was Norton Simon, Inc. In the mid-1960s, Simon had assembled a management team that combined consumables marketing know-how and skill in control of production of packaged foods and beverages. As the management showed its mettle, the founder had retired. Originally built by leveraged acquisitions, Norton Simon has the control over finances needed to support 15 percent growth from cash flow and conversion of assets. It was evident that the company had enhanced the efficiency of a group of companies that had been variable in earnings before they were acquired.

Superiority of Quality Stocks in 1971

Between January and November 1971, Standard & Poor's 425 Industrials Average was unchanged at 101. As rated by my method, 20 Grade I stocks increased in price almost 13 percent in the same period.

TABLE 14 — A
GRADE I STOCK INCREASE (1971)

	Price		Change
	January	November	
American Home Products	72	80	+11%
AMP, Inc.	57	57	0
Avon Products	90	94	+ 4
Bristol - Myers	65	64	− 2
Coca-Cola	83	108	+30
Eastman Kodak	75	84	+12
Emerson Electric	67	73	+ 9
IBM	320	298	− 7
International Flavors & Fragrances .	65	73	+12
Lubrizol	38	46	+21
Merck	96	114	+19
Minnesota Mining & Manufacturing	97	121	+25
Moore	34	33	− 3
J. C. Penney	57	66	+16
Pfizer	37	37	0
Procter & Gamble	58	72	+24
Scherning - Plough	65	81	+25
Simplicity Pattern	96	134	+40
Warner-Lambert	71	72	+ 1
Xerox	90	110	+22
Standard & Poor's 425 Industrials .	101	101	0

In Chapter 11, I explained that higher growth rate stocks of best quality tend to be underrated by the market. Because their P/E ratios do not fully discount growth, their prices usually advance at the same pace as earnings. The 20 Grade I stocks had earnings gains in 1971 in proportion to the price changes.

Conclusion

Stocks listed in Table 14-A were not the only attractive ones in late 1971. The examples were stocks we have been actively discussing. We saw our job as selecting specific stocks that should provide good investment results over the next few years. This is really my message. All the techniques explained are aimed at isolation of a few stocks.

Appendix

Following are the quality ratings of about 300 stocks in 25 different industries. An investor could conduct his own program from these lists and would be able to use stocks of different quality grades. (The first grouping contains 8 of the highest quality stocks, all in Grade I.)

The definitions of Columns 1 through 14 are as follows: 1) Dynamism; 2) Stability; 3) Reputation; 4) Management; 5) Organization; 6) Research; 7) Assets; 8) Return; 9) Plowback; 10) Debt/Equity; 11) Persistence; 12) Dividend; 13) Volatility; 14) Institutional Acceptance.

These lists of quality ratings are revised yearly by the author and are available at no charge by writing to Moore & Schley, Cameron & Co., 200 East Forty-second Street, New York, N.Y. 10017.

The Highest Quality

	1	2	3	4	5	6	7	8	9	10	11	12	13	14	Total	Grade
IBM	5	5	5	5	5	4	4	5	5	3	5	5	2	5	63	I
Eastman Kodak	4	5	5	5	5	3	3	4	4	5	4	5	3	5	60	I
Minnesota Mining & Mfg.	3	4	3	5	5	4	4	3	4	5	5	5	3	5	58	I
Coca-Cola	3	4	4	5	5	2	4	5	5	4	5	5	4	5	60	I
Avon Products	3	5	3	5	5	2	4	5	5	4	5	5	3	5	59	I
Merck	3	4	4	5	5	4	4	5	4	4	4	3	2	5	56	I
Moore Corp.	4	4	4	5	4	3	4	3	5	4	5	5	4	5	59	I
Xerox	5	5	5	5	5	5	5	4	5	0	5	5	2	5	61	I

These 8 stocks stand out from the rest of the list. Noteworthy is the fact that they score most of the points on financial operations. Avoidance of cyclical environments is typical. They benefit from institutional endorsement.

Aerospace-Aviation:

Erratic business ruins the financial scores.   Massive size is the only strength.

	1	2	3	4	5	6	7	8	9	10	11	12	13	14	Total	Grade
Beech Aircraft	3	0	1	2	3	2	3	0	0	0	0	1	0	3	18	V
Bendix	2	1	2	3	5	2	3	0	0	1	0	2	1	4	26	IV
Boeing	2	0	1	3	5	3	3	0	0	0	0	1	0	5	23	V
Cessna	3	0	1	3	3	2	3	0	0	0	0	1	1	4	21	V
Delta Airlines	3	1	2	3	5	2	4	0	5	0	0	3	2	5	35	III
MCDonnell Douglas	2	0	1	3	5	2	3	0	0	0	0	3	0	5	24	V
Northwest Airlines	3	1	2	3	3	2	4	0	0	0	0	3	1	5	27	IV
TRW	3	1	2	4	5	3	3	2	3	0	1	1	2	4	34	III
United Aircraft	2	1	1	3	5	4	3	0	3	0	0	2	0	5	29	V

Apparel & Textiles:

These companies participate in sluggish cyclical businesses. Quality is low.

	1	2	3	4	5	6	7	8	9	10	11	12	13	14	Total	Grade
Burlington Industries	1	1	1	3	5	2	3	0	0	0	0	3	2	5	26	IV
Interco	2	3	2	3	5	1	4	3	2	1	1	2	1	4	34	III
Jonathan Logan	2	2	1	4	4	2	3	3	5	0	5	2	2	3	38	III
Jostens	1	1	1	3	2	1	3	4	4	1	5	4	0	1	31	IV
Melville Shoe	2	3	2	5	4	2	4	4	5	1	2	2	1	4	41	III

Banking:

Stability and regularity are common threads with these companies, which are a shade above average in quality.   Differences
show up in financial strength and profit rates.

	1	2	3	4	5	6	7	8	9	10	11	12	13	14	Total	Grade
Bank America	3	4	3	3	5	2	3	2	2	0	4	2	5	5	43	II
Citizens & Southern	3	4	3	4	4	1	3	2	4	4	2	3	3	4	44	II
Cleveland Trust	2	4	3	3	3	1	3	0	3	5	3	3	4	1	38	III
Continental Illinois	2	4	3	3	4	1	2	1	1	5	3	3	4	5	41	III
First National City	2	4	3	4	5	2	3	1	1	3	4	3	4	5	44	II
Republic National Bank	2	4	3	3	4	1	3	1	1	2	4	4	4	5	41	III
Valley National Bank	3	4	3	3	4	2	3	2	3	4	3	4	4	3	45	II
Wachovia Corp.	3	4	3	3	3	1	3	2	4	5	3	3	5	2	44	II

Beverages & Foods:

Stability of markets, organization depth and financial consistency
are the strong points of this well accepted group of stocks.   They score
fairly high on quality as a group.

	1	2	3	4	5	6	7	8	9	10	11	12	13	14	Total	Grade
Anheuser-Busch	2	4	3	5	4	2	4	3	4	1	2	3	4	5	46	II
Beatrice Foods	1	4	3	2	3	2	1	4	4	1	4	3	2	3	37	III
Borden	1	4	3	2	4	1	2	0	0	0	0	3	2	5	27	IV
Campbell Soup	1	4	3	3	5	2	2	1	0	5	1	3	3	4	37	III
Carnation	1	4	3	3	2	2	3	2	3	4	4	2	2	1	36	III

Beverages & Foods (continued)

	1	2	3	4	5	6	7	8	9	10	11	12	13	14	Total	Grade
Coca-Cola	3	4	4	5	5	2	4	5	5	4	5	5	4	5	60	I
Consolidated Foods	1	4	3	2	3	2	1	3	3	1	4	4	1	5	37	III
CPC International	1	4	3	2	4	1	3	2	0	0	1	3	3	4	31	IV
Dr. Pepper	3	4	4	4	1	2	4	5	5	5	5	5	1	3	51	I
General Foods	2	4	3	3	5	3	4	3	0	1	3	4	4	5	44	II
General Mills	1	4	3	3	3	3	2	3	2	0	3	3	2	4	36	III
Gerber Products	1	4	3	4	3	1	3	3	3	4	1	5	3	2	40	III
Heublein	2	4	3	4	3	2	3	5	1	0	5	5	2	4	43	II
Kellogg	1	4	3	4	4	2	3	5	3	4	5	5	3	3	49	II
Kraftco Corp.	3	4	3	3	4	2	3	2	2	4	4	3	3	5	45	II
Norton Simon	3	3	3	4	3	3	3	1	1	0	0	0	0	5	29	IV
Pabst	2	4	3	4	1	1	4	1	5	5	1	3	2	4	40	III
Pepsico	3	4	4	4	5	1	4	4	5	0	4	3	3	5	49	II
Pillsbury	1	3	3	3	3	2	4	0	1	0	0	4	1	2	27	IV
Procter & Gamble	2	4	3	5	5	2	4	2	3	4	5	4	4	5	52	I
Quaker Oats Co.	1	4	3	4	3	3	4	1	2	1	2,	3	4	2	37	III
Schlitz	2	4	3	4	2	1	4	1	2	4	4	3	1	1	36	III
Standard Brands	2	4	3	4	4	1	3	1	2	0	5	4	3	3	39	III

Canadian Oils:

Industry growth is a major plus. Canadian oil companies have not yet developed profits in proportion to the massive capital invested.

	1	2	3	4	5	6	7	8	9	10	11	12	13	14	Total	Grade
Aquitaine Co.	4	5	2	1	1	2	4	1	5	1	2	0	0	4	32	IV
Canadian Superior	4	5	2	2	2	2	3	1	3	1	0	0	0	3	28	IV
Dome Petroleum	4	5	2	2	1	3	3	0	5	1	1	0	0	5	32	IV
Home Oil	4	5	2	0	1	2	3	0	0	0	0	3	0	3	23	V
Hudson's Bay Oil & Gas	4	5	2	3	2	3	3	4	1	0	4	1	2	3	37	III
Husky Oil	4	5	2	2	1	3	3	1	3	0	1	1	0	3	29	IV
Imperial Oil	3	5	2	4	4	3	3	1	0	3	2	3	2	5	40	III
Pacific Petroleums	4	5	3	4	3	2	4	0	0	0	4	2	1	4	36	III

Chemicals:

The group is about equal to the U.S. economy; cyclicality is the problem. Note that regularity helped the rating of Dow Chemical.

	1	2	3	4	5	6	7	8	9	10	11	12	13	14	Total	Grade
Allied Chemical	3	3	2	2	4	1	2	0	0	0	0	1	3	5	26	IV
Celanese	3	4	3	2	5	2	4	0	0	0	0	3	3	5	34	III
Dow Chemical	3	4	3	4	5	2	4	2	3	0	1	4	2	5	42	III
Dupont	3	4	3	4	5	2	4	2	3	3	0	2	1	5	41	III
Eastman Kodak	4	5	5	5	5	3	3	4	4	5	4	5	3	5	60	I
Ethyl Corp.	3	3	2	2	3	1	3	5	3	0	2	5	1	4	37	III
Lubrizol	3	4	4	5	3	4	3	5	5	4	5	2	1	4	52	I
Monsanto	3	4	3	3	5	2	4	0	2	0	0	3	1	5	35	III
Nalco Chemical	3	4	4	4	3	3	4	4	5	4	2	4	1	3	48	II
Pennsalt Chemical	3	3	3	3	4	2	4	1	0	1	0	2	0	4	30	IV
Rohm & Haas	3	4	3	3	4	2	3	0	3	1	0	3	2	3	34	III

Communication:

Although there is strong basic growth in communications, the dead hand of regulation prevents companies from performing or earning quality points.

	1	2	3	4	5	6	7	8	9	10	11	12	13	14	Total	Grade
General Tel. & Elec.	3	4	3	3	4	2	3	1	1	4	2	3	2	4	39	III
ITT	3	4	3	4	4	2	3	2	5	0	5	4	1	5	45	II

Computer & Office Equipment:

No industry has greater variety of qualities, and there are several that would measure to lower grades in other industries.

	1	2	3	4	5	6	7	8	9	10	11	12	13	14	Total	Grade
Addressograph	4	4	4	1	3	1	3	0	0	0	0	0	0	4	24	V
Burroughs	5	5	5	5	5	4	4	2	5	0	2	2	0	5	49	II
Control Data	3	2	3	2	4	2	4	0	0	0	0	0	0	5	25	V
Dennison	3	3	3	3	2	2	3	0	3	1	0	2	0	2	27	IV
Diebold	4	4	4	3	2	2	3	0	2	2	1	4	2	3	36	III
Digital Equipment	5	4	3	4	3	4	4	5	5	5	0	0	0	5	47	II
Honeywell	4	4	4	4	5	3	4	1	5	0	0	3	0	5	42	III
IBM	5	5	5	5	5	4	4	5	5	3	5	5	2	5	63	I
MMM	3	4	3	5	5	4	4	3	4	5	5	5	3	5	58	I
Mohawk Data	4	3	2	2	2	4	4	0	0	0	0	0	0	4	25	V
Moore Corp.	4	4	4	5	4	3	4	3	5	4	5	5	4	5	59	I

Computer & Office Equipment Contd.

	1	2	3	4	5	6	7	8	9	10	11	12	13	14	Total	Grade
National Cash Register	4	4	4	2	5	3	4	0	4	1	0	2	0	4	37	III
Pitney Bowes	4	4	4	2	4	2	3	0	1	1	0	3	2	4	34	III
Sperry Rand	4	3	3	3	5	3	3	0	5	1	0	1	0	5	36	III
Systems Engineering	3	2	3	1	1	4	4	0	0	2	0	0	0	0	20	V
Xerox	5	5	5	5	5	5	5	4	5	0	5	5	2	5	61	I

Computer Services:

This is a most dynamic industry with a short record, except for Automatic Data, which has been performing for 20 years.

	1	2	3	4	5	6	7	8	9	10	11	12	13	14	Total	Grade
Automatic Data	5	5	2	5	3	3	4	5	5	4	5	0	0	3	49	II
Computer Sciences	5	3	1	1	4	2	3	0	0	0	0	0	0	0	19	V
Computing & Software	5	3	1	3	2	2	3	5	5	1	0	0	0	3	33	IV
Electronic Data Systems	5	5	1	3	2	3	4	5	5	1	0	0	0	3	37	III
Planning Research	5	3	1	3	2	3	3	2	3	0	0	0	0	2	27	IV

Consumer Appliances:

Cyclicality really hurts the quality of this group, which had a good growth record and some fabulously profitable years.

	1	2	3	4	5	6	7	8	9	10	11	12	13	14	Total	Grade
Magnavox	3	0	2	3	3	2	3	3	3	3	0	4	1	5	35	III
Motorola	3	1	3	3	4	3	4	0	3	2	0	4	0	5	35	III
RCA	3	1	2	2	5	2	3	0	3	0	0	3	1	5	30	IV
Sunbeam	3	2	3	3	2	2	3	0	1	0	0	2	2	4	24	IV
Whirlpool	3	2	3	3	4	2	4	3	4	0	0	3	3	4	38	III
Zenith	3	0	2	2	4	2	3	1	0	5	2	3	2	5	34	III

Electrical:

Growth in consumption of electricity compensates to some degree for the irregularity in business of this group, whose cyclicality shows up in profits. Quality is about average. Emerson Electric shows what superior management can do in the field.

	1	2	3	4	5	6	7	8	9	10	11	12	13	14	Total	Grade
Cutler Hammer	2	1	2	2	2	2	2	0	0	1	0	2	0	3	19	V
Emerson Electric	3	2	3	5	4	2	4	5	5	3	4	4	2	4	50	II
General Electric	3	2	3	4	5	2	3	1	3	1	0	2	2	5	36	III
McGraw Edison	3	3	2	2	3	2	3	0	1	4	1	3	2	4	33	IV
Reliance Electric	3	2	2	2	3	2	3	0	3	0	0	1	1	3	25	IV
Square D	3	2	2	3	3	2	3	5	0	4	1	2	4	4	38	III
Westinghouse	3	3	2	3	5	3	3	0	4	0	0	2	3	5	33	IV

Electronic Components & Equipment:

Although there is a good deal of dynamics, these companies are buffeted by severe cyclical pressures. It is difficult even for excellent management to score high on quality.

	1	2	3	4	5	6	7	8	9	10	11	12	13	14	Total	Grade
Ampex	3	1	2	2	2	3	3	0	0	0	0	0	0	4	20	IV
AMP, Inc.	4	3	3	5	4	4	4	5	5	4	2	5	2	5	55	I
Corning Glass	3	2	4	3	5	3	4	1	3	3	0	2	2	3	38	III
Electronic Memories	4	2	2	2	2	2	4	0	0	0	0	0	0	3	21	V
Fairchild Camera & Inst.	3	3	2	1	2	3	3	0	0	0	0	0	0	3	20	V
General Instrument	3	1	2	1	3	2	4	0	0	0	0	0	0	4	20	V
P. R. Mallory	3	2	2	3	2	2	3	0	1	3	0	3	0	1	25	IV
North Amer. Philips	3	2	3	2	3	2	3	0	0	1	0	1	0	2	22	V
Raytheon	3	2	2	4	5	3	3	2	5	1	0	3	1	5	39	IV
Texas Instruments	4	3	3	5	5	5	4	1	5	1	0	3	0	4	43	II
Thomas & Betts	4	3	3	4	2	2	4	4	4	5	2	3	1	2	43	II

Health Aids & Toiletries:

This is the biggest category with high profit rates, growth persistence, research, little debt and acceptance. It includes almost half the Grade I stocks.

	1	2	3	4	5	6	7	8	9	10	11	12	13	14	Total	Grade
Abbott Labs	3	4	4	3	4	2	3	0	3	1	0	3	3	4	37	III.
American Home Prod.	3	4	4	5	5	2	4	5	3	4	4	4	4	5	56	I
Avon Products	3	5	3	5	5	2	4	5	5	4	5	5	3	5	59	I
Baxter Labs	4	4	4	4	3	3	4	2	4	0	3	4	1	4	44	II

Health Aids & Toiletries

	1	2	3	4	5	6	7	8	9	10	11	12	13	14	Total	Grade
Becton Dickinson	4	5	5	3	3	2	4	1	4	0	1	2	0	4	38	III
Bristol Myers	3	4	4	4	5	2	4	5	5	0	3	3	3	5	50	II
Chesebrough-Pond's	3	4	4	4	3	2	3	5	4	0	4	4	3	4	46	II
Max Factor	3	5	4	3	2	1	4	2	4	5	4	3	2	3	45	II
Gillette	3	3	3	4	5	2	3	5	4	2	2	2	2	5	45	II
IFF	4	5	4	4	3	4	3	5	5	4	4	5	3	4	57	I
Johnson & Johnson	4	5	5	5	4	3	4	4	5	4	5	5	0	4	57	I
Eli Lilly	3	4	4	4	4	4	4	5	5	4	3	3	0	5	52	I
Merck	3	4	4	5	5	4	4	5	4	4	4	3	2	5	56	I
PEPI, Inc.	3	4	4	3	2	3	3	0	3	4	0	0	0	1	30	IV
Pfizer	3	4	4	5	5	3	3	3	3	4	2	3	3	5	50	I
Revlon	3	5	4	3	3	2	3	5	5	1	2	3	2	4	45	II
Robins	3	4	4	4	2	2	3	5	5	0	5	3	1	4	45	II
Schering-Plough, Inc.	3	4	4	5	4	4	3	5	5	4	3	3	2	5	54	I
Searle	3	4	4	3	3	3	3	5	3	0	2	3	2	4	42	III
Sterling Drug	3	4	4	5	4	2	3	5	4	4	1	2	2	5	48	II
Syntex	3	2	4	2	2	3	4	2	4	5	0	2	0	4	37	III
Upjohn	3	4	4	5	4	3	3	2	2	4	1	3	1	4	43	II
Warner Lambert	3	4	4	4	4	2	3	5	4	4	2	5	3	5	52	I

Housing & Building:

Modular and mobile buildings are treated as part of the non-growth, cyclical housing industry. The forest products companies have a little more growth and consistency than housing, thanks to paper and large building markets. This is a relatively low grade group because of erratic profits in the main.

	1	2	3	4	5	6	7	8	9	10	11	12	13	14	Total	Grade
American Standard	1	1	1	2	3	1	3	0	0	0	0	1	0	4	17	V
Boise Cascade	2	1	3	2	3	1	4	0	0	0	0	2	0	5	23	V
Carrier	3	3	3	3	4	3	3	1	2	1	2	2	4	5	39	IV
Fedders	3	3	3	3	2	2	4	3	2	0	0	2	1	4	32	IV
Georgia Pacific	2	1	3	3	4	2	4	2	0	0	1	3	2	5	32	IV
Johns Manville	2	1	2	2	2	2	2	0	0	5	1	2	2	5	28	IV
Kaufman & Broad	1	0	1	2	3	2	3	5	0	0	0	2	0	5	24	V
Philips Industries	1	0	1	2	2	2	4	1	0	0	0	3	0	3	19	V
Redman Industries	1	0	1	2	1	2	4	4	5	4	0	1	0	4	29	V
Ryan Homes	1	0	1	2	0	2	4	5	5	4	0	0	0	4	28	IV
Skyline Corp.	1	0	1	4	2	2	4	5	5	5	5	2	0	4	40	III
U. S. Gypsum	1	1	1	1	3	1	2	0	5	4	0	1	3	5	28	IV
U. S. Plywood	2	1	3	2	3	2	3	0	0	1	0	3	2	5	27	IV
Weil McLain	1	0	2	2	1	2	4	5	4	3	0	2	0	1	26	IV
Weyerhaeuser	2	1	3	3	4	2	3	1	0	1	0	2	1	5	28	IV

Industrial Equipment & Machines

Cyclicality is the main quality defect in this category, where good engineering and effective management is the rule. Without the cycles the stock might rate a grade higher.

	1	2	3	4	5	6	7	8	9	10	11	12	13	14	Total	Grade
Babcock & Wilcox	3	2	2	1	4	3	3	0	0	1	0	1	0	5	25	V
Black & Decker	3	2	2	4	3	3	4	4	3	0	5	4	3	4	44	II
Carborundum	3	2	3	4	3	3	3	0	1	0	0	3	2	3	30	IV
Caterpillar Tractor	3	2	2	4	5	3	4	2	1	2	0	4	2	5	39	III
Clark Equipment	3	2	2	4	4	3	3	1	3	0	0	3	2	4	34	III
Combustion Engineering	3	4	3	4	4	2	4	3	3	1	1	3	2	4	41	III
Dresser Industries	2	2	2	3	4	2	4	4	3	0	0	3	2	4	35	III
Ex-Cell-O	2	1	3	3	3	2	3	0	3	1	0	2	2	3	28	IV
Fluor	2	0	1	3	2	2	4	1	5	3	0	0	0	4	27	IV
FMC Corp.	3	2	2	2	3	2	3	0	0	1	1	3	1	5	26	IV
Gardner Denver	3	2	2	5	3	3	4	4	4	4	1	4	3	3	45	II
Halliburton	3	2	2	3	4	2	4	3	5	1	0	3	2	4	38	III
Harvey Hubbell	3	2	2	4	3	3	3	5	4	4	3	3	3	0	42	III
Ingersoll Rand	3	2	2	4	5	2	4	5	2	3	2	2	4	4	44	II
Joy Manufacturing	2	1	2	2	2	2	3	0	1	1	0	1	1	4	22	V
J. Ray McDermott	2	1	1	2	2	2	4	1	0	0	0	3	0	4	22	V
Parker Hannifin	3	3	2	3	3	2	4	0	3	0	0	5	1	2	31	IV
Textron, Inc.	3	1	2	3	4	2	3	3	5	0	0	3	1	4	34	III
Warner & Swasey	2	1	2	3	2	3	4	0	2	4	0	3	1	1	28	IV

Instrumentation:

A full range of qualities is found among this glamor category. They are dynamic, but experience rough spots.

	1	2	3	4	5	6	7	8	9	10	11	12	13	14	Total	Grade
Cenco Instruments	4	3	3	4	3	2	4	3	3	0	1	3	0	3	36	III
Hewlett Packard	4	3	3	4	3	4	4	1	5	4	2	2	0	4	43	II
Leeds & Northrup	4	2	3	3	2	2	4	0	2	0	0	3	0	1	26	IV
Itek	2	2	1	2	1	4	3	0	0	4	0	0	0	1	20	V
Perkin-Elmer	4	2	3	4	2	4	4	2	5	2	4	0	0	3	39	III
Polaroid	4	4	5	3	3	5	4	1	5	5	2	3	0	5	49	II
Sanders	2	2	1	2	2	4	4	0	0	0	0	0	0	3	20	V
Schlumberger	3	3	2	4	4	3	4	2	5	4	2	3	2	3	44	II
Tektronix	4	2	2	3	2	4	4	0	5	4	0	0	0	4	34	III

Metals:

The quality measures on metals stocks show that we do not have a metals oriented economy. They have a lot of new plants, but little else to recommend them.

	1	2	3	4	5	6	7	8	9	10	11	12	13	14	Total	Grade
Alcoa	2	2	2	2	5	2	3	0	1	0	0	4	2	5	30	IV
American Smelting	2	0	1	3	3	2	3	0	0	4	0	4	1	4	27	IV
Armco	1	1	1	2	5	1	4	0	0	0	0	1	2	5	23	V
Bethlehem	1	1	1	2	5	1	4	0	0	1	0	1	1	5	23	V
Brush Wellman	3	2	2	3	2	3	4	0	3	4	0	0	0	2	28	IV
Englehard	2	2	2	2	2	2	3	3	4	1	1	3	0	4	31	IV
International Nickel	3	0	2	2	4	2	3	0	0	0	0	1	1	5	23	V
Kennecott Copper	1	0	1	2	3	0	3	0	0	1	0	1	0	5	17	V
National Steel	1	1	1	2	5	1	3	0	0	0	0	1	4	5	24	V
Revere Copper & Brass	1	0	1	1	3	1	4	0	0	0	0	1	0	3	15	V
Scovill	2	1	2	2	3	1	4	1	2	1	0	2	0	4	25	V

Motor Products:

Lacking growth or stability, there is no way to measure the motor group above lower medium grade.

	1	2	3	4	5	6	7	8	9	10	11	12	13	14	Total	Grade
Borg Warner	2	1	2	2	5	2	3	0	2	1	1	1	2	5	29	IV
Champion Spark Plug	2	2	2	4	3	1	4	5	4	3	2	3	1	4	40	III
Chrysler	1	0	1	1	5	1	3	0	0	1	0	0	1	5	19	V
Dana	1	0	1	3	3	1	3	0	1	1	0	2	3	3	22	V
Eaton Yale & Towne	2	1	1	3	4	2	4	2	2	1	0	3	1	4	30	IV
Firestone	2	2	2	3	5	1	3	0	2	0	1	3	3	5	32	IV
Ford	1	0	1	4	5	2	3	0	0	4	0	3	3	5	31	IV
General Motors	1	0	1	4	5	2	3	0	0	4	0	1	4	5	30	IV
General Tire	2	2	2	2	4	1	2	0	0	0	0	3	1	5	24	V
Goodyear	2	2	2	4	5	1	3	0	1	0	0	3	2	5	30	IV
Libbey Owens Ford	1	0	1	3	3	1	3	0	0	4	0	1	2	3	22	V
Monroe Auto Equip.	2	1	1	4	2	1	4	5	5	1	2	2	1	4	35	III
Purolator	2	3	2	4	2	2	4	3	5	0	4	3	3	1	38	III
Timken	1	0	1	2	3	1	2	0	0	5	0	1	3	3	22	V
Uniroyal	2	2	2	2	5	1	3	0	0	0	0	2	2	5	26	IV
White Motors	2	0	1	1	3	1	3	0	0	0	0	0	0	3	14	V

Packaging & Labels:

These companies have continuous consumption of products as the common theme that makes for stability.

	1	2	3	4	5	6	7	8	9	10	11	12	13	14	Total	Grade
American Can	2	2	3	2	5	1	3	0	0	0	0	2	4	4	28	IV
American Greeting	4	4	3	4	2	2	3	1	2	1	2	3	1	4	36	III
Avery Products	4	4	3	4	2	2	4	0	5	1	0	2	3	4	38	III
Continental Can	2	2	3	4	5	1	4	2	3	1	2	4	2	5	40	III
Crown Cork & Seal	2	4	3	4	3	2	4	3	4	2	5	0	0	4	40	III
Nashua Corp.	4	3	3	2	2	2	4	4	4	0	3	3	1	2	37	III
Owens Illinois	2	4	3	3	5	1	4	1	1	0	0	2	2	5	33	IV

Paper:

	1	2	3	4	5	6	7	8	9	10	11	12	13	14	Total	Grade
Crown Zellerbach	2	3	2	3	4	1	1	0	0	0	1	2	3	5	27	IV
Kimberly Clark	2	3	2	3	4	1	1	0	0	1	0	3	2	5	27	IV
St. Regis Paper	2	3	2	2	4	1	1	0	2	0	0	3	3	5	28	IV
Union Camp	2	3	2	4	3	1	1	0	2	0	1	3	3	5	30	IV

Petroleum:

Stability is the quality determinant for these big industrials, which earn more than any other group.

	1	2	3	4	5	6	7	8	9	10	11	12	13	14	Total	Grade
Amerada Hess	2	4	3	4	2	1	4	1	3	0	5	2	0	5	36	III
Atlantic Richfield	2	4	3	4	4	1	2	0	1	0	2	3	0	5	31	IV
Cities Service	2	4	3	2	3	1	2	0	2	1	2	3	0	5	30	IV
Continental Oil	2	4	3	3	5	1	3	0	2	0	2	3	2	5	35	III
Getty Oil	2	4	3	2	3	1	2	0	3	4	1	2	0	4	31	IV
Gulf Oil	2	4	3	3	5	1	2	0	2	1	2	1	2	5	33	IV
Kerr McGee	4	4	3	4	3	3	3	1	2	0	2	3	1	5	38	III
Louisiana Land & Expl.	3	4	4	4	2	2	4	5	5	3	4	4	1	5	50	II
Marathon Oil	2	4	3	3	3	2	3	1	2	0	2	3	1	5	34	III
Mobil Oil	2	4	3	5	5	2	4	1	3	3	4	4	2	5	47	II
Phillips Petroleum	2	4	3	3	5	3	2	0	1	0	0	3	2	5	33	IV
Royal Dutch	2	4	3	3	5	2	2	0	1	3	2	5	2	5	39	III
Shell Oil	2	4	3	3	5	2	3	0	2	1	1	3	1	5	35	III
Standard Oil--Calif.	2	4	3	4	5	2	3	0	3	3	2	3	3	5	42	III
Standard Oil--Indiana	2	4	3	4	5	2	3	0	3	1	3	3	1	5	39	III
Standard Oil--N. J.	2	4	3	5	5	2	3	2	1	3	2	3	1	5	41	III
Standard Oil--Ohio	2	4	3	4	4	1	3	2	1	3	0	4	0	4	35	III
Texaco	2	4	3	3	5	1	3	2	2	3	2	3	2	5	40	III
Union Oil-Calif.	2	4	3	3	4	2	3	0	3	1	0	4	1	4	34	III

Publishing:

Businesses of these companies are diverse and the range of performance is wide. Companies are not comparable in an industry sense.

	1	2	3	4	5	6	7	8	9	10	11	12	13	14	Total	Grade
Crowell Collier	3	3	3	2	3	1	3	0	1	0	0	0	0	4	23	V
Gannett	2	3	2	4	2	2	3	2	5	0	2	1	1	2	31	IV
Grolier	3	2	3	2	3	1	2	0	1	0	1	3	1	4	26	IV
Knight Newspapers	2	3	2	2	1	1	3	3	0	0	0	1	1	2	21	V
McGraw Hill	3	3	3	3	4	2	3	2	0	0	0	1	0	5	29	IV
New York Times	2	3	2	1	1	1	3	0	3	5	0	1	0	3	25	V
Prentice Hall	3	3	3	4	2	2	3	5	4	5	3	3	1	3	44	II
Simplicity Patterns	4	5	3	4	2	2	4	5	5	5	5	3	2	2	51	I
Time, Inc.	1	3	2	2	3	1	3	0	0	0	0	1	0	4	20	V
Times Mirror	2	3	2	4	3	1	4	3	4	1	1	3	2	4	37	III

Recreation:

Profit irregularity and tendency to over-aggressive financial policies hurts the quality of this group.

	1	2	3	4	5	6	7	8	9	10	11	12	13	14	Total	Grade
American Broadcasting	3	3	2	2	3	1	3	0	0	0	0	1	1	5	24	V
Brunswick	3	1	2	3	4	2	3	0	0	0	0	0	0	5	23	V
Capital Cities Bdcstg.	3	3	3	3	1	1	3	5	5	0	2	0	0	4	33	IV
Columbia Broadcasting	3	3	2	3	3	1	3	4	4	0	0	4	1	5	36	III
Walt Disney	3	4	2	4	3	3	4	1	5	1	1	3	0	4	38	III
Loews	1	2	2	4	3	1	2	3	0	0	2	1	0	5	26	V

Retail Trade:

The basic industry's moderate growth and competition make high quality scoring a major achievement.   It is a middle grade group of stocks.

	1	2	3	4	5	6	7	8	9	10	11	12	13	14	Total	Grade
Allied Stores	3	4	3	2	4	0	2	0	0	0	0	3	0	4	25	V
Arlan's	3	4	3	1	2	0	3	0	0	0	0	0	0	2	18	V
Associated Dry Goods	3	4	3	4	5	1	4	0	0	1	2	3	2	4	36	III
Broadway Hale	4	4	3	5	4	1	4	4	1	0	2	2	3	4	41	III
Federated Dept. Stores	4	4	3	5	5	1	3	2	2	3	2	3	2	5	44	II
Gimbel Bros.	3	4	3	3	4	1	3	0	1	2	0	3	0	5	32	IV
Grant	3	4	3	4	5	1	4	2	3	0	1	3	1	4	38	III
Hart, Schaffner & Marx	2	4	3	3	4	1	3	0	0	0	0	3	1	3	27	IV
Interstate Stores	3	4	3	2	3	1	3	0	0	0	0	0	0	4	23	V

Retail Trade (continued)

	1	2	3	4	5	6	7	8	9	10	11	12	13	14	Total	Grade
Kresge, S.S.	3	4	3	5	5	2	4	4	3	1	3	3	1	5	46	II
Kroger Co.	2	4	3	2	4	1	1	1	3	1	0	3	2	5	32	IV
Lane Bryant	3	4	3	3	3	1	3	2	3	4	2	3	3	1	38	III
Macy, R.H.	3	4	3	3	5	2	2	0	1	0	4	3	2	5	36	III
Marcor	4	4	3	2	4	0	3	0	0	0	0	2	1	5	28	IV
Marshall Field	3	4	3	2	4	1	3	0	0	3	1	2	2	4	32	III
May Dept. Stores	4	4	3	2	4	1	3	1	0	0	1	2	0	4	29	V
Mercantile Stores	4	4	3	5	4	1	4	2	3	1	4	2	3	1	41	III
Murphy, G.C.	3	4	3	2	3	1	3	0	0	1	2	2	2	3	29	IV
New Process	4	4	3	4	2	1	2	5	5	5	3	5	0	3	46	II
Penney, J. C.	4	4	3	5	5	1	4	4	4	1	2	3	3	5	48	II
Petrie Stores	4	4	3	4	2	1	3	5	5	5	5	1	1	2	45	II
Safeway	2	4	3	2	4	1	1	1	3	4	2	3	2	5	37	III
Sears, Roebuck	4	4	3	5	5	2	4	2	3	3	4	4	3	5	51	II
Woolworth	3	4	3	3	5	1	2	0	3	3	2	2	2	5	38	III
Zayre	3	4	3	2	3	1	4	1	5	0	2	0	0	3	31	IV

Services:

        Services span the quality range.   Some of the most profitable companies appear in this group.

	1	2	3	4	5	6	7	8	9	10	11	12	13	14	Total	Grade
American Express	3	4	3	5	5	2	3	5	0	5	5	5	2	4	51	I
American Motor Inns	2	3	2	3	3	2	3	1	1	0	1	0	0	1	22	V
ARA Services	2	4	2	5	4	2	4	5	5	0	5	2	2	4	46	II
Dun & Bradstreet	3	4	4	4	5	2	3	5	3	5	4	5	3	4	54	I
Friendly Ice Cream	2	4	2	4	3	3	5	1	5	4	4	1	0	3	41	III
Hilton Hotels	2	2	2	2	3	1	3	0	3	0	1	2	0	4	25	V
Holiday Inns	2	3	2	3	4	2	4	3	5	0	5	3	0	5	41	III
Host International	2	3	2	2	3	2	3	3	5	0	5	4	3	3	40	III
Howard Johnson	2	4	2	4	4	2	4	1	5	4	2	1	1	4	40	III
Manpower	3	3	2	3	2	2	4	2	0	4	0	3	0	1	29	IV
Marlennan	2	4	2	4	2	2	3	5	0	4	4	4	2	3	41	III
Marriott Corp.	2	3	2	4	3	2	4	4	4	0	5	0	0	4	37	III
McDonald's Corp.	2	4	2	5	3	2	4	5	5	0	5	0	0	5	42	III
Ramada Inns	2	3	2	4	1	2	4	3	3	3	0	1	0	4	32	IV
Sambo's Restaurants	2	4	2	4	3	3	5	0	5	0	1	0	0	2	31	IV
Transamerica	2	3	2	2	4	1	3	0	1	1	2	3	0	5	29	IV
Warner Communications	2	3	1	3	3	2	4	5	5	0	0	2	0	5	35	IV

Glossary

Accelerated amortization. Write-off of fixed assets in a period shorter than expected service life of asset. In some cases, the amounts are larger in the first years of an amortization schedule.

Accruals. Expenses charged against current operations but not requiring cash payment, therefore, until some future date.

Amortization. Process of gradually extinguishing, over a period of time, a liability, deferred charge, or capital expenditure.

Book value. (1) Of an asset: value at which the asset is carried on the company's books. (2) Of a stock or bond issue: value of the assets available for that issue, as stated on the books, *after deducting all prior liabilities*. Book value is generally stated at so much per share or so much per $1,000 bond. Some services *exclude* intangibles (goodwill) in computing book value. Book value so defined usually is lower than costs less amortization, and it does not correctly reflect the full amount paid for property. It gives the impression that the company developed its earning power with less investment than was the case.

Capital assets or fixed assets. Assets of a relatively permanent nature that are held for use or income rather than for sale or direct

313

conversion into salable goods or cash. Chief capital assets are: real estate, buildings, and equipment, often referred to together as "plant account" or "property account." Intangible assets such as goodwill and patents are also capital assets.

Capital expenditures. Expenditures or outlays (payments) of cash or its equivalent that are undertaken to increase or improve capital assets.

Capital structure. Division of the capitalization between bonds, preferred stock, and common stock. When common stocks represent all or the bulk of the capitalization, the structure may be called conservative; when common stock represents a small percentage of the total, the structure is called speculative.

Capitalizing expenditures. Certain kinds of expenditures may at the company's option be treated either as *current* expense or *capital* expenditure. The capital expenditure appears on the balance sheet as an asset, which is generally written off gradually over a period of years — for example, intangible drilling costs (oil), development expense (mines, manufacturing companies), organization expense, or expense of floating bond or stock issues.

Cash equivalents. Assets held in lieu of cash, which are convertible into cash in a short period of time. Examples are time deposits, U. S. government bonds, and other marketable securities.

Cash flow. The amount of dollars available after payment of all current expenses; it usually consists of net income, depreciation and amortization, and other additions to reserves that do not require current disbursement of cash. Cash flow is the money available for payment of dividends, repayment of debt for added investment in assets for operation of the business.

Cash plowback. Retained earnings plus depreciation, amortization, and other reserve strengthening, total cash flow less dividends. Cash plowback adjusted for retirements: the amount of the cash plowback is reduced by the amount of book retirements of worn-out facilities. Because realizations on assets sold must be added back, this is a rather cumbersome statistic for most analysts to work with.

Cash plowback return. This is a measure originated by the author to compare the cash plowback to the gross operating assets of the company. Its purpose is to show the increase in assets represented by the cash plowback as a percent of the assets at the beginning of the year. Inferences about the rate of future growth may be possible with use of this technique. (See Chapter 6.)

Cash plowback return index. This index is derived by compounding the yearly percentage value for a series of years' cash plowback returns.

	1949	1950	1951	1952	1953	1954	1955	1956	1957	1958
Percentage of CPR . .		9	6	5	7	9	11	10	8	5
Index	100	109	116	122	130	142	158	174	188	197

Certified report. Corporate report (balance sheet, income statement, and/or surplus statement), which a CPA, as a result of independent audit, certifies to be in conformance with generally accepted accounting principles. Certification does not mean that every item is absolutely correct.

Consolidated statement. Corporate or certified report that combines the separate statement of the corporation and its subsidiaries. Such consolidated reports eliminate all intercompany accounts and show an entire group of companies as if they were a single enterprise.

Consolidation. Merging of two or more companies into one.

Constant dollars. These are dollars adjusted for inflation — a statistical measure to help relate the decline in buying power of the dollar to the value of assets is needed. We want to know if the growth in value or earnings associated with a stock compensate for inflation and provide a satisfactory return. Based on experience from 1960 to 1970, the combination of dividends and gain in value had to equal more than 4 percent a year to offset inflation.

Statisticians use a group of commodities as the basis for a constant dollar measurement. For instance, shelter, food, and clothing for a family of four had the same value for the family in 1970 as in 1950 but cost twice as many dollars. For the 1970 family savings account to equal $1,000 in the 1950 savings account, one must have $2,000 in the bank.

Contingency reserves. Reserves set up out of earnings or surplus to indicate a possible future loss or claim against the corporation, likelihood of which is open to question. Usually regarded as part of surplus, but occasionally indicate probable as well as merely possible losses or claims.

Controlled company. Company whose policies are controlled by another company through ownership of 51 percent or more of its voting stock. The Securities and Exchange Commission frequently holds that one company controls another when with less than 50 percent of the other's voting stock it is able to elect a majority of its directors with support of other stockholders.

Conversion parity or conversion level. Price of the common stock, which is equivalent to a given quotation for a convertible issue, or vice versa. For example, if a preferred stock is convertible into 3 shares of common stock and sells at $90, conversion parity for common would be $30. If common is selling at $25, conversion parity for preferred would be $75. Also known as conversion value of preferred stock.

Convertible bonds. Bonds that are convertible into other securities at a prescribed price or ratio at the option of the holder. Usually convertible into the common stock of the corporation, but sometimes convertible into preferred stock or even into other bonds. The holder has the privilege of additional profits if the enterprise is successful.

Current assets. Cash, cash equivalents, receivables due within one year, and inventories.

Current liabilities. Recognized claims against the enterprise that are considered to be payable within one year.

Debentures. Bonds that are general obligations of the company but not a specific claim on property.

Deferred maintenance. Delayed repairs, needed to keep plant in good running condition. This measure of equipment neglect usually does not appear in corporate reports, although its existence frequently is suggested by maintenance expenditures drastically lower than those of earlier years. Most noticeable in income accounts of railroads.

Demand deposits. Bank deposits subject to withdrawal by check. In investment analysis, they are of interest as one of the measures of domestic money supply, being the equivalent of cash. The rate of growth in total money supply is a factor in the strength in prices of stocks and bonds.

Depletion. Reduction in the value of a wasting asset due to removal of part of the asset, such as mining ore, pumping petroleum reserves, or cutting timber. Usually, depletion is expensed through operating statements on a unit of production basis, which means that an estimate of the total reserves is made before production; depletion is charged in proportion to production of the estimated original reserves; the amount of depletion is based on the cost to discover and develop the ore or other material.

Depreciation. Loss in value of a capital asset due to wear that cannot be compensated for by ordinary repairs, or to allowance for an asset's becoming obsolete before it has been completely exploited. Purpose of bookkeeping charge for depreciation is to write off original cost of an asset by equitably distributed charge against operations over its entire useful life. Chapter 5 contains a discussion of inadequacy of depreciation in an economy with currency inflation.

Depreciation reserve. Valuation reserve reflecting the total book depreciation to date and, therefore, indicating the expired portion of the useful life of assets to which it pertains. A $200,000 depreciation reserve against a $1 million asset indicates, not that the asset's present resale value is $800,000, but rather that about 20 percent of the asset's cost has been expensed. Because of inflation, the reserve is seldom meaningful as measure of money set aside to replace worn-out equipment. The number years in which an asset is depreciated is often close to the actual useful life of an asset.

Development expense. (1) Cost of developing manufacturing or other processes or products to make them commercially usable. New enterprises frequently treat such items as deferred assets; established and successful enterprises more frequently treat them as current expense. (2) The cost of opening up an oil or mining property — in most cases treated as a deferred asset.

Dilution. From the standpoint of a convertible issue, an increase in the number of common shares without a corresponding increase in the company's assets. Most convertible issues are protected against this contigency by an antidilution clause that reduces the conversion price in the event of dilution.

Earned growth. A measure of the ratio between retained earnings in a year and the book value of the stockholder equity at the start of the year. The earnings less dividends paid in cash are divided by the book value to derive a percent measure, which is the percent increase in book value. Since most companies have about the same average rate of earnings as a percent of book value over a decade, earned growth as defined here is usually a good measure of average long-term growth.

Earned on net worth, or earned on equity. The reported net income as a percent of stockholder's equity capital. The capital usually is the book figure at January 1, although many analysts use average capital in a year. This ratio is the most important of all stock analysis statistics, since it is a direct measure of management success in employing stockholder capital. U. S. industry normally earns about 11 percent on stockholder capital. A lower rate is unsatisfactory. Net income equal to 20 percent of equity is very good.

Earning power. A rate of earnings that is considered as normal or reasonably probable for a company or particular security. Should be based on past record and on reasonable assurance that the future will be reasonably consistent with or similar to the past. Hence, companies with highly variable records or especially uncertain futures may not logically be thought of as having a well-defined earning power. However, the term is often loosely used to refer to the average earnings over any given period, or even the current earnings rate.

Earnings leverage. The effects of rises and declines in a business operating rate relative to its capacity and break-even levels. It is particularly evident in companies whose plant investment is a big factor in costs and where direct labor is a small part of costs. A big plant investment is said to cause high fixed costs, particularly in a year of slow sales. However, when volume is high the plants can turn out much more goods, with incremental costs being mainly more materials; the positive effects become visible through earnings leverage.

Earnings yield. Ratio of the market price to the annual earnings. Example:. A stock earning $4 annually and selling at $50 shows an earnings yield of 8 percent. Earnings yield is the reciprocal of the more commonly used P/E ratio. It is useful mainly for comparing bond yields to stocks. *Barrons* bond-stock ratio is calculated by comparing bond yields to the earnings yield.

Effective debt. Total debt of a company, including the principle value of annual lease or other payments that are equivalent to interest charges (such may not appear as part of the funded debt). It may be calculated by capitalizing fixed charge at an appropriate rate. With long-term bond issues, which carry abnormally high or abnormally low coupon (interest) rate, the effective debt may be thought of as higher or lower than the face value. This measure is used in analysis of retail and hotel chains that enter into long-term leases on properties used for stores and hotels.

Equity. The interest of the stockholders in a company as measured by the capital and surplus. Also the protection afforded a senior issue by reason of the existence of a junior security.

Equity securities. (1) Any stock issue — preferred or common. (2) A common stock or any issue equivalent to that through having an unlimited interest in the assets and earnings of the company (after previous claims, if any).

Eurodollars. American currency on deposit in European banks. It is of interest to investors because of effects on international money markets and interest rates on securities as well as loans. Banks pay interest on these deposits and make loans against them. The borrowers, in turn, make deposits that can lead to further loans. Most central banks have ability to control expansion of loans in their national currencies by reserve requirements. Eurodollar loans have been harder to control. U. S. balance of payments deficits have contributed to the increase in Eurodollar deposits.

Expenditures versus expenses. Expenditures are outlays of cash or its equivalent; usually, they involve no concurrent charge against operations or earnings (for example, capital expenditures). Expenses are costs — that is, charges against current operations or earnings; frequently they do not involve concurrent cash expenditure (accruals, depreciation).

FIFO (first in, first out). Usual way of determining cost of inventory on hand. Sales are deemed to be made against the earliest acquired items; hence, inventory remaining represents the latest acquired.

Fiscal year. Twelve-month period selected by a corporation as the basis for computing and reporting profits. Usually ends December 31, in accordance with the calendar year. Many merchandising company fiscal years end January 31 to facilitate inventory taking after the close of the most active season, and some meat packers' fiscal years end October 31 for the same reason.

Fixed assets. *See* Property account.

Fixed charges. Interest charges and other deductions equivalent thereto: rentals, guaranteed dividends, subsidiary preferred dividends rating ahead of parent company charges, and amortization of bond discount (annual allowance to write off discount on bonds sold).

Funded debt. Debt represented by securities — that is, by formal written agreements evidencing borrower's obligation to pay a specified amount at a specified time and place with interest at a specified rate; includes bonds, debentures, and notes, but not bank loans.

General reserves. In financial companies, part of earned surplus may be designated as general reserves to identify part of surplus not considered available for dividends. General reserves normally are not required for loan losses or for insurance disasters. The purpose of this segregation of surplus is to impress customers with the financial strength of the company.

Goodwill. Intangible asset that usually represents premium over book assets paid for acquired subsidiaries. Companies carry goodwill as an asset when they consider that some advantage is held, such as brand name, reputation, strategic location, or special connections. In many cases, goodwill is not accurately portrayed on balance sheets; usually it is carried as $1. (See Pooling of interests for further discussion.)

Gross income. Sometimes used as the equivalent of gross sales. More often represents an intermediate figure between gross sales and net income. When the company markets or processes goods or services for others, it may report as gross income the fees it earned but not the full value of goods or property handled.

Gross operating assets. Consists of fixed assets at cost (before depreciation), working capital, and other assets such as investments.

Gross property. Original cost of existing plant and equipment still in use.

Gross revenues or gross sales. Total business done, without deducting costs or expenses.

Index of earned growth. This index is derived by compounding the yearly values of earned growth to construct a trend line that can be compared to the actual earnings.

Intangible assets. Assets acquired by cash expenditure or investment, which are not readily saleable but whose value is derived from influence on future company revenues.

Intrinsic value. This is a concept value behind a security issue, contrasted with its market price or book value. Generally, it is an indefinite concept, but sometimes the balance sheet and earnings record supply dependable evidence that the intrinsic value is substantially higher or lower than market price. In a way, it is a value that a third party thinks buyer and seller should use in exchange of property if one were not getting advantage over the other.

Inventories. Current assets representing the present stock of finished merchandise, goods in process of manufacture, raw materials used in manufacture, and sometimes miscellaneous supplies such as packing and shipping material. Usually stated at cost or market value, whichever is lower. Some problems in determining market value of inventory are explained in Chapter 5.

Inventory turnover. Cost of goods sold divided by year-end inventory. See Chapter 5.

Investment return. The compounded percent of annual increase in market value plus the cash dividend yield.

Leasehold obligation. The obligation or liability, inherent in a leasehold, to pay rent for a specified period of years.

Leverage. The condition that makes for wide changes in per-share earnings and market value, arising because a company's common stock has relatively heavy fixed costs or deductions (interest and/or preferred dividends) ahead of it. Small percentage changes in gross earnings or operating costs, or total asset values in the case of investment funds, will affect the earnings and market price of the common stock in much greater ratio. A leverage stock usually sells at a small aggregate figure in proportion to the total amount of senior securities.

Liabilities. Recognized claims against an enterprise. In its common and narrower sense, it includes only creditors' claims — that is, excluding surplus and proprietorship reserve accounts. In its broader sense, it includes all items on the right side of the balance sheet.

Liability reserve. Reserve or claim against an enterprise representing a liability whose existence is unquestioned but whose exact amount cannot as yet be determined (for example, loss reserves of an insurance company).

LIFO (last in, first out). A method of valuing inventory on hand intended to minimize inventory profits and losses. Sales are deemed to be made against the most recently acquired items. Hence, inventory remaining represents those acquired earliest.

Liquid assets. Same as current assets, but sometimes applied to current assets excluding inventory (quick assets).

Liquidating value. The amount that would be available for a security if the business were wound up and the assets turned into cash. It is usually less than book value, because allowance must be made for shrinkage in the value of the various kinds of assets if sold during a short period.

Loan Loss Reserves. Banks charge earnings by an amount sufficient to set up a reserve for uncollected loans. It is usually about 2 percent of loans and appears on the balance sheet as a deduction from loans.

Low carrying values. Usually applies to the balance sheet value of nonconsolidated investments, whose market value is much greater than cost. It is not an accounting term and is usually used by investors as an argument that a stock has greater assets than it reports.

Margin of profit. Operating income divided by sales. Depreciation usually is included in the operating expenses, while income taxes usually are excluded. Nonoperating income received and interest charges paid are not included in the operating income total.

Market share. The output of a company as a percentage of U. S. production. For example, GM has 55 percent of the passenger car market; IBM, 66 percent of the computer market; Sears, Roebuck & Company, 6 percent of retail sales.

Marketability. The facility with which a security may be bought and sold. Good marketability requires a continuous close relation between bid and offering prices sufficient to permit ready purchase or sale in fair volume.

Merger. A combination in which one company absorbs one or more other companies.

Money supply. Currency in circulation, demand deposits, and savings accounts. Sometimes it includes personal and corporate holdings of short-term Treasury securities and even life insurance values.

Net current assets (working capital). Current assets less current liabilities.

Net fixed assets. Property, plant, and equipment account at cost less the depreciation reserve.

Net quick assets. Net current assets, excluding inventory and receivables.

Net working capital. Equals current assets (cash, accounts receivable, inventories) minus current liabilities (accounts payable, taxes payable, short-term borrowing).

Net worth. The amount available for the stockholders as shown by the books and made up of capital, surplus, and such reserves as are equivalent to surplus. It is ordinarily used to include intangible assets as they appear on the books, and to that extent it differs from the book value of the stock issues as calculated by statistical services.

Obsolescence. The loss of value of a capital asset resulting from new manufacturing developments or inventions that render the asset commercially unusable. Also, the accounting charge (usually part of the depreciation charge) to adjust for the probable future loss in value resulting from these causes.

Operating margin. Operating earnings as a percentage of sales before deduction of depreciation, interest, and income tax.

Operating ratio. Operating expenses (including depreciation but excluding income taxes) as a percent of revenues. In the case of railroads, the ratio is found by dividing total operating revenue (or gross revenue) into operating expenses, excluding taxes. In the case of public utilities, it is generally defined as the ratio of operating expenses, including taxes and depreciation, to the total revenue. The same is true of industrials, except that some authorities do not include depreciation, and most do not include income taxes in operating expenses.

P/E ratio. *See* Price-earnings ratio.

Plant account. *See* Property account.

Pooling of interests. A method for combining financial statements of companies being merged. See Chapter 5 for discussion.

Pre-opening expenses. In retailing, new stores are partially staffed months before store openings. Normally, such expenses are absorbed against other company operations as incurred. When they are large in a short period, the company may make mention of them in reports to stockholders.

Pre-tax profit margin. Profit before income tax as a percentage of sales.

Preferred stock. Stock that has prior claim on dividends (and/or assets in the case of dissolution of the corporation) up to a certain definite amount before the common stock is entitled to anything.

Price-earnings ratio. Market price divided by the current annual earnings per share. Example: Stock selling at 84 and earning $7 per share has a price-earnings ratio of 12 to 1 (or is said to be selling at 12 times earnings).

Property account. This is an assets account, sometimes called fixed assets, plant account, or capital assets. It represents assets that are used to produce goods or services. The account may be stated at cost (gross property) or after deduction of reserves for depreciation and amortization (net property). Modern corporation reports normally show the property account net of reserves and show the gross property and the reserves as subheadings.

Corporations have differing policies with respect to definitions of assets included in the property account. Certain companies include in property items that may be treated as current expense by other companies and that are eligible deductions under income tax regulations. See Chapter 5 for discussion.

Prospectus. A document that describes a new security issue, especially the detailed description that must be supplied to intending purchasers under the Securities Act of 1933.

Quick assets. Sometimes used to mean current assets but preferably, means current assets excluding inventory.

Registration statement. The forms filed by a corporation (or foreign governmental body) with the Securities and Exchange Commission in connection with an offering of new securities or the listing (registration) of outstanding securities on a national securities exchange. The prospectus, supplied to intending purchasers of a new issue, contains most but not all of the information given in the registration statement.

Relative P/E; relative yield, relative dividend, relative earnings. In these ratios the P/E, yield, dividend, and earnings, respectively, are compared to the concurrent figures for one of the market averages. (See Chapter 11 for full discussion.)

Reserves. Offsets against total or specific asset values, set up on the books to: (1) reduce or revalue assets; (2) indicate the existence of liabilities, generally of uncertain amount; or (3) earmark part of surplus for some future use. *See* Valuation reserves, Liability reserve. Properly speaking, reserves represent not assets but claims against or deductions from assets.

Source and application of funds. This is a memorandum table supplied in annual reports to show how much cash the corporations obtained during the year from profits, depreciation, assets, sales, securities issues, and additions to deferred reserves. The application list shows dividend payments, capital investments, debt retirement, sale of assets, and change in working capital as a balancing item. It is important for analysts in judging the adequacy of a corporations cash flow to finance its projects.

Start-up expense. After completion of a new factory, there are usually costs beyond the normal expense of labor, materials, power, supervision, and maintenance. Items include training of workers, adjustment of machinery, raw materials used in trial runs, and so on. It is normal in conservative accounting to absorb such costs against total company operations at the time they occur. Some companies treat such costs as part of the investment in new plants and write them off over some number of months or years.

Start-up expense is not a regular accounting item but is used in reports to stockholders when management wants to identify factors that led to profits lower than might have been expected. When new machinery does not perform so well as its designers proposed, start-up expenses can be large.

Stock dividends. Dividends payable in the form of stock of the declaring company but not necessarily of the same class as the shares that receive the stock dividend.

Subsidiary. A company controlled by another company (called parent company) through ownership of at least a majority of its voting stock.

Surplus. The excess of the total net worth or stockholders' equity over the total of par or stated value of the capital stock and excess usually results from earnings retained in the business; this part frequently is labeled "earned surplus" or "profit and loss surplus" to indicate its source. That part of surplus arising from other sources (for example, write-ups of fixed asset values, write-downs of the par or stated value of capital stock issues, or sale of stock at a premium) frequently is labeled "capital surplus."

Tangible assets. Assets either physical or financial in character — for example, plant, inventory, cash receivables, investments. *See* Intangible assets.

Time deposit. Money on deposit with a bank withdrawable at the end of a short period instead of on demand and generally drawing interest.

Total return. A theoretical measure to indicate projected return to a stockholder from the effects of growth in company earnings and dividends plus the cash dividend paid. In this book, it is used to help judge the level of the stock market and the relative prices of stocks compared to the averages. It is popular in the academic field for interpreting stock prices to business college students. It is used to some extent by investment managers in a rule-of-thumb style. *See* Chapter 11 for discussion.

Valuation reserves. Reserves set up to: (1) indicate a diminution in present value of the assets to which they pertain; or (2) provide for a reasonably probable failure to realize value. Example of (1): depreciation and depletion reserves; reserve to reduce securities owned to market value. Example of (2): reserve for bad accounts.

Warrants. (1) Stock purchase warrants or option warrants. A right to purchase shares of stock, generally running for a longer period of time than the ordinary subscription rights given shareholders. These warrants often are attached to other securities, but they may be issued separately or detached after issuance. Nondetachable warrants cannot be dealt in separately from the security with which they were issued and can be exercised only on presentation with the original security. Option warrants often are issued in re-organizations or granted to management as additional compensation and incentive. (2) A name given to certain kinds of municipal obligations.

Working capital. The net current assets. Found by deducting current liabilities from the current assets.

Write-off (Write-down). The accounting procedures of reducing the book figures for assets without actually disposing of them by sale or collection. The write-offs or write-downs may apply to inventory that cannot be sold at prices to recover the cost; they can be recognition that accounts receivable cannot be collected or that some equipment is really useless although not fully depreciated. In the best accounting practice, such costs are taken each year in the normal course of business. In companies in which annual write-offs or write-downs in one year, and it may be implied that this was an unusual expense. Usually, a large item in one year means that normal expenses of past years were not recognized as they occurred. In reporting write-offs of some magnitude, companies may take it all out of latest period earnings, they may go back and adjust prior year reports, or they may bypass the profit and loss statement by charging it against surplus, which overstated past profits.

Yield. The return on an investment, expressed as a percentage of cost. "Straight yield" or "current yield" is found by dividing the market price into the dividend rate in dollars (for stocks) or interest rate (for bonds). It ignores the factor of maturity or possible call at a price higher or lower than the market. "Amortized yield" or "yield to maturity" (of a bond) takes into account the eventual gain or loss of principal value to be realized through repayment at maturity. When callable before maturity, the amortized yield might be lower if it is assumed that call takes place. The true amortized yield should be the lowest shown on any assumption about call.

Index

A

AMP Incorporated, 76, 104, 124, 230

Abbott Laboratories, 171-172, 226

Accelerated depreciation, 161

Accelerated write-off, 62-63

Accounting practices, 54-72, 75
  accrued profits, 66-67
  California savings and loans, 55
  foreign earnings, 59-60
  full-cost accounting, 72
  human resources, 55
  inventory, 63
  pooling of interests, 57-59
  profits, 68-72

Accrued profits, 66-68

Acquisitions, 80

Aerospace industries, 15, 124

Aggressive investing, 203

Air conditioning industry, 117, 122

Aircraft Owners' and Pilots' Association, 206

Airlines industry, 6-7, 9, 24-25, 60-61, 125-127
  marketing, 25
  pilots' association, 271
  profits, 68-72

Alberta Conservation Commission, 154-155

Alberto-Culver Co., 173

Alliance Tire & Rubber Co., Ltd., 206-209

Aluminum Co. of America, 86-87, 114

American Brands, Inc., 59
American Electric Power Co.,
    Inc., 70
American Express Co., 168,
    195-196
American Home Products
    Corp., 172-173, 207
The American Investor, 202
American Stock Exchange, 179,
    201-202
  growth companies, 204-212
American Telephone & Tele-
    graph Co., 124, 178, 281
Ames Department Stores, Inc.,
    206, 209
Angelica Corp., 206, 209
Annual reports, 11
Annuities, 66-67
Antibiotics, 170
Antitrust laws, 179-180
Appliances industry, 285
Arab Oil Review, 267
Aramco, 156
Arctic Enterprises, Inc., 206, 209
Asarco, 114
Assets, 56-57
Associated Baby Services, Inc.,
    206, 209
Atlantic Richfield Co., 19, 151-
    153
Augat Inc., 206, 209
Automatic Data Processing, Inc.,
    98-100, 187, 189
Automobile industry, 6-7, 109,
    118-119, 285
Automotive supply industry, 146
Avemco Corp., 206, 209
Avon Products, Inc., 11, 26,
    74-76, 82-84, 173, 214, 284

Banking industry, 9, 14-15,
    139-144, 285, 287
  bank credit, 274-276
  and credit expansion, 18
  use of capital debt, 49-51
Bankruptcy, 125-126, 272-273
Barclays Bank, 183
Barge industry, 6-7, 127
Barron's, 17, 216, 231
Baxter Laboratories, Inc.,
    171-172
Bear market, 10, 91, 96, 202
Becton, Dickinson & Co., 171
Bethlehem Steel Corp., 22
Beverage industry, 133, 137-138,
    287
Boeing Co., 20, 36-37
Bonds, 275-276
  interest rates, 217
  safety of, 217
  yields, compared to stocks, 215
Book value, 21-22, 47, 56-57,
    77-78, 141-144
Bradford Computer & Systems,
    Inc., 186, 208-209
Brand names, 136-137, 145
Bristol-Myers Co., 172-173
Brunswick Corp., 286
Building industry
  growth stocks, 117-118
  materials suppliers, 6-7, 117,
    270-271
Bull market, 12, 107, 118
Burns, Arthur, 277
Burroughs Corporation, 19,
    65-66, 177-178, 180-183, 186
Business cycles, 41, 284-286
Business equipment leasing
    industry, 67-68
  computers, 174, 178, 190

B

Bad debt reserves, 55
Balloon payments, 66

C

California Computer Products,
    Inc., 190

California savings and loan associations, 55
Canadian Pacific, 129
Capital
  gains trading, 80
  growth, 2
  industry dependence, 110
  preservation, 2
Capital Cities Broadcasting Corp., 47-49, 57-58, 104, 229
Capitalism, 3-9
  and military governments, 5
Carnation Co., 206, 210
Cars and trucks industries, 6-7, 109, 118-119, 285
Cash
  dividends, 2, 11, 54, 162, 213, 249
  flow and leverage, 36, 45-49, 150-151
  plowback and stock value, 23-24, 46, 69-70, 74, 80-108, 150-151, 184
  plowback return, 30, 75-77
Caterpillar Tractor Co., 119
Celanese Corp., 38-39
Cenco Instruments Corp., 80-82
Charting stock performance, 265
Chemicals industry, 15, 24, 38-39, 91, 93-94, 112-114, 195, 285
  processing, 60-61
Chesebrough-Pond's Inc., 173
Chrysler Corporation, 19
Cincinnati Milacron Inc., 119
Circle K Corp., 206, 209-210
Clairol Inc., 173
Clark Equipment Co., 119
Cleveland Electric Illuminating Co., 162
Clothing patterns industry, 167, 192
Coal producers, 150, 158
Coca-Cola, 11, 19, 76, 100, 214 228

Competition, 9, 38-41, 180-185, 197
Computer industry, 57, 80, 167, 174-191
  accounting practices, 55
  accrued profits accounting, 67-68
  business applications, 178, 183-185
  competition in, 180-185
  inventory control application, 230
  leasing, 174, 178, 190
  office equipment companies, 27, 167, 185-186
  problems of, 175-176
  products suppliers, 15, 167
  services suppliers, 9, 98, 167, 186-190
Computer Sciences Corp., 187-189
Conglomerates, 268-269, 275-276
Conservatism, 1
Consolidated Freightways, Inc., 118
Consumable products industries, 132-138
Consumer products industry, 122
Continental Oil Co., 158
Control Data Corp., 177, 185
Convertible preferred stocks, 78
Corinthian Broadcasting Corp., 196
Corning Glass Works, 122
Cosmetics industry, 84-86, 167-168, 173-174
Credit information industry, 167, 196
Creole Petroleum Corp., 155
Current yield, 2, 26-27
Cyclicality, 15, 29, 32, 91, 96 109-131, 134, 184, 284-286
  and stock quality, 15-16

D

Data General Corp., 186
Datamation, 230
Debt
  and capital, 30
  in judging smaller companies,
    204
  long-term, 26
  ratio and stock value, 25-26
  short-term, 26, 53
  and stock quality, 35-53
Defense contracts, 96, 124, 182
Deflation, 278
Delta Air Lines, Inc., 100
Delta Corporation of America,
    208-209
Democratic administrations,
    277-278
Depreciation
  accounting, 60-61
  straight-line, 62
Devaluation, 216
Digital Equipment Corp., 100,
    104, 177, 185
Diminishing return, 82
Diversification, 168-169, 173
Dividends, 2, 11, 54, 151, 213
  and discounts and premiums,
    221-222
  record of, 30
  relative, 241-263
  and stock quality, 26-27
Dollar cost averaging, 173
Dome Petroleum Ltd., 42-45
Dow Badische Co., 39
Dow Chemical Co., 39, 113
Dow Jones & Co., 216
Dow Jones Industrials Average,
    13, 23, 113, 119, 133-135,
    139, 151, 179, 194, 209-210,
    214-215, 227, 229, 231-232,
    245-251, 263, 283-285
Drug industry, 15, 84-86, 91,
    167-173, 286

Dry process duplicating, 194
Dun & Bradstreet, Inc., 167, 196
Dynamism, 28-29

E

E. I. du Pont de Nemours & Co.,
    24, 76, 110-111, 125, 129
  product pricing, 111
Earnings, 30, 144, 151
  earned growth, 77-78, 88
  leverage, 24
  and net worth, 30
  and stock quality, 22
  and stock value, 26
Eastern Air Lines, Inc., 126
Eastern Gas & Fuel Associates,
    158
Eastman Kodak Co., 11, 17, 22,
    26, 32, 76, 106, 167, 191-192
Economy
  expanding, 278
  restrained, 278
  war, 278
Eisenhower, Pres. Dwight D.,
    277-278
Electric and electronic compo-
    nents industries, 15, 100,
    109, 121-125
Electric power industry, 14-15,
    158
Electronic data processing
    industry, 60-61
Electronic Data Systems Corp.,
    186-187, 189-190
Emerson Electric Co., 76
Engelhard Minerals & Chemicals
    Corp., 115
Entertainment industry, 15
Entrepreneurial management,
    8-9, 132-133, 166
  identifying qualities of, 4-5,
    203, 212

Environmental problems
    and industry, 8, 12, 18-19, 133,
    198-200
    pollution control electronics,
    125
Eurodollars, 279
Ex-Cell-O Corp., 119
Expense deferral accounting, 60,
    63

F

Max Factor & Co., 173
Fairchild Publications, Inc.,
    48-49, 57-58
Featherbedding, 128
Fedders Corp., 118
Federal Power Commission,
    153, 163
Federal Reserve Board, 275-280
Financial Analysts Society
    Accounting Committee, 72
Firestone Tire & Rubber Co.,
    119
Food and Drug Administration,
    138, 169-170
Food industry, 14, 133, 145, 287
Forbes, 17
Ford, Henry II, 20
Ford Motor Co., 20, 118
Forecasting, 202-203
    company growth, 73-108
    dividend growth, 250
    stock performance, 10-11, 285
Foreign
    earnings, 59-60
    markets, 112-113, 123, 170
    subsidiaries, 82
Forest products industries, 14,
    24, 51-53, 270-271
The Franklin Mint, Inc., 61
Franklin National Bank, 49-51
Fuel-energy industries, 132,
    148-158

Fund American companies, 195

G

Garamycin, 170
Gas pipeline industry, 158,
    164-166
G. E. — Bull, 183
General Electric Co., 26, 119,
    123, 183-184, 286
General Foods Corp., 136
General Mills, Inc., 136
General Motors Corp., 15, 118,
    128, 178
General Telephone & Electronics
    Corp., 124
Genuine Parts Company, 119
Georgia-Pacific Corp., 51-53,
    100, 229, 270
Gerber Products Co., 136
Geronimo Hilton, 270
Gerstacker, Carl, 39
The Gillette Co., 173
Globe Security Systems, 206,
    209
Goodwill accounting, 48, 58-59
Goodyear Tire & Rubber Co.,
    119
W. T. Grant Co., 286
Great Society programs, 278
Gross National Product, 275
Growth, 28-29, 46-47, 73-108
    capital, 2
    companies, 62-63, 76
    earned, 77-78
    in earnings per share, 30
    emerging companies, 201-212
    forecasts, 73-108
    industries, 13-14, 167-200
    rates for industries, 13-14,
    167-200
    stocks, 26, 100-108, 118,
    201-212
Gulf Oil Corp., 156
Gulf, Mobile & Ohio R.R., 129

H

Hammer, Dr. Armand, 266-267
Hartz Mountain Products, 207-208
Heck's, Inc., 206, 209
Helene Curtis Industries, Inc., 173
Hercules Incorporated, 91, 93-94, 113
Hersch, Ira, 286
Hewlett-Packard Co., 125
Highway transport industry, 129-131
Hilton Hotels Corp., 25, 270
Holiday Inns, Inc., 25
Honeywell Inc., 65, 177-178, 180, 183-184, 228, 286
Hospital supplies industry, 167-168, 286
    drug suppliers, 172
    patient monitoring equipment, 186
Hotel-motel industry, 24-25, 269-270
House of Fabrics, Inc., 206, 209-210
Household products industry, 133, 285
Housing industry, 117-118
    modular homes, 9
Howard Johnson Co., 230
Harvey Hubbell, Inc., 207, 209

I

Illinois Central Industries, Inc., 129
Illusion
    ffect on investors, 264-273
    individual investor
        bond yield   9 15
        and apitalism, 3-9
        and company maturity   13-15

conservative viewpoint, 1
    and cyclical industries, 15-16
    and dividend yield, 26-27
    forward-looking viewpoint, 1
    and illusion, 264-273
    long-term debt and stock quality, 35-53
    magazines for, 17
    portfolio management, 282-289
    speculation, 27, 88, 91, 151, 201-202
    and stable industries, 15-16
    and stock ownership, 2
    stock price and return, 213-263
    timing purchases, 210, 285
Industrial equipment industry, 122-124, 285
Industrial materials industry, 109-118
    capital intensiveness, 110
    product development, 110
Industry
    accounting practices, 54-72, 75
    business cycles, 41, 284-286
    competition, 9, 38-41, 180-185, 197
    cyclicality, 15, 29, 32, 91, 96, 109-131, 134, 184, 284-286
    depreciation, 60-62
    and environmental problems, 8, 12, 18-19, 125, 133, 198-200
    growth rates, 13-14, 167-200
    maturity, 5-6, 13
    regulation of, 6, 8-9, 68-72, 126-127, 132-133, 158-166
    socialist tendencies in, 5
    and unions, 5-6, 119, 128-129, 158
Inflation, 2, 14, 145, 278
Infonet, 188
Institutional investors, 28, 31-32
Insurance industry, 55, 66-67, 139, 195, 275

Interest rates, 215-216
  related to stock prices,
    274-281
International Business Machines
  Corp., 11, 17, 26, 31-32, 65,
    70, 76, 100, 173-174, 177-184,
    190-191, 194, 214, 227, 250,
    273, 284
  Service Bureau Corp., 187
International Flavors & Fra-
    grances Inc., 173
International Harvester Co., 118
International Telephone and
    Telegraph Corp., 124
Interstate Commerce Commis-
    sion, 6, 128
Inventory
  accounting, 63
  control, 176, 230

J

Johns-Manville Corp., 229
Johnson & Johnson, 172-173
Johnson, Pres. Lyndon B.,
    277-278

K

Kaufman & Broad, Inc., 117
Kellogg Co., 136
Kennecott Copper Corp.,
    114-115, 158
Kern County Land Company,
    59
Kerr-McGee Corp., 168, 195, 227
Walter Kidde & Co., Inc., 206,
    209
K-Mart Stores, 148
Kraftco Corp., 287
S. S. Kresge Co., 19, 100,
    146-148

L

Law of diminishing return, 82
Leadership
  in business, 4
  and empire building, 4
  environment and oppor-
    tunity for, 5
  and pollution problems, 8,
    12, 198-200
  in a social group, 3-4
  sources of, 5-6
  in stock companies, 4
Learson, T. Vincent, 179
Leasing companies
  business equipment, 67-68
  computer, 174, 178
Levenstein, Ernest, 286
Levitz Furniture Corp., 207,
    209-210
Life insurance industry, 9, 60,
    139
Eli Lilly and Co., 170-172
Linocin, 170
Long-term debt, 26, 80
Louisiana Land & Exploration
    Co., 153, 227
"Love" cosmetics, 169
Low-tax countries, 59-60
The Lubrizol Corp., 113, 168,
    194

M

Machines and machinery indus-
    tries, 15, 109, 119-121
R. H. Macy & Co., Inc., 228
Magnavox Co., 122
Mammoth Mart, Inc., 207, 209
Management, 84, 98, 146
  depth, 29

entrepreneurial, 8-9, 132-133,
166, 203, 212
and stock quality, 17-19
top, 29
Marantz equipment, 208
Market domination, 146-147
Market paper, 276
Marketing, 6, 84, 133, 168-169,
• 182-183, 196
and cash flow, 24-25
Markup, 273
Marriott Corp., 25, 45-47
Masco Corp., 117
Maturity
measuring, 28-29
and stock quality, 13-15
McDonald's Corp., 230
McLean Trucking Co., 41, 130
Melville Shoe Corporation, 100
Memorex Corp., 100, 190
Merck & Co., Inc., 11, 172-173,
214, 226
Metals and mining industries,
24, 114-116, 285
copper, 114-115
Minnesota Mining & Mfg. Co.,
11, 76, 113, 168, 191,
196-200, 214
anti-pollution leadership,
198-200
Mobil Oil Corp., 153, 156
"Moneymakers", 203, 212
Moneymarkets, 274-281
Money supply and demand,
274-280
Monroe Auto Equipment Co.,
119
Moody's Investors Service, Inc.,
15-16, 196
Moore Business Forms, Inc., 191
Mortgage insurance and banking,
139
Motorola, Inc., 100, 114,
124-125, 230
Multi-growth Company,
167-168, 196-200

N

Nalco Chemical Co., 113, 287
National CSS, Inc., 188
National Cash Register Co., The,
177-178, 180, 185
National Cities Corp., 287
Natomas Company, 267-268
Natural gas, 154-155
pipeline companies, 164-166
Net worth
earnings on, 30
return on and stock value,
22-23
New Process Co., 207, 209-210
New York Stock Exchange, 11,
192, 202, 207, 275, 283
Nixon, Pres. Richard M.,
277-278
Norton Simon, Inc., 287
Nuclear fuel industry, 167, 195

O

Occidental Petroleum Corp.,
158, 266-267
Oil & Gas Journal, 266
Oil industry, 6-7, 60-61, 149-157
accounting practices, 55
concessions, 150
offshore production, 195
stock prices, 265-268
Oil Industry Survey, 268
ONLINE Systems, 188
Outlook, 231
Overpricing of stocks, 12, 122,
189-190

P

Pacific Petroleums Ltd., 153, 266
Pamida, Inc., 207, 209
Pan American World Airways,
Inc., 36-38

Parke, Davis & Co., 171
Parker-Hannifin Corp., 100
Pataphysics, 264
Patent protection, 91, 167
J. C. Penney Co., Inc., 76, 86,
    88-89, 91, 146, 228
Performance
    in a bull market, 12
    higher grade stocks, 11-12
    lower grade stocks, 11-12
Personal portfolio and savings,
    280-289
Petrie Stores Corp., 26, 207, 209
Petroleum modifiers industry,
    167, 194
Pfizer Inc., 84-86, 169-170, 172,
    286
Phelps Dodge Corp., 115
Phillips Petroleum Co., 266,
    268
Photography industry, 167,
    191-192
Physical assets, 30
    and stock quality, 20-21
The Pittston Co., 158
Planning Research Corp., 187
Polaroid Corp., 76, 104, 167,
    191-193
Pollution control
    costs, 51, 162-163
    industry, 125, 287
    technology, 210
    3M Company leadership role,
        198-200
Pollution problems,
    and industry, 8, 12
    noise, 126
    sulfur, 158
Pooling of interests accounting,
    57-59
Powers, John, 86
Preferred stocks, 275-276
Premium stock price, 219, 220
    221
Prentice-Hall, Inc., 207, 209-210
Preservation of capital, 2

Price
    cycle, 133
    -earnings ratio, 220-221,
        231-232
    multiple, 11
Procter & Gamble Co., 24, 76
Product development, 110
    impact on sales, 19-20, 29
    innovation, 180-181
    and stock quality, 19-20
Profits, 54, 62, 113, 150-151,
    167-168, 177-179, 183-185,
    194
    and accounting practices,
        68-72
    in judging smaller companies,
        203-204
    recognition of (cash or
        accrual), 56
    of regulated industries, 68-72
Prudential Building Mainte-
    nance Corp., 207, 209-210
Public Service Electric & Gas Co.,
    159
Publishing industry, 6-7
    services, 17, 29
Purolator, Inc., 119

Q

Q-Tips, 173
Quaker Oats Co., 136
Quality of stocks, 2, 10-34, 218
    premiums and discounts,
        219-221
    and rate of return, 219-221
    ratings, 32-34
    scoring tables, 28-34

R

RCA Corp., 124, 177 178, 180,
    184
Railroads industry, 6, 60-61,
    127-129

profits, 68-72
Rank-Xerox, 195
Rapidata, 188
Raytheon Co., 96-98, 183
Real estate industry, 60-61
Recession, 41, 173
  resistance to, 144
Recreation vehicles, 207
Recycling, 200
Regulated industries, 6, 8-9,
    126-127, 132-133, 158-166
  profits of, 68-72
Relative dividend, 241-263
Relative graphics, 232-241
Relative price-earnings ratio,
    223-231
Relative stock prices, 218-223
Relative yield, 133-135, 241-263
Republican administrations,
    277-278
Reputation and stock quality,
    16-17
Research-Cottrell, Inc., 125,
    207, 209
Retail Credit Co., 196
Retail trade industries, 6-7, 15,
    24, 86, 88-91, 132, 144-148,
    286
  and credit expansion, 18
Retained earnings, 21-22, 213
  = book value ratio, 77-78
Return
  on cash plowback, 30
  on equity, 21-22, 46-47
  on investment, 11, 151, 283
  on net worth, 22-23
Revenue-capital ratio, 188-189
Revlon, Inc., 173
Rex-Noreco, Inc., 207, 209
Richardson-Merrell Inc., 172
Riley Stoker Corp., 125
Roadway Express, Inc., 41, 130
Roosevelt, Pres. Franklin D.,
    277-278
Royal Dutch Petroleum Co.,
    156, 178, 268

Rupp Industries, Inc., 207, 209
Ryan Homes, 117, 286

S

STP Corp., 207, 209
Sales
  effect of convenience features,
    14
  product development impact,
    19-20
St. Louis — San Francisco RY.,
    129
Sales mix, 145
Sasic, George, 286
SCAM Instruments, 125
Schering-Plough Corp., 170,
    172-173
Scientific Data Systems, 177
G. D. Searle & Co., 169, 171-172
Sears, Roebuck and Co., 76,
    145-147
Securities brokerage and
    underwriting, 139
Service Bureau Corp., 187
Short-term debt, 26, 53
The Signal Companies, Inc., 118
Simplicity Pattern Co., Inc.,
    168, 192
Sinclair Oil, 151-153
Sinequan, 170
Skyline Corp., 117
Smith Kline & French Labora-
    tories, 91-92, 169, 171-172
Sony equipment, 208
Speculation, 27, 88, 91, 151,
    201-202
Sperry Rand Corp., 94-96,
    177-178, 180, 184, 228
Stability, 29
  and stock quality, 15-16
Stable industries, 15
Standard Brands Incorporated,
    136, 228
Standard industry classification,
    16-17

Standard Oil Co. (New Jersey),
154-156, 158, 178, 267-268
Standard Oil Co. of California,
156
Standard & Poor's Corp., 16,
106, 136, 143, 157, 172, 214,
288
statistical services, 16, 231, 241
Staples industries, 132-166
Sterling Drug Inc., 169-170,
172-173
Sternco Industries, Inc., 207-210
Stock options, 86
Stock price, 45, 121, 218-223
= book equity ratio, 22
effect of debt, 35-53
and interest rates, 274-281
market evaluation, 21-22
relative, 218-223
and return, 213-263
valuation hypothesis, 104-108
volatility of, 31
Stock promotions, 264
Stock returns, 213-215
Stocks
and bond yields, 215
book value, 21, 47, 77-78
capital gains trading, 80
convertible preferred, 78
determining quality, 2, 10-34,
202, 219, 282-283
growth, 26, 100-108, 118,
201-212
higher-grade, 11-12
individual investor ownership,
2
institutional investor acceptance, 31-32
investment return, 11
lower grade, 11-12
overpriced, 12, 122, 189-190
preferred, 275-276
price volatility, 31, 184
price and return, 213-263
pricing by the market, 21-22,
104,108

timing purchases, 210, 285
utility compared to industrial,
164
Strikes, 119
Suave Shoe Corp., 208-209
Superscope, Inc., 208-209
Supersonic transport (SST), 20
Supply cycle, 133

T

Talwin, 170
Teamsters Union, 129
Tecumseh Products Co., 117
Tektronix, Inc., 100
Telephone industry profits,
68-72
Tenneco Corporation, 58-59,
70-72, 166
Texaco Inc., 153-154, 156
Texas Instruments, Inc., 39-41,
78-80, 124, 181, 185-186, 230
Texas Utilities Co., 26
Textile industry, 24
Time sharing computer network,
174-175, 181-182, 184, 188
Times-Mirror Co., 229
Timing of stock price moves,
285
Tobacco industry, 138
Trade balance, 112-113, 279
Trans World Airlines, Inc., 38
Transportation equipment
industries, 130
Transportation industries,
60-61, 109, 125-131
Triangle Publications, Inc., 49
Trucking industry, 6-7, 118, 127,
129-131
Truman, Pres. Harry, 277
Turn around, 137
Tymshare, 188

U

Unions, 5-6, 119, 128-129, 158
    strikes, 119
U.S. Congress, 189
U.S. Food and Drug Administra-
    tion, 138
U.S. Treasury securities, 274-277
Univac computers, 94, 184-185
University Computing Co., 188-
    189
Upjohn Co., 169-170, 172
Utilities industry, 60-61, 132-
    133, 158-166
    debt ratio in, 26
    earnings in, 26
    profits, 68-72

V

Valle's Steak House, 208-209
Valuation hypothesis, 104-108
Value Line, 15, 58, 268
    statistical services, 16
Varian Associates, 186
Vaseline, 173
Venice Industries, Inc., 208-209
Vetco Offshore Industries, Inc.,
    208-209
Viatron Corporation, 272-273
Volatility
    of stock price, 31, 184
    and stock quality, 27-28

W

The Wall Street Journal, 231
Warner-Lambert Company, 172
Westinghouse Electric Corp., 123
Weyerhaeuser Co., 270
Whirlpool Corporation, 122
J.H. Whitney & Company, 196
Woolco stores, 88

F. W. Woolworth Co., 86, 88,
    90-91, 207
World markets, 112-113
Write-off, 62-63

X

Xerox Corp., 76, 167, 177,
    194-195

Y

Yield, 133-135, 241-263, 284

Z

Zenith Radio Corp., 122